American Sea Fencibles
in the War of 1812

Heritage Books by the Society of the War of 1812
in the State of Ohio:

Transcribed by Harrison Scott Baker

*American Prisoners of War Held at Bermuda,
Cape of Good Hope and Jamaica During the War of 1812*

*American Prisoners of War Held at Barbados,
Newfoundland and New Providence During the War of 1812*

*American Prisoners of War Held at Halifax
During the War of 1812, Volume I and II*

Transcribed by Eric Eugene Johnson

American Prisoners of War Held at Dartmoor During the War of 1812

*American Prisoners of War Held in Montreal
and Quebec During the War of 1812*

*American Prisoners of War Held at Plymouth
During the War of 1812*

*American Prisoners of War Held at Quebec
During the War of 1812, 8 June 1813–11 December 1814*

*American Prisoners of War Paroled at Dartmouth,
Halifax, Jamaica and Odiham During the War of 1812*

*American Sea Fencibles in the War of 1812:
United States Sea Fencibles, State Sea Fencibles*

Black Regulars in the War of 1812

Black Regulars and Militiamen in the War of 1812

Forgotten Americans Who Served in the War of 1812

Ohio and the War of 1812: A Collection of Lists, Musters and Essays

Ohio's Regulars in the War of 1812

Heritage Books by the Society of the War of 1812
in the State of Maryland:

Maryland Regulars in the War of 1812
Transcribed by Eric Eugene Johnson; Foreword by Christos Christou

American Sea Fencibles in the War of 1812

United States Sea Fencibles
State Sea Fencibles

Eric Eugene Johnson

Society of the War of 1812
in the
State of Ohio

HERITAGE BOOKS
2018

HERITAGE BOOKS
AN IMPRINT OF HERITAGE BOOKS, INC.

Books, CDs, and more—Worldwide

For our listing of thousands of titles see our website
at
www.HeritageBooks.com

Published 2018 by
HERITAGE BOOKS, INC.
Publishing Division
5810 Ruatan Street
Berwyn Heights, Md. 20740

Copyright © 2018 Society of the War of 1812 in the State of Ohio

All rights reserved. No part of this book may be reproduced or transmitted in any form or by any means, electronic or mechanical, including photocopying, recording or by any information storage and retrieval system without written permission from the author, except for the inclusion of brief quotations in a review.

International Standard Book Number
Paperbound: 978-0-7884-5827-9

The Contents

The Introduction	1
United States Sea Fencibles	3
New York Sea Fencibles	10
The Other States Sea Fencibles	14
The Scorecard	17
U.S. Sea Fencibles Roster	19
State Sea Fencibles Roster	68
U.S. Sea Fencibles Companies	136
State Sea Fencibles Companies	145
The Bibliography	163

American Sea Fencibles in the War of 1812

The Introduction

The U.S. Corps of Sea Fencibles, which served during the War of 1812, was a unique branch of the U.S. Army. With most of the nation's merchant ships tied up in the ports along our eastern seaboard due to the British blockade during the war, there were plenty of unemployed sailors who needed jobs. The sea fencibles were heavy artillery companies which helped man our major forts along the east coast.

Various states also created their own sea fencibles companies which protected the ports and harbors of their cities. These sea fencibles companies were modeled after the U.S. Corps of Sea Fencibles.

The U.S. Corps of Sea Fencibles consisted of U.S. Army officers and seamen in the enlisted ranks. They were a very unique corps which not only operated heavy canons but they could also man harbor gunboats and serve as infantry when needed.

The term 'fencible' is usually not associated with the American military but fencible units were raised by the United States during the Revolutionary War through the end of the War of 1812. This term is found in the British military system beginning in the early 1700's through the Napoleonic Wars when describing a certain type of military unit.

Simply, fencibles were locally raised military units used as garrison troops in order to free combat troops for oversea duties. Most of these fencibles were raised once hostilities started and then disbanded after the signing of a treaty of peace. These fencibles units were a part of the regular British army, subject to the same rules and regulations.

In the British Empire, fencibles were raised locally to defend the colonies. Upper and Lower Canada and the Maritime Provinces raised many fencible regiments and battalions, which served commendably during the War of 1812. These fencibles were combat units. In most cases, the term 'fencibles' is used as part of the unit's numeric designation and name.

Only one type of American military organization used the term 'fencibles' in their military designation and that was the U.S. Corps of Sea Fencibles. Also, Congress, under the Act of 5 July 1813, converted the 40th through the 44th Regiments of U.S. Infantry into fencible regiments. These regiments could only serve in the defense of the seaboard of the United States and they could not be sent to the other parts of the country or into foreign territories. This restriction was used to help recruit men who otherwise probably would not have joined the army.

The 41st through the 43rd Regiments of U.S. Infantry were actually artillery regiments assigned to forts along the eastern seaboard. They had incorporated state sea fencibles units and other state artillery companies when they were formed. After the war these three regiments merged into the U.S. Corps of Artillery. The remaining two fencible regiments, the 40th and 44th Regiments of U.S. Infantry, merged into the new infantry regiments that were created after the war. The 40th U.S. Infantry saw combat in the District of Maine while the 44th U.S. Infantry participated in the Battle of New Orleans.

The other fencible organization created by Congress during the War of 1812 was the U.S. Flotilla Service. This service was not a part of the navy but it was still under the control of the Secretary of the Navy. Four captains and twelve lieutenant positions were authorized for this service with the same relative rank and authority as the same grade in the navy.

The gunboats and barges of the Baltimore Flotilla, the Potomac Flotilla, and the New York Flotilla, operated by the U.S. Navy, were turned over to the U.S. Flotilla Service. Captain Joshua Barney took command of the Chesapeake Bay unit made up of the former Baltimore and Potomac flotillas while Captain Jacob Lewis commanded the New York unit. Lewis had been in commanded on the U.S. Navy's naval flotilla service in New York City.

Many of the states created sea fencibles companies before, during and after the War of 1812. These companies were independent militia companies, attached to a local militia regiment, which could serve as infantry, heavy artillery, or as a gunboat crew. They were raised from men living in a major port and they were stationed at the fort guarding their port's harbor.

Most militia sea fencibles companies were named after their cities, thus, we have the Boston Sea Fencibles and the Portsmouth Sea Fencibles. Other companies were named after their commanding officers and many of these companies were indistinguishable from other militia companies.

The State of New York raised twelve companies of sea fencibles which consisted of over 2,100 men for the defense of New York City. The state had plans to establish these companies along Lake Ontario and the Niagara River but these plans never materialized.

The U.S. Corps of Sea Fencibles and the various state sea fencibles are one of the least understood military organizations which ever served our nation. They were very successful in their recruiting efforts and in the duties that they performed.

Eric E. Johnson

United States Corps of Sea Fencibles

Ten companies of U.S. Sea Fencibles were authorized under the Congressional Act of 26 July 1813[1] to serve for one year guarding the ports and harbors on our nation's eastern seaboard. These companies could be used on both land or on water in order to perform their missions. Most of the sea fencibles companies served as heavy artillery units at the forts protecting the ports in which was located a major U.S. naval base and/or naval shipbuilding yard.

By the provisions of this act, the corps could be retained until the end of the war. The corps did survive for two years although the make up of the corps was different in each year. Some companies were not renewed for a second year while new companies were formed in the second year.

These companies were unique in that the officers were army officers and the enlisted men were naval personnel. The companies were made up of a captain, a 1st lieutenant, a 2nd lieutenant and a 3rc lieutenant in the officer's ranks. The enlisted consisted of the warrant officer's rank of a boatswain plus six gunners and six quarter gunners along with ninety seamen.

As fencibles, the corps was recruited in and around the ports in which the men served. They could not be sent to any other areas of the country. No field officers, that is, majors or colonels, were appointed or commissioned for this corps. Each company was independent from the other sea fencibles companies and each company was assigned to the commanding officer of the fort in which the company served.

Even though this corps was a U.S. Army organization, it was decided to use unemployed civilian seaman for the enlisted ranks. However, the Corps' officers recruited any one who wanted to serve. All enlistments were for one year and the men who wanted to serve for a second year, had to re-enlist.

The U.S. Corps of Sea Fencibles was a separate corps of the U.S. Army. They were not a part of the U.S. Volunteer Corps which was another war-time branch of the U.S. Army. Each of these corps were created separately by Congress and each had a unique mission along with a separate budget.

The men were protected under the military pension laws during the War of 1812. If injured or wounded in the line of duty, the men could receive a military pension. If a man had been killed or died in the line of duty, then the heirs could received the man's half pay per month for five years.

The men were not eligible for military land bounties until 1855 although some men received bounty lands prior to this date since they had served previously in the militia or in federal service. The men, or their widows, who lived past 1871 qualified for service pensions. Under the Act of 27 February 1815, the U.S. Corps of Sea Fencibles was disbanded.[2]

An Act to Authorize the Raising a Corps of Sea Fencibles

Be it enacted by the Senate and House of Representatives of the United States of America in Congress assembled, that the President of the United States be, and he is hereby authorized to raise for such term as he may think proper, not exceeding one year, as many companies of sea fencibles as he may deem necessary, not exceeding ten, who may be employed as well on land as on water, for the defense of the ports and harbors of the United States.

Section 2. And be it further enacted, that each of the said companies of sea fencibles shall consist of one captain, one first, one second, and one third lieutenant, one boatswain, six gunners, six quarter gunners, and ninety men.

Section 3. And be it further enacted, that the commissioned officers shall receive the same pay and rations as officers of the same grade in the army of the United States; that the boatswains, gunners, quarter gunners, and men shall receive the same pay and

---

[1] *Public Statutes at Large of the United States of America*, volume III, (Boston: Charles C. Little and James Brown, 1846), Thirteenth Congress, Session I, Chapter XXVII, pp. 47-48, 26 July 1813, "an act to authorize the raising a corps of sea fencibles."

[2] *Ibid.*, Session III, Chapter LXIV, 27 February 1815, page 219, "an Act to repeal certain acts therein mentioned."

rations as warrant officers of the same grade and able seaman receive in the service of the United States.

Section 4. And be it further enacted, that the officers, warrant officers, boatswains, and men raised pursuant to this act, shall be entitled to the like compensation in case of disability incurred by wounds or otherwise in the service of the United States, as officers, warrant officers, and seamen in the present naval establishment, and shall be subject to the rules and articles which have been or may hereafter be established by law, for the government of the army of the United States.

Section 5. And be if further enacted, the this act shall be and continue in force during the present war between the United States of American, and their territories, and the United Kingdom of Great Britain and Ireland, and the dependencies thereof.

Section 6. And be if further enacted, that in the recess of the Senate, the President of the United States is hereby authorized to appoint all the officers proper to be appointed under this act, which appointments shall be submitted to the Senate at their next session for their advise and consent.

Section 7. And be if further enacted, that the sum of two hundred thousand dollars be, and the same is hereby appropriated to carry this act into effect, to be paid out of any money in the Treasury not otherwise appropriated.

Approved, July 26, 1813

Captain John S. Davis' Company
Fort Constitution, Portsmouth, NH

John S. Davis was commissioned as a captain on 27 June 1814 and served until discharged on 15 June 1815. He had previously served as a lieutenant in the Portsmouth Sea Fencibles, a militia company assigned to the 1st New Hampshire Militia Regiment.[3] A roster of Davis' company can be found in the *Military History of the State of New Hampshire*.[4]

This company of U.S. Sea Fencibles was assigned to Fort Constitution in Portsmouth, New Hampshire, with the mission of protecting the city and its port. Portsmouth also had a major U.S. naval base and shipyard. The fort was originally built in 1631 as Fort William and Mary but fell into disuse before the Revolutionary War. The army took over the fort in 1794 and then rebuilt the facility between 1807 and 1808. The fort became a 36-gun brick fortification with a new name, Fort Constitution. The fort remained active until 1948 when the land was divided into a state park and a U.S. Coast Guard Station.

Captain Peleg Barker's Company
Fort Phoenix, Fairhaven, MA

Peleg Barker was commissioned as a captain on 11 July 1814 and he served until discharged on 15 June 1815. Barker raised his company in the Fairhaven area of Massachusetts which is across the river from New Bedford, home of a major U.S. naval base.

The company was stationed at Fort Phoenix in Fairhaven. This fort was originally a six-gun battery named Fort Fearing, which protected New Bedford during the American Revolution. It was rebuilt and re-named in 1798, and was again re-built into a 12-gun fort in 1808. The fort was used until after World War II and it is now a part of the Fort Phoenix Beach State Reservation.

---

[3] *Laws of the State of New Hampshire passed from December session 1805 to June session 1810,* (Isaac Hill Printers: Concord, NH, 1811), pp. 12-14, 8 Jun 1808, An Act to incorporate a military company in the town of Portsmouth in said State by the name of the Portsmouth Sea Fencibles, John S. Davis, lieutenant.

[4] *Military History of the State of New Hampshire. Part II, War of 1812-1815,* (C. E. Potter, McFarland & Jenkins: Concord, NH, 1866), page 129, roster of Captain John S. Davis' Company, U.S. Sea Fencibles.

A recruiting notice for this company was re-published by the *Presto Press* of Mattapoisett, Massachusetts, in 1969: [5]

> Recruiting – Rendezvous. Captain Peleg Barker of the Corps of Sea Fencibles to be raised for the defense of New Bedford, informs the public that he invites all true friends of the country to enlist. The term of service, one year; to pay and rations, the same as in the United States Navy, to be paid monthly.

Captain Benjamin Pearce's Company
Fort Greene, Newport, RI

Benjamin Pearce was commissioned as a captain on 2 August 1814 and served until discharged on 15 June 1815. He raised his company in the Newport, Rhode Island, area. The company was stationed at Fort Greene in Newport, which was a 12-gun battery during the War of 1812. The site is now a city park.

Captain Noah Terry's Company
Sag Harbor Fort, Sag Harbor, NY

Noah Terry was commissioned as a captain on 18 June 1814 and served until discharged on 15 June 1815. His company was raised in Suffolk County, Long Island, New York, in order to keep the British navy from entering Long Island Sound. The company was stationed at the Sag Harbor Fort in Sag Harbor, New York, during the last year of the war.

The fort was originally a British fortified supply depot during the American Revolution. A new fort was built in 1813 and it consisted of six guns. It had a 3,000-man garrison, mostly manned by New York sea fencibles and militia.

The journal of Second Lieutenant Pardon T. Tabor of Terry's company was published in *The Sag-Harbor Express* in 1891.[6] The journal contains a muster roll of company plus the following statements:

> Enlisted in Capt. Noah Terry's Company of Sea Fencibles, the 3rd day of August, 1814, as lieutenant for 12 months. Discharged from the United States service after the return of peace 3rd day of April 1815.
> Celebrated the return of peace, February 23rd, 1813 (sic). While firing the salute there were two men killed, by accident. While loading one of the eighteen pounders, the cartridge took fire while ramming down the charges. One of them was killed immediately, the other lived about two hours. Names of the men: John Pierson, Nathaniel Baker. They were both buried in one grave: both belonged to Capt. Noah Terry's Company of Sea Fencibles.

Captain Lemuel Morris' Company
Fort Gates, Sandy Hook, NJ

Lemuel Morris was commissioned as a captain on 4 August 1813 and served until discharged on 15 June 1815. Morris had served as a secretary and as a chaplain on the U.S. Frigate *President* under Captain

---

[5] *Presto Press*, Mattapoisett, MA, volume XVII, number 9, 26 Feb 1969, page 14, History of Fort Phoenix, by Donald R. Bernard, part XV.

[6] *The Sag-Harbor Express*, Sag Harbor, Suffolk County, NY, Thursday, 30 Apr 1891, volume XXXII, number 42, page 1, column 5, Journal of Pardon T. Tabor, muster roll of Captain Noah Terry's Company of Sea Fencibles, page 1, column 4.

William Bainbridge between 1809 and 1810, and on the U.S. Frigate *Adams* in 1813 under Captain Charles Morris, before being commissioned in the Sea Fencibles.[7]

Morris raised his company in the New York City area and the company was stationed on the west battery of Fort Gates at Sandy Hook, New Jersey. The fort on Sandy Hook helped protect the entrance to the New York harbor. The fort was built in 1813 and consisted of a garrison of 800 men with thirty-two cannons.

On 7 July 1814, Captain Morris had seventy-eight men under his command at Fort Gates while sixty of his men (from Hudson, New York) were attached to the 41st Regiment of U.S. Infantry under the command of First Lieutenant Theophilus Beekman.[8] The 41st Infantry was a fencibles regiment raised by the army for the protection of New York City.

Captain Matthew Simmons Bunbury's Company
Captains John Gill and William H. Addison's Companies
Fort McHenry, Baltimore, MD

Baltimore raised two companies of U.S. Sea Fencibles for service at Fort McHenry. Matthew Simmons Bunbury was commissioned as a captain on 1 October 1813 and he served until discharged on 15 Jun 1815. John Gill was commission as a captain on 25 Nov 1813 but his commission was cancelled by the U.S. Senate on 17 March 1814.

> **Honor to the Brave!**
>
> **SEA FENCIBLES,**
> *And only for Twelve Months.*
> Where an honorable situation now offers to all young men, whose hearts are inspired with love for their country. There is no situation which offers more advantages at this eventful crisis, than the SEA FENCIBLES, and that in defence of the Ports and Harbors of the United States, only. Come then my
> **Brave Patriots,**
> embrace this opportunity of tendering your services to your beloved country. Repair immediately to my *Standard* Water st. No. 21, near Cumberland Row, or to the Barracks, Liberty street, Old Town, where you have an opportunity of crowning yourselves with the laurels of your country, and receive *Twelve Dollars* in advance, and *Twelve Dollars* per month in addition to Navy Rations.
> JOHN GILL, Capt. U. S. S. F.
> feb 11   d1m

American Commercial and Daily Advertiser, February 11, 1814, Baltimore, MD

William H. Addison was commissioned as a captain on 27 Apr 1814 replacing Captain Gill. Addison died on 9 December 1814. He had previously been commissioned as an ensign in the 38th Regiment of

---

[7] Davenport, Charles Benedict, *Naval Officers, Their Heredity and Development*, (Carnegie Institution of Washington: Washington, DC, 1919), page 136.

[8] Guernsey, R. S., *New York City and Vicinity during the War of 1812-1815*, volume II, (Charles L. Woodward, Bookseller: New York, NY, 1895), pp. 138-139.

U.S. Infantry before joining the U.S. Sea Fencibles. A listing of the officers and men who served in these two companies is listed in *The British Invasion of Maryland 1812-1815*.[9]

Originally, Captain Bunbury's company was assigned to Fort Babcock, located one and a half miles west of Fort McHenry while Captain Addison's company manned Fort Covington which was located two miles west of Fort McHenry.[10] Fort Babcock, built in 1813, was a six-gun earthwork while Fort Covington, also built in 1813, was a 10-gun brick fort.

Before the Battle of Fort McHenry on 13 September 1814, both companies were moved to the 10-gun water battery below Fort McHenry. This fort was built in 1798 and it operated thirty guns plus the water battery. This fort was owned by the U.S. Army until 1933 and it is now a national park. Both companies participated in this famous battle.

Captain John Nicholson's Company
Captain John DuBose's Company
Captain Frederick Brooks' Company
Captain McQueen McIntosh's Company

Three companies of U.S. Sea Fencibles were raised in North Carolina during the War of 1812. Frederick Brooks was commissioned as a captain on 7 Aug 1813 and he was dismissed from the service on 14 Feb 1815. His company was raised in Beaufort County, North Carolina, with his recruiting headquarters was in Washington. The company was stationed at Fort Hampton in Beaufort and some of the men also served on the Albemarle Sound and the Currituck Sound in northeastern North Carolina.

Prior to his service in the U.S. Sea Fencibles, Brooks was a captain in the Beaufort Militia Regiment. He served a tour of duty as a captain in the 2nd North Carolina Detached Regiment before being commissioned in the U.S. Sea Fencibles.[11] After Brooks was dismissed, it appears that McQueen McIntosh took command of his company. McIntosh was commissioned on 22 November 1814 and he served until discharged on 15 June 1815.

The second company of sea fencibles was raised by John Nicholson in Bladen County, North Carolina. The recruiting headquarters was located in Elizabethtown. Nicholson was commissioned as a captain on 1 August 1813 and he died on 5 April 1814.

Before receiving a commission in the U.S. Sea Fencibles, Nicholson was a captain in the Bladen Militia Regiment. He served a tour of duty as a captain in the 4th North Carolina Detached Regiment before joining the U.S. Sea Fencibles.[12]

The third company of sea fencibles was raised by John DuBose who was commissioned as a captain on 4 August 1813. The company was raised in Sumter County with its recruiting headquarters located at Willow Grove. It appears that after the death of Nicholson, the second and third companies merged under DuBose. He resigned his commissioned on 20 September 1814. The second and third companies operated along the coast of southeastern North Carolina primarily protecting the Wilmington area.

---

[9] Marine, William M., *The British Invasion of Maryland 1812-1815*, (Society of the War of 1812 in Maryland: Baltimore, MD, 1913).

[10] Whitehorne, Joseph A., *The Battle for Baltimore 1814*, (The Nautical & Aviation Publishing Company of America: Baltimore, MD, 1997), pp. 44, 168, 172.

[11] *Muster Rolls of the Soldiers of the War of 1812 detached from the Militia of North Carolina in 1812-1814*, (North Carolina Adjutant General's Office: Raleigh, 1851), page 10, Captain Frederick Brooks' Company.

[12] *Ibid*, page 24, Captain John Nicholson's Company.

Captain Thomas M. Newell's Company
Fort Jackson, Savannah, GA

Thomas M. Newell was commission as a captain on 1 August 1813 and he was discharged on 1 August 1814. His company was raised in the Savannah, Georgia, area and may have been stationed at Fort Jackson, which was a 6-gun brick fort built in 1810 at Savannah. The recruiting headquarters was located in Savannah and a recruiting station was located at St. Mary's, Georgia.

Captain Newell and Thomas Spalding (legal aide to Brigadier General John Floyd, commander of the 1st Brigade of the Georgia Militia) were appointed by General Floyd to negotiate the return of 702 slaves plus private property which were taken by Rear Admiral George Cockburn, Royal Navy, when his forces captured Cumberland Island off the coast of Georgia after the ratification of the Treaty of Ghent.[13]

At the time, Admiral Cockburn did not know that the war had ended. The slaves had either been taken into British military service or freed and then sent to other British colonies.

The Discharging of the Sea Fencibles

After the War of 1812, the Act of 3 March 1815[14] established the peacetime army by consolidating all of the existing infantry regiments into eight new infantry regiments, plus a rifle regiment and two artillery regiments totaling 10,000 men.

All other branches of the army raised during the War of 1812 were not retained in the peacetime army. These branches included the sea fencibles plus the U.S. Rangers, the U.S. Corps of Artificers, the U.S. Volunteers, the Canadian Volunteers, and the U.S. Flotilla Service. All officers who were discharged under this act received an additional three-month pay.

Twenty Dollars Reward.

Deserted from Fort M'Henry on the 12th inst. ANTHONY GREEN, a private in the Sea Fencibles; born in Pennsylvania, five feet seven inches high; dark complexion; dark eyes; and dark hair.

Also, ERASTUS HOOPER; born in Massachusetts, 24 years of age; five feet 8½ inches high; light complexion; grey eyes, and light brown hair. A reward of ten dollars will be given for either of the above deserters on their being delivered at Fort M'Henry, or to any officer commanding in the U. S. service.

M. S. BUNBURY.
Capt U. S. S. Fencibles, Fort M·H.
april 23   d6t

American Commercial and Daily Advertiser, April 23, 1814, Baltimore, MD

---

[13] *British and Foreign State Papers 1816-1817*, British Foreign Office, (James Ridgway and Sons: Piccadilly, England, 1836), Correspondence with Great Britain, relative to the restitution of certain slaves, captured during the war, pp. 276-291.

[14] *Public Statutes at Large of the United States of America*, volume III, (Boston: Charles C. Little and James Brown, 1846), Thirteenth Congress, Session III, Chapter LXXIX, pp. 224-225, 3 March 1815, "an act fixing the military peace establishment of the United States."

U.S. Sea Fencibles in 1813

Captain Matthew Simmons Bunbury	Baltimore, MD
Captain John Gill	Baltimore, MD
Captain Lemuel Morris	Sandy Hook, NJ
Captain John Nicholson	Bladen County, NC
Captain Thomas M. Newell	Savannah, GA
Captain Frederick Brooks	Beaufort County, NC
Captain John DuBose	Sumter County, NC

U.S. Sea Fencibles in 1814

Captain Matthew Simmons Bunbury	Baltimore, MD
Captain William H. Addison	Baltimore, MD
Captain John S. Davis	Portsmouth, NH
Captain Peleg Barker	Fairhaven, MA
Captain Benjamin Pearce	Newport, RI
Captain Noah Terry	Sag Harbor, NY
Captain Lemuel Morris	Sandy Hook, NJ
Captain McQueen Mcintosh	Bladen County, NC
Captain John DuBose	Sumter County, NC

New York Sea Fencibles

The State of New York organized the largest sea fencibles force during the War of 1812 to protect the New York City area. With the Royal Navy ravishing the Chesapeake Bay area and the coast line of New England, particularly the District of Maine, the state government assumed in 1814 that New York City would be the next target of the British war machine.

The sea fencibles, both the state sea fencibles and the U.S. Corps of Sea Fencibles, were probably the most successful military organization raised during the war. The sea fencibles had no problems recruiting men since these companies could only served in the areas where they were recruited. The sea fencibles companies raised in New York City would stay in this city and could not be sent north to fight the British along the northern New York border.

The New York State Militia ordered the organization of sea fencibles for New York City on 29 August 1814.[1] The Neptune Corps of Sea Fencibles, first organized during the Revolutionary War, was re-activated for duty in the city.[2] But on 24 October 1814, the state legislature passed an act authorizing the raising a state corps of sea fencibles.[3] This corps would replace the Neptune Corps.

Captain James T. Leonard, U.S. Navy, commander of the U.S. Navy's flotilla boats in New York harbor, also had a company of U.S. Sea Fencibles at Sandy Hook, New Jersey, which protected the entrance to New York harbor. Another company of U.S. Sea Fencibles was being formed in Sag Harbor, Long Island, New York.

An ACT to authorise the raising a corps of Sea Fencibles

I. Be it enacted by the people of the state of New York, represented in Senate and Assembly, That the governor of the state of New York be, and he is hereby authorized to raise for three years, unless sooner discharged, twenty companies of sea fencibles, who may be employed as well on the land as on the water, for the defence of the port and harbor of New York.

II. And be it further enacted, That each of the said companies of sea fencibles, shall consist of one captain, one first, one second, and one third lieutenant, one boatswain, six gunners, six quarter gunners, two musicians and ninety privates.

III. And be it further enacted, That the said companies of sea fencibles shall be formed into battalions, regiments and a brigade, or organised in such a manner as shall be deemed best adapted to promote the objects of this act, and that officers of such grade, and as many as may be deemed necessary, shall be appointed to command the said battalions, regiments and brigade of sea fencibles.

IV. And be it further enacted, That the several companies of sea fencibles which have been raised, shall be considered, and they are hereby declared to be a part of the corps authorised to be raised by this act, and the raising of the said companies is hereby ratified and confirmed.

V. And be it further enacted, That the governor of the state of New York be, and he is hereby authorised to appoint by brevet, all officers of the said corps of sea fencibles, who

---

[1] Guernsey, R. S., *New York City and Vicinity during the War of 1812-1815*, volume II, (Charles L. Woodward, Bookseller: New York, NY, 1895), page 246.

[2] *Ibid.*, pp. 206-207.

[3] *Laws of the State of New York Passed at the Thirty-Eighth Session of the Legislature*, (J. Buel, Printer to the State: Albany, NY 1815), thirty-eighth session, chapter XVII, pp. 21-22.

shall hold their respective commissions until the council of appointment shall have appointed the officers for the said corps, in pursuance of the constitution and laws of this state.

VI. And be it further enacted, That the commissioned officers of the said corps shall receive the same pay, rations, forage and allowances, as officers of the same grade in the army of the United States; that the boatswains, gunners and quarter gunners shall receive the same pay as warrant officers of the same grade in the navy of the United States, and shall receive the same rations as sergeants in the army of the United States; that the musicians and privates shall receive the same pay as musicians and able seamen receive in the navy of the United States, and shall receive the same rations as musicians and privates receive in the army of the United States; and it shall be lawful to pay the boatswains, gunners, quarter gunners, musicians and privates of the said corps, one month's pay in advance at the time of enlistment.

VII. And be it further enacted, That the said corps of sea fencibles may be ordered into the service of the United States in lieu of an equal number of militia which may be required by the government of the United States, for the defence of the port and harbor of New-York.

VIII. And be it further enacted, That when the corps of sea fencibles to be raised as aforesaid, shall be in the service of the United States, they shall be subject to the rules and articles which have been, or may be hereafter established by the laws of the United States, for the government of the army of the United States; that when the said corps shall be in the service of the state of Newark, they shall be subject to the same rules and regulations; and the governor of the said state shall be, and he is hereby authorised and directed to exercise all the power and authority which, by the said rules and articles, are required to be exercised by the president, of the United States.

Passed October 24, 1814.

The New York State Sea Fencibles were modeled on the U.S. Corps of Sea Fencibles, except two musicians were added to each company. Only twelve companies, organized into three battalions, were raised in New York. Initially, a brigade of 2,160 men were authorized for the New York City area while a battalion of 540 men was scheduled to be raised for service on Lake Niagara.[4] It appears that the Lake Niagara battalion was never raised.

The first three companies were commanded by Captains James T. Leonard, Pexcel Fowler and Josiah Ingersoll.[5] Leonard's company occupied Fort Diamond, located on an island in the Narrows between Staten Island and Brooklyn. Fowler's company was stationed at Fort Lewis and adjoining blockhouses on the Brooklyn shore at the Narrows. Ingersoll's company manned the blockhouse on Rockaway Peninsula on the south shore of Queens. Ingersoll's men also manned two gun barges at the blockhouse.

Both Leonard and Fowler would be promoted to the rank of major and command battalions in the state sea fencibles. A total of sixty-six officers, 158 non-commissioned officers and 1,065 enlisted men would serve in the New York State Sea Fencibles.[6]

Captain Ingersoll's company consisted of a captain, first lieutenant, third lieutenant, a boatswain, two gunners, two quarter gunners, a purser's steward and sixty privates.[7] The company was issued sixty

---

[4] *Documents of the Senate of the State of New York*, 127th Session, Volume VIII, Number 2, Part 5, 1904, (Oliver A. Quayle, State Printers: Albany, NY, 1904), page 546.

[5] Guernsey, *New York City*, pp. 330-331.

[6] *Ibid.*, page 566.

muskets, sixty cartridge boxes, sixty-five cutlasses, 1000 musket cartridges, 500 musket flints, twenty pistols, 100 pistol flints, a flag, twenty mess pans, and sixty hammocks. Although assigned to man the artillery pieces at the blockhouse and to operate the gunboats, the company could serve as infantry when needed.

Fort Gates
Sandy Hook, New Jersey

Six of the twelve New York sea fencibles companies were stationed at Fort Gates at Sandy Hook, New Jersey. Fort Gates helped protect the entrance to the New York harbor. The fort was built in 1813 and consisted of a garrison of 800 men and thirty-two artillery pieces.

Major James T. Leonard commanded a battalion of four companies under the commands of Captains Alexander Robinson, William Russell, Francis Costigan and Robert Perry. Assigned to the fort were two other New York sea fencibles companies under the commands of Paul Burrows, Junior, and John Cunningham.

Decatur Blockhouse
Rockaway Peninsula, Queens, New York

Captain Josiah Ingersoll's company was stationed at the Decatur Blockhouse on the Rockaway Peninsula, which guarded the entrance to the New York harbor. It was also called the Rockaway Blockhouse. The blockhouse was probably located near present day 137th Street.

Hell Gate
East River, New York

Major Charles W. Wooster's battalion was assigned to the Hell Gate area on the East River between the Bronx and Queens. Captain Isaac Silliman's company occupied the blockhouse at Hurl Gate while Captain John M. Randlett's company manned the blockhouse on Mill Rock.

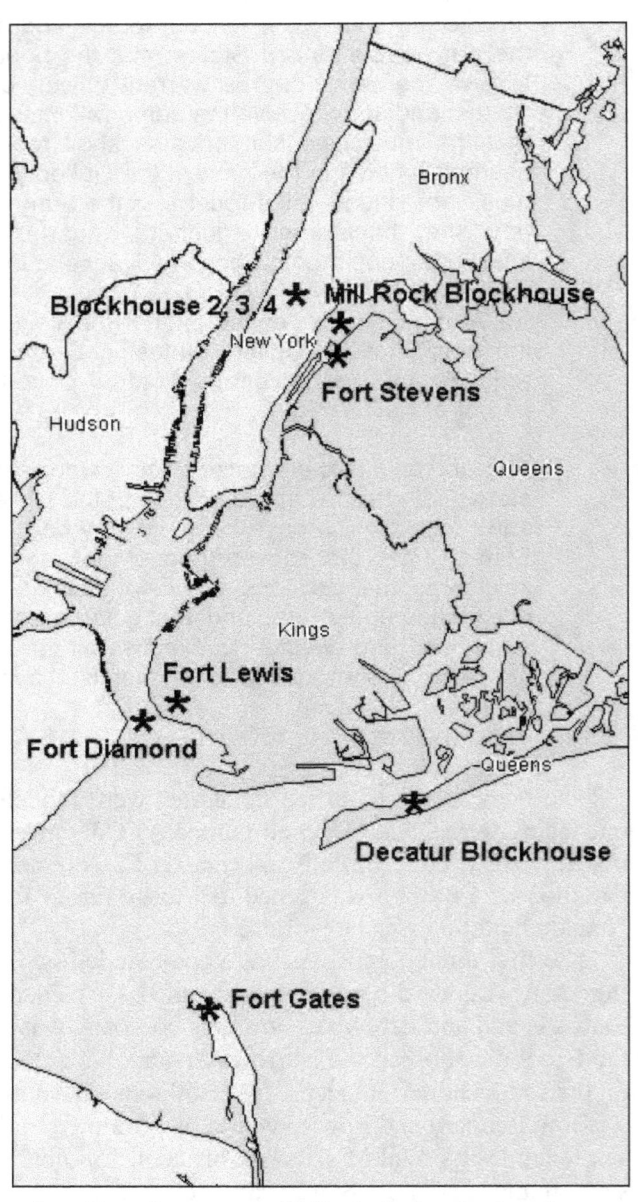

Captain John O. Roorbach's company was stationed at Fort Stevens at Hallet's Point in the Queens. Lieutenant Benjamin G. Dayton's detachment was assigned to the prison ship on the East River. It is assumed that the prison ship was holding British prisoners of war.

---

[7] *Documents of the Senate of the State of New York*, 127th Session, Volume VIII, Number 2, Part 5, 1904, (Oliver A. Quayle, State Printers: Albany, NY, 1904), page 508.

Manhattan Blockhouses
Manhattan, New York

Major Pexcel Fowler's battalion manned Blockhouse Numbers 2, 3 and 4 in the northern part of Manhattan Island. His two companies were commanded by Captains Benjamin A. Muzzy and James Breath.

New York Sea Fencibles Companies

Captain Christopher Colles' Company
Captain John Cunningham' Company
Captain Josiah Ingersoll' Company
Captain Paul Burrows' Company

Major Fowler's Detachment
    Captain Benjamin Muzzy's Company
    Captain James Breath's Company
    Captain Pexcil Fowler's Company

Major Leonard's Battalion
    Captain Alexander Robinson's Company
    Captain Francis Costigan's Company
    Captain James Leonard's Company
    Captain Robert Perry's Company
    Captain William Russell's Company

Major Wooster's Battalion
    Captain Isaac Silliman's Company
    Captain John Randlet's Company
    Captain John Roorbach's Company
    Lieutenant Benjamin Dayton's Detachment

The Other State Sea Fencibles

Captain William Marshall's Sea Fencibles
Portsmouth, New Hampshire

Captain William Marshall of the 35th New Hampshire Militia Regiment was detached from his regiment in the spring of 1813 and ordered to form a sea fencibles company for the protection of Portsmouth.[1] The company was activated on 27 May 1813 and it was discharged on 27 November 1813. The company was stationed at Little Harbor at the entrance to the Piscataqua River.

On the day of discharge, Captain Marshall and fourteen men received extended duty until 31 December 1813. The muster rolls of Captain Marshall's company can be found in the *Military History of New Hampshire*.

Captain Jeremiah Stickney's Sea Fencibles
Newburyport, Massachusetts

Captain Jeremiah Stickney raised a company of sea fencibles for the protection of Newburyport, Massachusetts in 1814.[2] This company was stationed at Plum Island at the entrance to the Merrimac River. They probably manned the 5-gun battery at Fort Philip. The muster roll of Captain Stickney's company can be found in the *History of the Marine Society of Newburyport, Massachusetts*.

Boston Sea Fencibles
Captain Nehemiah W. Skillings

The Boston Sea Fencibles was organized on 25 July 1814 in Boston, Massachusetts under the command of Captain Nehemiah W. Skillings. The unit was made up of masters and mates of vessels to serve as an artillery company.[3]

The company was stationed at Fort Strong in East Boston. The fort was actually a state militia earthwork near present day Brophy Memorial Park. An excerpt from the *Proceedings of the Bostonian Society* states:

> Captain Nehemiah W. Skillings, *captain*; Captain Winslow Lewis, *first lieutenant*; Captain Charles Tracy, *second lieutenant*; Captain Nathaniel Snow, *third lieutenant*; Captain Joseph Lewis, *treasurer and clerk*.
> *Sergeants*: Captain Joseph Callender, *orderly*; Captain William Newman, *second sergeant*; Captain Russell Glover, *third sergeant*; Captain Henry Russell, *fourth sergeant*. *Corporals*: Captains Edward Howe, Charles Knapp, Caleb Curtis, and Edward S. Scott.
> In August 1814, the Selectmen granted leave for the temporary erection of a new gun-house on the ground at the floor of the "Old Common" for the accommodation of the artillery of the Sea Fencibles and New England Guards, to be taken down at the close of the war.
> September 10th, the Fencibles paraded, and marched through the town of South Boston, with four pieces of heavy artillery, each piece drawn by four horses, with

---

[1] *Military History of the State of New Hampshire. Part II, War of 1812-1815*, (C. E. Potter, McFarland & Jenkins: Concord, NH, 1866), pp. 94 and 99, rosters of Captain William Marshall's Company.

[2] Bayler, William H. and Oliver O. Jones, *History of the Marine Society of Newburyport, Massachusetts*, 1906, pp. 496-497, sea fencibles.

[3] *Proceedings of the Bostonian Society at the Annual Meeting, January 10, 1899*, (Order of the Society: Old State House, Boston, 1899), pp. 44 and 47.

caissons, etc. Their uniform was a neat blue jacket and trousers, and they were armed with cutlasses and pikes. They encamped and dined at South Boston Point, and fired thirty-two rounds at two targets, placed at the distance of a mile. "Every shot would have hulled a frigate; no battery firing at a target had ever excelled it in the vicinity."

It appears that the officers and non-commissioned officers were all unemployed ship's masters. The enlisted personnel would probably have been the men from their ships.

Captain Isaac Lyman's York Sea Fencibles
York, District of Maine

A detachment from Captain Isaac Lyman's York Sea Fencibles, under the command of Sergeant John S. Thompson, was called out during the summer of 1814 to help defend Fort Edward at the mouth of the York River in York, District of Maine. The Fort Edward was a Massachusetts state militia fort.

In 1825, the Maine State Auditor petitioned the U.S. Treasury Department to have the men from Thompson's detachment paid for their war services.[4] Twenty-one men, including Thompson, served between 25 July 1814 and 25 October 1814. The muster roll of this detachment can be found in the *Records of the Massachusetts Volunteer Militia*.[5]

Captain Gershom Bradford's Sea Fencibles
Duxbury, Massachusetts

Major General Nathaniel Goodwin of the Massachusetts Militia requested a detachment of men from Captain Gershom Bradford's Duxbury Sea Fencibles for duty as guards for the Duxbury harbor during the fall of 1814.[6] A roster has not been found for this detachment.

HQ Plymouth 19 Oct 1814

You will detach from the company under your command one sergeant and ten privates, to do duty as row-guards for the harbor of Duxbury and its vicinity, and put them on duty the 20th instant.

There are ten men more wanted for sentinels on the shore; if you can furnish them from you company you will do it, and return their names to me; they will be under the command of the sergeant you will detach for the row-guard. If you cannot accomplish this, you will inform me that I may order otherwise.

Nath. Goodwin, Major General, 5th Division

Captain Gershom Bradford of the Sea Fencibles in Duxbury

---

[4] *American State Papers*, Military Affairs, Volume III, (Gales & Seaton: Washington, DC, 1860), pp. 167-184, 19th Congress, 1st Session, number 291, Rules for the Adjudication of Claims for Militia Services, and Report of Third Auditor on the Claim of Massachusetts, Supplementary Report Number 1, Treasury Department, Third Auditor's Office, 25 Apr 1825.

[5] *Records of the Massachusetts Volunteer Militia*, Brigadier General Gardner W. Pearson, (Wright & Potter Printing Co.: Boston, MA, 1913), page 311.

[6] *American State Papers*, Military Affairs, Volume III, (Gales & Seaton: Washington, DC, 1860), Copies of Orders, 5th Division, Major General Goodwin, page 38, No. 64 – Division Orders.

Captain Elisha Field's Sea Fencibles
Northfield, Massachusetts

The *History of the Connecticut Valley in Massachusetts* states that a sea fencibles company, under the command of Captain Elisha Field, was organized at the beginning of the war and was stationed at Fort Independence in Boston Harbor.[7] A roster of the men in this company has not been found. The book states:

> When the War of 1812 broke out Northfield was the headquarters of the 15th Division Massachusetts Militia, commanded by Maj. Gen. John Nevers of Northfield. Shortly after the beginning of hostilities, Capt. Elisha Field opened a recruiting office in Northfield and organized a company known as the "Sea Fencibles." Afterward stationed at Fort Independence, in Boston Harbor.

---

[7] *History of the Connecticut Valley in Massachusetts*, Volume II, (Louis H. Everts: Philadelphia, PA, 1879), History of Franklin County, page 660.

The Scorecard

This chapter will explain the data fields, abbreviations, terms and phrases used in creating the rosters of sea fencibles.

Data Field	Explanation
Rank	The highest known military rank is listed for each seaman. The ranks of third lieutenant and ensign were discontinued by the U.S. Army after the War of 1812. **Officer ranks:** Captain First Lieutenant Second Lieutenant Third Lieutenant **Enlisted ranks:** Boatswain Gunner Quarter Gunner Musician Seaman or Private Servant or waiter Other ranks are listed in the rosters
Other regiment(s)	If a seaman was transferred to or from another regiment or regiments, the name of the regiments are listed in this field.
Company	The company commander's name, or the name of a battalion or state company.
Age	Age of the seaman at the time of his enlistment or commissioning
Height	Height of the seaman in feet and inches.
Birth Place	The enlistment rosters list the birth of a seaman by state or country, county and city.
Trade	Civilian trade of a seaman at the time of enlistment.
Commissioning date	Date that an officer was commissioned into the sea fencibles.
Enlistment date	Date that an enlisted man entered service.
Enlistment Place	The place of enlistment by state, county and city.
Enlistment Period	The U.S. Corps of Sea Fencibles had one year enlistments while most states had three-month enlistments.
Discharged	The date of discharge and location with other comments.

Pension　　　　　　　　　I-9999 – Invalid
　　　　　　　　　　　　　　IC-9999 – Invalid's Certificate
　　　　　　　　　　　　　　IF-9999 – Invalid's File
　　　　　　　　　　　　　　IO-9999 – Invalid's Original
　　　　　　　　　　　　　　MC-9999 – Minor's Certificate
　　　　　　　　　　　　　　MO-9999 – Minor's Original
　　　　　　　　　　　　　　SC-9999 – Survivor's Certificate
　　　　　　　　　　　　　　SF-9999 – Survivor's File
　　　　　　　　　　　　　　SO-9999 – Survivor's Original
　　　　　　　　　　　　　　WC-9999 – Widow's Certificate
　　　　　　　　　　　　　　WF-9999 – Widow's File
　　　　　　　　　　　　　　WO-9999 – Widow's Original

Bounty Number　　　　　BLW 999999-999-99

　　　　　　　　　　　　　　BLW = Bounty land warrant number
　　　　　　　　　　　　　　-999- = number of acres issued for the warrant
　　　　　　　　　　　　　　-12 or -14 or -42 or -50 or -55 = Years of the Land Bounty Acts

Comments　　　　　　　　Any additional comments for a seaman.

Terms and phases

Land bounty to "name of heirs" heirs at law of "name of seaman"
　　This phase lists the name of the heir or heirs (by law) who received the land bounty of a deceased seaman.

Surgeon's Certificate of Disability
　　A surgeon could issue a "Surgeon's Certificate of Disability" to a wounded, sick or injured seaman and this would released the seaman from the service. The seaman's enlistment would end and he was still entitled to all his back pay, bonuses and land bounties.

Deserted
　　This term denotes seamen who left their companies and who did not return to duty. In early 1815, many seamen simply left their companies without permission and returned home. These men were not entitled to their enlistment benefits.

U.S. Sea Fencibles Roster

Adams, Aaron - Seaman - Company: John Davis - Age: 21 - Height: 5' 8 1/2" - Born: Herkimer, Hillsborough County, NH - Trade: Tobacconist - Enlistment date: 25 Jul 1814 - Place: Portsmouth, NH - Period: 1 Year - Discharged on 29 Mar 1815.

Adams, John - Seaman - Company: Frederick Brooks - Age: 19 - Height: 5' 4 3/4" - Born: Charleston, SC - Trade: Mariner - Enlistment date: 24 Feb 1814 - Place: Washington, NC - Period: War.

Adams, John - Seaman - Company: John DuBose - Age: 21 - Height: 5' 8" - Born: Black River, SC - Enlistment date: 24 May 1814 - Place: Willow Grove, SC - Period: 1 Year.

Adams, William - Quarter Gunner - Company: John DuBose - Enlistment date: 27 Jan 1814 - Place: Willow Grove, SC - Period: 1 Year - Deserted on 27 Jan 1814.

Adams, William P. - First Lieutenant - Company: John Davis - Born: Massachusetts - Period: 1 Year - Commissioned as a 1st lieutenant on 21 Jun 1814; resigned on 31 Jan 1815.

Addison, William H. - Captain - Company: William Addison - Other regiment: 38th US Infantry - Born: Maryland - Pension: Wife Anna, Old War WF-15507, Navy WF-1040 Rejected - Commissioned as an ensign, 38th U.S. Infantry, on 20 Sep 1813; commissioned as a captain, U.S. Sea Fencibles, on 27 Apr 1814; died on 9 Dec 1814.

Alben, Zerah - Seaman - Company: Noah Terry - Age: 20 - Height: 5' 6 1/2" - Born: Brookhaven, NY - Trade: Comb maker - Enlistment date: 10 Aug 1814 - Place: Sag Harbor, NY - Period: 1 Year - Deserted.

Aldridge, Howell - Seaman - Company: Noah Terry - Age: 21 - Height: 5' 9" - Born: Riverhead, NY - Trade: Cordwainer - Enlistment date: 20 Jul 1814 - Place: Sag Harbor, NY - Period: 1 Year - Discharged at Sag Harbor, NY, on 5 Apr 1815.

Alford, Jacob - Musician - Company: William Addison - Pension: Land bounty to Elizabeth Alford, widow of Jacob Alford - BLW 54798-160-55.

Alford, Thomas - Seaman - Company: John Gill - Age: 21 - Height: 5' 7" - Born: Baltimore - Enlistment date: 8 Jan 1814.

Allan, James - Seaman - Company: John Nicholson.

Allen, John M. - Private.

Anderson, James - Seaman - Company: Frederick Brooks - Age: 18 - Height: 5' 8 1/2" - Born: Beaufort, Beaufort County, NC - Trade: Farmer - Enlistment date: 7 Feb 1814 - Place: Washington, NC - Period: 1 Year.

Anderson, Stephen B. - Seaman - Company: Noah Terry - Age: 21 - Height: 5' 6" - Born: Philadelphia - Trade: Cordwainer - Enlistment date: 21 Jul 1814 - Place: Sag Harbor, NY - Period: 1 Year - Discharged on 5 Apr 1815.

Andrews, John - Seaman - Company: Lemuel Morris - Age: 29 - Height: 5' 5 1/4" - Born: Ireland - Enlistment date: 14 Jan 1814 - Deserted on 12 Jun 1814.

Andrews, Nathaniel - Seaman - Company: Lemuel Morris - Age: 26 - Height: 5' 5" - Born: New York, NY - Trade: Mariner - Enlistment date: 10 Jul 1814 - Place: New York - Period: 1 Year - Discharged on 25 Mar 1815.

Anthmans, Emanuel - Seaman - Company: Frederick Brooks - Age: 20 - Height: 5' 4" - Born: New York, NY - Trade: Seaman - Enlistment date: 19 Feb 1814 - Place: Washington, NC - Period: 1 Year.

American Sea Fencibles in the War of 1812

Antone, Joseph - Seaman - Company: Lemuel Morris - Age: 21 - Height: 5' 2 3/4" - Born: Norfolk, VA - Enlistment date: 14 Jan 1814 - Period: 1 Year - Discharged at Fort Gates, NJ, on 14 Jan 1815.

Archibald, Samuel - Seaman - Company: Frederick Brooks - Age: 21 - Height: 5' 6" - Born: Beaufort, Beaufort County, NC - Trade: Farmer - Enlistment date: 7 Feb 1814 - Place: Washington, NC - Period: 1 Year.

Archibald, William - Seaman - Company: Frederick Brooks - Age: 22 - Height: 5' 9 1/2" - Born: Beaufort, Beaufort County, NC - Trade: Seaman - Enlistment date: 7 Feb 1814 - Place: Washington, NC - Period: 1 Year.

Arnold, Ambrose - Seaman - Company: Frederick Brooks - Age: 20 - Height: 5' 6 1/2" - Born: Beaufort, NC - Trade: Farmer - Enlistment date: 8 Feb 1814 - Place: Washington, NC - Period: 1 Year.

Arnold, George Washington - Seaman - Company: Frederick Brooks - Age: 23 - Height: 5' 9 1/2" - Born: Pitt County, NC - Trade: Farmer - Enlistment date: 15 Feb 1814 - Place: Washington, NC - Period: 1 Year.

Askew, Charles - Seaman - Company: John Gill - Age: 29 - Height: 5' 11" - Born: Baltimore City - Enlistment date: 3 Jan 1814.

Atkins, George - Seaman - Company: Lemuel Morris - Deserted on 14 Jun 1814.

Aull, James - Seaman - Company: John Gill - Age: 21 - Height: 5' 6 1/2" - Born: Washington, DC - Enlistment date: 3 Jan 1814 - Under aged.

Azzalell, Dolphus - Private.

Bachelder, William - Seaman - Company: John Davis - Enlistment date: 22 Jul 1814 - Discharged on 29 Mar 1815.

Bailey, Arthur - Seaman - Company: Frederick Brooks - Age: 25 - Height: 5' 9 3/4" - Born: Woolwich, ME - Trade: Sailor - Enlistment date: 7 Feb 1814 - Place: Washington, NC - Period: 1 Year.

Bailey, Bethel - Gunner.

Bailey, Esma - Seaman - Company: Simmones Bunbury.

Baisard, James - Private.

Baker, Asa H. - Seaman - Company: John Gill - Age: 24 - Height: 5' 7 1/2" - Born: Baltimore City - Enlistment date: 8 Jan 1814.

Baker, Clothier H. - Gunner - Company: Noah Terry - Age: 24 - Height: 5' 7 3/4" - Born: Freetown, Bristol County, MA - Trade: Cooper - Enlistment date: 20 Jul 1814 - Place: Sag Harbor, NY - Period: 1 Year - Discharged at Sag Harbor, NY, on 5 Apr 1815.

Baker, John - Seaman - Company: Noah Terry - Age: 19 - Height: 5' 10" - Born: Southold, NY - Trade: Seaman - Enlistment date: 25 Jul 1814 - Place: Sag Harbor, NY - Period: 1 Year - Discharged at Sag Harbor, NY, on 5 Apr 1815.

Baker, Nathaniel - Seaman - Company: Noah Terry - Died on 23 Feb 1815 from a discharge of a cannon while in the act of ramming a cartridge.

Barbine, Charles - Seaman - Company: Simmones Bunbury.

Barell, Francis - Private.

Barfield, Asa - Seaman - Company: John DuBose - Age: 36 - Height: 5' 9" - Born: Greene, Lenoir County, NC - Trade: Farmer - Enlistment date: 15 Nov 1813 - Place: Willow Grove, SC - Period: 1 Year - Re-enlisted in the 43rd US Infantry.

American Sea Fencibles in the War of 1812

Barker, Peleg - Captain - Company: Peleg Barker - Commissioned as a captain on 11 Jul 1814; discharged on 15 Jun 1815.

Barnal, John - Private.

Barnett, John - Seaman - Company: Lemuel Morris.

Barnhart, Henry - Seaman - Company: William Addison.

Barras, Waratit - Private.

Barren, Francis - Private.

Barrett, Horatio - Seaman - Company: Frederick Brooks - Age: 18 - Height: 5' 2" - Born: Pitt County, NC - Trade: Farmer - Enlistment date: 3 Feb 1814 - Place: Washington, NC - Period: 1 Year.

Barstow, Solomon - Seaman - Company: Peleg Barker - Age: 17 - Height: 5; 3" - Born: Pembroke, Plymouth County, MA - Trade: Mariner - Enlistment date: 7 Nov 1814 - Place: Fairhaven, NY - Period: 1 Year.

Bartlett, William - Private.

Barton, John - Private.

Barwick, William - Seaman - Company: John DuBose - Age: 21 - Height: 5' 10 1/2" - Born: Sumter District, SC - Enlistment date: 29 Dec 1813 - Place: Willow Grove, SC - Period: 1 Year.

Bates, John - Seaman - Company: Peleg Barker - Age: 21 - Height: 5' 7" - Born: Bristol, MA - Trade: Mariner - Enlistment date: 5 Oct 1814 - Place: Fairhaven, MA - Period: 1 Year.

Bates, John - Seaman - Company: Benjamin Pearce - Enlistment date: 13 Sep 1814 - Period: 1 Year - Discharged at Fort Greene, RI, on 27 Mar 1815.

Bates, Joshua T. - Seaman - Company: Peleg Barker - Age: 27 - Height: 5' 7 1/2" - Born: Bristol, MA - Trade: Shipwright - Enlistment date: 11 Nov 1814 - Place: Fairhaven, MA - Period: 1 Year - Pension: Wife Priscilla W. Record, WO-6602, WC-3383; married in 1805 in Plymouth, MA; sailor died on 24 Sep 1870, Mattapoisett, MA - BLW 29237-80-50 & 48395-80-55 - Discharged on 26 Mar 1815.

Baxter, Benjamin - Seaman - Company: Benjamin Pearce - Enlistment date: 7 Nov 1814 - Period: 1 Year - Discharged at Fort Greene, RI, on 27 Mar 1815.

Bayner, Richard - First Lieutenant - Company: Frederick Brooks - Commissioned as a 1st lieutenant on 7 Aug 1813; resigned on 31 Jan 1815.

Beacham, Thomas - Private.

Beachman, Jesse - Seaman - Company: Frederick Brooks - Age: 22 - Height: 5' 4 1/2" - Born: Hyde County, NC - Trade: Farmer - Enlistment date: 12 Mar 1814 - Place: Washington, NC - Period: 1 Year.

Bean, Obadiah - Seaman - Company: John Davis - Enlistment date: 21 Jul 1814 - Discharged on 29 Mar 1815.

Beebe, Edward - Seaman - Company: William Addison.

Belford, Isabel - Seaman - Company: Lemuel Morris.

Bell, Releaser - Seaman - Company: Frederick Brooks - Age: 22 - Height: 6' 2" - Born: Hyde County, NC - Trade: Carpenter - Enlistment date: 1 Mar 1814 - Place: Washington, NC - Period: 1 Year.

Bell, Mathew - Gunner - Company: Frederick Brooks - Age: 21 - Height: 5 10 1/2" - Born: Hyde County,

NC - Trade: Farmer - Enlistment date: 7 Feb 1814 - Place: Washington, NC - Period: 1 Year.

Beloit, William - Seaman - Company: William Addison.

Bennett, Edward - Seaman - Company: Noah Terry - Age: 26 - Height: 5' 5" - Born: Easthampton, NY - Trade: Seaman - Enlistment date: 20 Jul 1814 - Place: Sag Harbor, NY - Period: 1 Year - Discharged at Sag Harbor, NY, on 5 Apr 1815.

Bennett, Freeman - Seaman - Company: Simmones Bunbury.

Bennett, Gamily - Seaman - Company: Noah Terry - Age: 25 - Height: 5' 7" - Born: Easthampton, NY - Trade: Weaver - Enlistment date: 27 Aug 1814 - Place: Sag Harbor, NY - Period: 1 Year - Discharged at Sag Harbor, NY, on 5 Apr 1815.

Bennett, Lester - Seaman - Company: Noah Terry.

Bennett, Samuel - Seaman - Company: Noah Terry - Age: 20 - Height: 5' 10 1/2" - Born: Easthampton, NY - Trade: Seaman - Enlistment date: 21 Jul 1814 - Place: Sag Harbor, NY - Period: 1 Year - Discharged at Sag Harbor, NY, on 5 Apr 1815.

Bennett, William H. - Seaman - Company: John DuBose - Age: 21 - Height: 5' 10 1/2" - Born: Charleston, SC - Enlistment date: 1 Dec 1813 - Place: Willow Grove, SC - Period: 1 Year.

Berkline, Peter - Private.

Berry, Isaac - Seaman - Company: John Davis - Age: 18 - Height: 5' 8 1/2" - Born: Newport, MA - Trade: Farmer - Enlistment date: 19 Sep 1814 - Place: Portsmouth, NH - Period: 1 Year - Discharged on 29 Mar 1815.

Bare, Charles - Seaman - Company: Simmones Bunbury - Pension: Old War IF-12458 Rejected.

Bigelow, William H. - Seaman - Company: Frederick Brooks - Age: 27 - Height: 5' 10 1/2" - Born: Comminuting, MA - Trade: Carpenter - Enlistment date: 3 Feb 1814 - Place: Washington, NC - Period: 1 Year - Pension: Wife Susanna, WO-22742 - BLW 18985-160-50.

Boons, Caleb - Quarter Gunner.

Biseman, David - Gunner - Company: McQueen McIntosh.

Blunt, Joseph - Seaman - Company: Simmones Bunbury.

Bongers, Peter C. - Seaman - Company: William Addison.

Bonner, John - Third Lieutenant - Commissioned as a 3rd lieutenant on 7 Aug 1813; discharged on 1 Jul 1814.

Bosley, Thomas - Servant - Company: Simmones Bunbury - Discharged at Fort McHenry on 24 Mar 1815.

Bowers, Daniel - Seaman - Company: John Gill - Age: 28 - Height: 5' 6" - Born: Baltimore, MD - Enlistment date: 1 Jan 1814 - Place: Baltimore, MD - Period: 1 Year.

Boyd, John - Gunner - Company: Simmones Bunbury - Age: 26 - Height: 5' 5 1/4" - Born: Ireland - Enlistment date: 4 Jan 1815 - Period: 1 Year - Discharged on 24 Mar 1815.

Bradford, Henry - Gunner - Company: Peleg Barker - Age: 28 - Height: 5' 10" - Born: Duxbury, Plymouth County, MA - Trade: Mariner - Enlistment date: 2 Sep 1814 - Place: Fairhaven, MA - Period: 1 Year.

Bradford, William - Seaman - Company: John Gill - Age: 33 - Height: 5' 9" - Born: Salem, Salem County, NJ - Enlistment date: 1 Jan 1814.

Brady, William - Quarter Gunner - Company: Lemuel Morris - Age: 28 - Height: 5' 6" - Born: Philadelphia - Trade: Mariner - Enlistment date: 30 Apr 1814 - Place: New York - Period: 1 Year - Discharged at New York on 25 Mar 1815.

Brant, Solomon - Seaman - Company: Thomas Newell - Age: 30 - Height: 5' 5 1/2" - Born: New Haven, CT - Enlistment date: 12 Feb 1814 - Place: Savannah, GA - Period: 1 Year.

Brantly, James - Private.

Bredging, Andrew - Seaman - Company: Lemuel Morris - Age: 33 - Height: 5' 5 1/4" - Born: Amsterdam - Enlistment date: 24 Jan 1814 - Period: 1 Year - Discharged on 2 Feb 1815.

Bridges, James - Private.

Briggs, Jonathan - Seaman - Company: Benjamin Pearce - Discharged on 24 Dec 1814.

Briggs, Spencer - Second Lieutenant.

Brinkman, John - Seaman - Company: Simmones Bunbury.

Britts, John F. - Seaman - Company: Frederick Brooks - Age: 17 - Height: 5' 3" - Born: Beaufort, NC - Trade: Farmer - Enlistment date: 8 Feb 1814 - Place: Washington, NC - Period: 1 Year.

Brook, William - Seaman - Company: Simmones Bunbury - Age: 45 - Height: 5' 7 1/2" - Born: Annapolis - Enlistment date: 11 Mar 1814 - Period: 1 Year.

Brooks, Frederick - Captain - Company: Frederick Brooks - Commissioned as a captain on 7 Aug 1813; dismissed on 14 Feb 1815.

Brooks, Stephen - Seaman - Company: Frederick Brooks - Age: 20 - Height: 5' 7 1/4" - Born: Currituck, NC - Trade: Seaman - Enlistment date: 25 May 1814 - Place: Washington, NC - Period: 1 Year.

Broughton, John - Seaman - Company: John Davis - Enlistment date: 8 Aug 1814 - Pension: Wife Sarah A. Sherburne, WO-12650, WC-7796; married on 10 Mar 1824 in Portsmouth, NH; seaman died on 3 Mar 1869 in Portsmouth, NH - BLW 96960-40-50; BLW 2779-120-55 - Discharged on 19 Oct 1814.

Brown, Barnabas - Quarter Gunner - Company: John Nicholson - Age: 38 - Height: 6' 1/2" - Born: Bladen, NC - Trade: Farmer - Enlistment date: 3 Feb 1814 - Place: Elizabeth Town, NC - Period: 1 Year - Pension: Land bounty to Ann Brown, widow of Barnabas Brown - BLW 54285-160-55 - Also served in Captain John Nicholson's company.

Brown, Daniel - Gunner - Company: Noah Terry - Age: 37 - Height: 6 1/4" - Born: Southold, NY - Trade: Seaman - Enlistment date: 20 Jul 1814 - Place: Sag Harbor, NY - Period: 1 Year - Discharged at Sag Harbor, NY, on 5 Apr 1815.

Brown, David - Boatswain - Company: Noah Terry - Age: 33 - Height: 5' 9 1/2" - Born: Southold, NY - Trade: Seaman - Enlistment date: 20 Jul 1814 - Place: Sag Harbor, NY - Period: 1 Year - Discharged at Sag Harbor, NY, on 5 Apr 1815.

Brown, Francis - Private.

Brown, James - Servant - Company: Simmones Bunbury - Enlistment date: 1 Nov 1814 - Period: 1 Year - Discharged at Fort McHenry on 24 Mar 1815.

Brown, John - Seaman - Company: Simmones Bunbury - Enlistment date: 26 Jan 1814 - Period: 1 Year - Discharged on 24 Jan 1815.

Brown, John - Seaman - Company: John Nicholson - Age: 26 - Height: 5' 1 1/4" - Born: New York - Trade: Farmey - Enlistment date: 17 Jan 1814 - Place: Elizabeth Town, NC - Period: 1 Year.

Brown, John - Seaman - Company: Lemuel Morris - Age: 22 - Height: 5' 6 1/2" - Born: Ireland - Enlistment date: 23 Nov 1813 - Place: New York - Period: 1 Year - Discharged on 7 Nov 1814 on Surgeon's Certificate of Disability.

Brown, John - Seaman - Company: Simmones Bunbury - Age: 33 - Height: 5' 1/2" - Born: Bucktown, PA - Enlistment date: 24 Dec 1813 - Place: Baltimore - Period: 1 Year - Discharged on 23 Dec 1814.

Brown, Leander - Seaman - Company: Noah Terry - Age: 19 - Height: 5' 6" - Born: Southold, NY - Trade: Seaman - Enlistment date: 31 Aug 1814 - Place: Sag Harbor, NY - Period: 1 Year - Discharged at Sag Harbor, NY, on 5 Apr 1815.

Brown, Noah - Seaman - Company: Frederick Brooks - Age: 19 - Height: 5' 10 1/4" - Born: Beaufort, NC - Trade: Farmer - Enlistment date: 7 Feb 1814 - Place: Washington, NC - Period: 1 Year.

Brown, Orin D. - Seaman - Company: Noah Terry - Age: 20 - Height: 5' 6" - Born: Southold, NY - Trade: Seaman - Enlistment date: 2 Sep 1814 - Place: Sag Harbor, NY - Period: 1 Year - Discharged at Sag Harbor, NY, on 5 Apr 1815.

Brown, Peter - Seaman - Company: Lemuel Morris - Age: 27 - Height: 5' 9" - Born: France - Trade: Mariner - Enlistment date: 22 Jun 1814 - Place: New York - Period: 1 Year - Discharged on 25 Feb 1815.

Brown, Samuel - Seaman - Company: Noah Terry - Age: 19 - Height: 5' 10" - Born: Southampton, NY - Trade: Seaman - Enlistment date: 22 Jul 1814 - Place: Sag Harbor, NY - Period: 1 Year - Discharged at Sag Harbor, NY, on 5 Apr 1815.

Brown, Thomas - Seaman - Company: John Davis - Age: 18 - Height: 5' 1 1/2" - Born: Kittery, ME - Trade: Farmer - Enlistment date: 25 Jul 1814 - Place: Portsmouth, NH - Period: 1 Year - BLW 5251-80-55 - Discharged on 29 Mar 1815.

Brown, Thomas - Seaman - Company: Lemuel Morris - Age: 40 - Height: 5' 3" - Born: Yorkshire, England - Trade: Mariner - Enlistment date: 18 Apr 1814 - Place: New York - Period: 1 Year - Discharged on 25 Mar 1815.

Brown, Thomas - Seaman - Company: John Nicholson - Age: 28 - Height: 5' 7 3/4" - Born: Bladen, NC - Enlistment date: 30 Jan 1814 - Place: Elizabeth Town, NC - Period: 1 Year.

Brown, Thomas - Quarter Gunner - Company: Simmones Bunbury - Age: 33 - Height: 5' 5" - Born: Cecil County, MD - Enlistment date: 5 Nov 1813 - Period: 1 Year - Discharged on 5 Nov 1814.

Brownell, Isaac - Seaman - Company: Benjamin Pearce - Enlistment date: 4 Dec 1814 - Period: 1 Year - Discharged at Fort Greene, RI, on 27 Mar 1815.

Brownell, Lawton - Seaman - Company: Benjamin Pearce - Enlistment date: 9 Nov 1814 - Period: 1 Year - Discharged at Fort Greene, RI, on 27 Mar 1815.

Bryam, Eliab - Gunner - Company: Noah Terry.

Bumpus, Etsiel - Seaman - Company: Benjamin Pearce - Enlistment date: 13 Sep 1814 - Period: 1 Year - Pension: Land bounty to Lucy Bumpus, widow of Etsiel Bumpus - BLW 30349-80-50 - Discharged at Fort Greene, RI, on 26 Mar 1815.

Bumpus, Perez - Seaman - Company: Benjamin Pearce - Enlistment date: 2 Dec 1814 - Period: 1 Year - Discharged at Fort Greene, RI, on 26 Mar 1815.

Bumpus, Warren - Seaman - Company: Benjamin Pearce - Enlistment date: 6 Dec 1814 - Period: 1 Year - Discharged at Fort Greene, RI, on 26 Mar 1815.

Bumpus, Willard - Seaman - Company: Benjamin Pearce - Enlistment date: 13 Sep 1814 - Period: 1 Year - Pension: SO-25214, SC-19117 - BLW 30351-80-50; BLW 16712-80-55 - Discharged at Fort

Greene, RI, on 26 Mar 1815.

Bunbury, Matthew Simmones - Captain - Company: Simmones Bunbury - Commissioned as a captain on 1 Oct 1813; discharged on 15 Jun 1815.

Burnham, Dudley - Seaman - Company: John Davis - Enlistment date: 21 Sep 1814 - Discharged on 29 Mar 1815.

Burrall, Lewis - Private.

Bursley, Samuel C. - Private.

Bussel, George - Gunner - Company: Simmones Bunbury.

Butler, William - Private.

Buzzard, Michael - Seaman - Company: John Gill - Age: 22 - Height: 6' - Born: Baltimore City - Enlistment date: 2 Jan 1814.

Caffrey, John R. - Seaman - Company: John Gill - Enlistment date: 26 Dec 1813.

Calm, John - First Lieutenant - Company: Peleg Barker - Born: Germany - Commissioned as a 1st lieutenant on 22 Jul 1814; discharged on 15 Jun 1815.

Cameron, Alexander - Seaman - Company: Lemuel Morris - Age: 21 - Height: 6' 1" - Born: Batavia, NY - Enlistment date: 16 Dec 1813.

Cammell, Richard - Gunner - Company: Lemuel Morris - Age: 22 - Height: 5' 9 1/2" - Born: Barnstable, MA - Enlistment date: 8 Nov 1813 - Period: 1 Year - Absent since 8 Nov 1814.

Campbell, Richard - Seaman - Company: Lemuel Morris - Age: 27 - Height: 5' 6" - Born: Ireland - Enlistment date: 22 Dec 1813.

Carberry, John - Seaman - Company: Lemuel Morris - Age: 38 - Height: 5' 3 1/2" - Born: New York City - Trade: Mariner - Enlistment date: 23 Apr 1814 - Place: New York - Period: 1 Year - Discharged on 25 Mar 1815 on Surgeon's Certificate of Disability.

Carey, Dennis - Seaman - Company: John Gill - Age: 40 - Height: 5' 7" - Born: Derry, County Derry, Ireland - Enlistment date: 6 Jan 1814.

Carlisle, Edward - Seaman - Company: John Nicholson - Age: 18 - Height: 5' 4" - Born: Columbus, NC - Trade: Farmer - Enlistment date: 14 Feb 1814 - Place: Elizabeth Town, NC - Period: 1 Year.

Carlisle, Jesse - Seaman - Company: John Nicholson.

Carlisle, Robert - Seaman - Company: John Nicholson - Age: 21 - Height: 5' 8" - Born: Columbus, NC - Trade: Farmer - Enlistment date: 14 Feb 1814 - Place: Elizabeth Town, NC - Period: 1 Year.

Carlisle, Robert - Seaman - Company: McQueen McIntosh - Enlistment date: 1 May 1814 - Pension: Wife Sarah A. Falkner, WO-34464, WC-20255; married on 3 Aug 1846 in Russell County, AL; seaman died on 7 Dec 1878 in Choctaw County, AL - BLW 21235-160-50; BLW 30455-80-50 Cancelled - Discharged on 14 Feb 1815.

Carny, John - Seaman - Company: Thomas Newell - Age: 32 - Height: 5' - Born: Savannah, GA - Trade: Sailor - Enlistment date: 27 Jan 1814 - Place: Savannah, GA - Period: 1 Year.

Carr, George - Seaman - Company: John Gill - Age: 29 - Height: 5' 6 1/2" - Born: Baltimore City - Enlistment date: 5 Jan 1814.

Carroll, David - Sergeant - Company: McQueen McIntosh.

Carter, Frederick - Seaman - Company: John Nicholson - Age: 23 - Height: 5' 7" - Born: Duplin, NC -

Trade: Farmer - Enlistment date: 9 Feb 1814 - Place: Elizabeth Town, NC - Period: 1 Year.

Cartwright, Henry N. - Private - Company: John Nicholson.

Cary, Dennis - Seaman - Company: William Addison.

Case, Hyman St. - Private.

Case, Samuel H. - Seaman - Company: Noah Terry - Age: 27 - Height: 5' 8 1/2" - Born: Southampton, Suffolk County, NY - Trade: Seaman - Enlistment date: 1 Sep 1814 - Place: Sag Harbor, NY - Period: 1 Year - Discharged at Sag Harbor, NY, on 5 Apr 1815.

Cason, William - Seaman - Company: Frederick Brooks - Age: 21 - Height: 5' 6 3/4" - Born: Hyde County, NC - Trade: Farmer - Enlistment date: 9 Jun 1814 - Place: Washington, NC - Period: 1 Year.

Caspost, Jeremiah - Seaman - Company: John Gill - Age: 47 - Height: 5' 6" - Born: Philadelphia - Enlistment date: 3 Jan 1814.

Cassady, Andrew - Seaman - Company: Lemuel Morris - Age: 18 - Height: 5' 3" - Born: New York, NY - Trade: Mariner - Enlistment date: 2 Apr 1814 - Place: New York - Period: 1 Year - Discharged on 25 Mar 1815.

Castillaw, Henry - Gunner's Mate - Company: Thomas Newell - Age: 22 - Height: 6' - Born: Savannah, GA - Trade: Sailor - Enlistment date: 27 Jan 1814 - Place: Savannah, GA - Period: 1 Year.

Caswell, Daniel - Seaman - Company: Peleg Barker - Age: 17 - Height: 5' 5" - Born: Pembroke, MA - Trade: Mariner - Enlistment date: 14 Nov 1814 - Place: Fairhaven, MA - Period: 1 Year.

Cathcart, Robert - Seaman - Company: Lemuel Morris - Age: 39 - Height: 5' 8 1/2" - Born: Nantucket, MA - Trade: Mariner - Enlistment date: 20 Jun 1814 - Place: New York - Period: 1 Year - Deserted at Sandy Hook, NJ, on 22 Jan or 8 Feb 1815.

Champean, Jeremiah - Seaman - Company: John Nicholson.

Champeon, James - Private - Company: John Nicholson.

Chaves, Asgad - Seaman - Company: John Nicholson - Age: 21 - Height: 5' 9" - Born: Bladen, NC - Trade: Farmer - Enlistment date: 7 Sep 1814 - Place: Elizabeth Town, NC - Period: 1 Year.

Chaves, John - Seaman - Company: John Nicholson - Age: 23 - Height: 5' 9" - Born: Bladen, NC - Trade: Farmer - Enlistment date: 16 Feb 1814 - Place: Elizabeth Town, NC - Period: 1 Year.

Childes, James - Seaman - Company: John Gill - Age: 39 - Height: 5' 9" - Born: Baltimore - Enlistment date: 29 Dec 1813.

Claridge, Stephen T. - Seaman - Company: John Davis - Age: 18 - Height: 5' 7 /4" - Born: Portsmouth, NH - Enlistment date: 15 Jul 1814 - Period: 1 Year - Discharged on 15 Oct 1814 as a minor, claimed by his father.

Clark, David E. - Seaman - Company: John Davis - Age: 20 - Height: 5' 4 3/4" - Born: Plymouth, Grafton County, NH - Trade: Farmer - Enlistment date: 19 Aug 1814 - Place: Portsmouth, NH - Period: 1 Year - Discharged on 29 Mar 1815.

Clark, James M. - Seaman - Company: William Addison.

Clark, Needham - Private - Company: John Nicholson.

Clark, Peter - Seaman - Company: John Gill - Age: 22 - Height: 5' 7" - Born: Baltimore City - Enlistment date: 10 Jan 1814.

Clarke Jr., Ebenezer - Seaman - Company: Benjamin Pearce - Enlistment date: 17 Oct 1814 - Period: 1

Year - Discharged at Fort Greene, RI, on 27 Mar 1815.

Clarke Sr., Ebenezer - Gunner - Company: Benjamin Pearce - Enlistment date: 26 Aug 1814 - Period: 1 Year - Discharged at Fort Greene, RI, on 27 Mar 1815.

Clarke, Stephen - Quarter Gunner - Company: Benjamin Pearce - Enlistment date: 27 Aug 1814 - Period: 1 Year - Discharged at Fort Greene, RI, on 27 Mar 1815.

Clarke, Thomas L. - Seaman - Company: Frederick Brooks - Age: 24 - Height: 5' 3" - Born: Newbern, NC - Trade: Seaman - Enlistment date: 19 Feb 1814 - Place: Washington, NC - Period: 1 Year.

Clarkson, John - Seaman - Company: Lemuel Morris - Age: 36 - Height: 5' 5 1/2" - Born: Philadelphia - Trade: Mariner - Enlistment date: 20 Jun 1814 - Place: New York - Period: 1 Year - Discharged on 25 Mar 1815.

Clements, George - Boatswain - Company: John DuBose - Age: 24 - Height: 5' 9" - Born: Portsmouth, NH - Enlistment date: 27 Jan 1814 - Place: Willow Grove, SC - Period: 1 Year.

Clements, Peter - Seaman - Company: Lemuel Morris - Age: 45 - Height: 5' 6 1/2' - Born: Albany, NY - Enlistment date: 8 Jan 1814 - Period: 1 Year - Discharged at Fort Gates, NJ, on 8 Jan 1815.

Cline, David - Seaman - Company: McQueen McIntosh.

Clinton, James - Quarter Gunner - Company: Lemuel Morris - Age: 27 - Height: 5' 3 1/2" - Born: Boston - Trade: Mariner - Enlistment date: 29 Apr 1814 - Place: New York - Period: 1 Year - Discharged at New York on 25 Mar 1815.

Coats, Thomas G. - Private.

Cochran, John - Seaman - Company: Lemuel Morris - Age: 24 - Height: 5' 9" - Born: Ireland - Enlistment date: 8 Nov 1813 - Discharged on 18 Jan 1815.

Coffin, Daniel - Seaman - Company: Lemuel Morris - Age: 28 - Height: 5' 5" - Born: Hudson, NY - Trade: Mariner - Enlistment date: 20 Jun 1814 - Place: New York - Period: 1 Year - Discharged on 25 Mar 1815.

Cole, Benjamin - Seaman - Company: Lemuel Morris - Age: 46 - Height: 5' 6 1/4" - Born: England - Enlistment date: 26 Jan 1814 - Period: 1 Year - Discharged on 26 Jan 1815.

Cole, Jacob - Gunner - Company: Frederick Brooks - Age: 38 - Height: 5' 9" - Born: Beaufort, Beaufort County, NC - Trade: Farmer - Enlistment date: 3 Feb 1814 - Place: Washington, NC - Period: 1 Year.

Coleman, Jonas - Private - Company: John Nicholson.

Coleman, Joseph - Seaman - Company: John Nicholson.

Coles, John - Private.

Coles, Thaddeus - Seaman - Company: Noah Terry - Age: 24 - Height: 5' 8" - Born: Southold, Suffolk County, NY - Trade: Seaman - Enlistment date: 1 Aug 1814 - Place: Sag Harbor, NY - Period: 1 Year - Discharged at Sag Harbor, NY, on 5 Apr 1815.

Coles, William - Quarter Gunner - Company: Noah Terry - Age: 24 - Height: 5' 5" - Born: Oyster Bay, Queens County, NY - Trade: Blacksmith - Enlistment date: 25 Jul 1814 - Place: Sag Harbor, NY - Period: 1 Year - Discharged at Sag Harbor, NY, on 5 Apr 1815.

Collins Jr., Samuel - Seaman - Company: Noah Terry - Age: 19 - Height: 5' 5" - Born: Chatham, MA - Trade: Rope maker - Enlistment date: 20 Jul 1814 - Place: Sag Harbor, NY - Period: 1 Year - Discharged at Sag Harbor, NY, on 5 Apr 1815.

Collins, Samuel - Seaman - Company: Noah Terry - Age: 34 - Height: 5' 10" - Born: Providence, RI - Trade: Seaman - Enlistment date: 30 Jul 1814 - Place: Sag Harbor, NY - Period: 1 Y - Discharged at Sag Harbor, NY, on 5 Apr 1815.

Coly, Wright - Seaman - Company: John Nicholson - Age: 23 - Height: 5' 5 1/2" - Born: Sampson, NC - Trade: Farmer - Enlistment date: 14 Feb 1814 - Place: Elizabeth Town, NC - Period: 1 Year.

Concklin, John - Seaman - Company: Simmones Bunbury - Enlistment date: 27 Sep 1814 - Period: 3 Mos.

Conger, David - Gunner - Company: Lemuel Morris - Age: 41 - Height: 5' 7 1/2" - Born: Newark, NJ - Enlistment date: 1 Jan 1814 - Period: 1 Year - Discharged at Sandy Hook, NJ, on 8 Jan 1815.

Congleton, George - Seaman - Company: Frederick Brooks - Age: 18 - Height: 6' 1/2" - Born: Beaufort, NC - Trade: Sailor - Enlistment date: 3 Feb 1814 - Place: Washington, NC - Period: 1 Year.

Connally, James - Seaman - Company: Simmones Bunbury - Age: 23 - Height: 5' 8" - Born: Ireland - Enlistment date: 6 Jul 1814 - Period: 1 Year.

Connally, John - Seaman - Company: Simmones Bunbury - Enlistment date: 6 Jul 1814 - Period: 1 Year - Discharged at Fort McHenry on 24 Mar 1815.

Connaway, Charles - Private.

Conrad, John - Seaman - Company: John Gill - Age: 21 - Height: 5' 8" - Born: New York City - Enlistment date: 4 Jan 1814 - Period: 1 Year - Discharged on 3 Jan 1815.

Cook, Johnson - Seaman - Company: John Nicholson - Age: 21 - Height: 5' 4" - Born: Robeson, NC - Trade: Farmer - Enlistment date: 1 Mar 1814.

Cook, Samuel - Seaman - Company: John Gill - Enlistment date: 23 Dec 1813.

Coomes, John - Gunner - Company: Simmones Bunbury - Age: 30 - Height: 5' 6 3/4" - Born: Trieste, Austria - Enlistment date: 16 Nov 1814 - Discharged on 28 Jul 1815.

Cooper, Elias M. - Seaman - Company: Noah Terry - Age: 38 - Height: 5' 8" - Born: Southampton, Suffolk County, NY - Trade: Cordwainer - Enlistment date: 25 Jul 1814 - Place: Sag Harbor, NY - Period: 1 Year - Discharged at Sag Harbor, NY, on 5 Apr 1815.

Cooper, Hezekiah - Seaman - Company: William Addison.

Cooper, John - Seaman - Company: Simmones Bunbury - Age: 23 - Height: 5' 7 1/4" - Born: Baltimore - Enlistment date: 9 Apr 1814 - Period: 1 Year - Discharged at Fort McHenry on 24 Mar 1815.

Cooper, Joseph - Private - Company: John Nicholson.

Cooper, Josiah - Seaman - Company: John Nicholson - BLW 65237-160-55.

Cooper, Samuel - Seaman - Company: Lemuel Morris - Age: 22 - Height: 5' 6 1/2" - Born: Norfolk, VA - Trade: Mariner - Enlistment date: 16 Jun 1814 - Place: New York - Period: 1 Year - Deserted at Sandy Hook, NJ, on 8 Feb 1815.

Corcheran, John - Seaman - Company: Lemuel Morris - Age: 24 - Height: 5' 9" - Born: Ireland - Enlistment date: 8 Nov 1813 - Discharged on 18 Jan 1815.

Corcoran, John - Seaman - Sentenced to death by General Court-Martial, execution to take place on 4 May 1814 at New Utrecht, NY.

Cordery, Isaac - Seaman - Company: Simmones Bunbury - Age: 22 - Height: 5' 6 1/2" - Born: Salisbury, CT - Enlistment date: 25 Feb 1814 - Period: 1 Year - Discharged on 24 Feb 1815.

Corey, John O. - Quarter Gunner - Company: Noah Terry - Age: 21 - Height: 5' 7" - Born: Southold,

Suffolk County, NY - Trade: Farmer - Enlistment date: 21 Jul 1814 - Place: Sag Harbor, NY - Period: 1 Year - Discharged at Sag Harbor, NY, on 5 Apr 1815.

Corey, Stephen - Seaman - Company: Noah Terry - Age: 20 - Height: 5' 8" - Born: Southold, Suffolk County, NY - Trade: Seaman - Enlistment date: 28 Jul 1814 - Place: Sag Harbor, NY - Period: 1 Year - Discharged at Sag Harbor, NY, on 5 Apr 1815.

Corherson, John - Private.

Cornwall, Hewlett - Seaman - Company: Noah Terry - Age: 21 - Height: 5' 10" - Born: Southampton, Suffolk County, NY - Trade: Seaman - Enlistment date: 3 Aug 1814 - Place: Sag Harbor, NY - Period: 1 Year - Discharged at Sag Harbor, NY, on 5 Apr 1815.

Cottingham, Michael - Waiter.

Cottingham, William - Seaman - Company: Lemuel Morris - Age: 25 - Height: 5' 9" - Born: Ireland - Trade: Mariner - Enlistment date: 3 Mar 1814 - Place: New York - Period: 1 Year - Discharged on 3 Mar 1815.

Couturier, John Julius - First Lieutenant - Commissioned as a 1st lieutenant on 4 Aug 1813; discharged on 15 Jun 1815.

Coward, John - Private.

Cowdery, Isaac - Private.

Craig, John - Seaman - Company: John Gill - Age: 37 - Height: 5' 1/2" - Born: Dorchester County, MD - Enlistment date: 5 Jan 1814 - Period: 1 Year - Deserted on 6 Oct 1815.

Craig, John - Seaman - Company: Lemuel Morris - Age: 35 - Height: 5' 9" - Born: Maryland - Trade: Mariner - Enlistment date: 18 May 1814 - Place: New York - Period: 1 Year - Discharged on 25 Mar 1815.

Crawford, William - Seaman - Company: Frederick Brooks - Age: 18 - Height: 5' 7" - Born: Baltimore - Trade: Sailor - Enlistment date: 8 Feb 1814 - Place: Washington, NC - Period: 1 Year.

Crea, Hugh - Seaman - Company: Simmones Bunbury - Age: 29 - Height: 5' 11" - Born: Baltimore City - Enlistment date: 27 Nov 1813 - Period: 1 Year - Discharged on 26 Nov 1814.

Creamer, James - Seaman - Company: Frederick Brooks - Age: 22 - Height: 5' 8 1/4" - Born: Beaufort, NC - Trade: Farmer - Enlistment date: 28 Jun 1814 - Place: Washington, NC - Period: 1 Year - Pension: Wife Sarah McRay; WO-11819, WC-14425; married on 18 Mar 1814 in Pitt County, NC; seaman died on 19 Mar 1870 in Floyd County, IN - BLW 3580-160-55 - Discharged on 3 Aug 1815.

Cribb, Jonathan - Seaman - Company: John Nicholson - Age: 36 - Height: 5' 11" - Born: Marion, SC - Trade: Sail maker - Enlistment date: 1 May 1814 - Place: Elizabeth Town, NC - Period: 1 Year - Pension: Wife Sarah Smith, WO-40884, WC-31331; married on 29 Apr 1816 in Columbus County, NC; seaman died on 15 Mar 1855 in Appling County, GA - BLW 78190-160-55 - Discharged on 14 Feb 1815.

Cribb, Shadrach - Seaman - Company: John Nicholson - Age: 35 - Height: 5' 7" - Born: Marion, SC - Trade: Farmer - Enlistment date: 23 Jan 1814.

Crocker, James - Seaman - Company: William Addison.

Crowell, Mark S. - Seaman - Company: Noah Terry - Age: 21 - Height: 5' 11" - Born: Southampton, Suffolk County, NY - Trade: Seaman - Enlistment date: 21 Jul 1815 - Place: Sag Harbor, NY - Period: 1 Year - Discharged at Sag Harbor, NY, on 5 Apr 1815.

Crowell, Paul - Seaman - Company: Noah Terry - Age: 37 - Height: 5' 6" - Born: Southampton, Suffolk County, NY - Trade: Seaman - Enlistment date: 3 Aug 1814 - Place: Sag Harbor, NY - Period: 1 Year - Discharged at Sag Harbor, NY, on 5 Apr 1815.

Culberhouse, Charles - Private.

Cullin, Terrance - Seaman - Company: Lemuel Morris - Age: 32 - Height: 5 6 1/4" - Born: Ireland - Enlistment date: 27 Jan 1814 - Period: 1 Year - Discharged on 10 Mar 1815.

Cumming, James J. - First Lieutenant - Commissioned as a 1st lieutenant on 1 Aug 1813; discharged on 15 Jun 1815.

Cummings, Robert - Seaman - Company: Lemuel Morris - Age: 25 - Height: 5' 5 1/2" - Born: New Castle, England - Enlistment date: 15 Jan 1814 - Period: 1 Year - Discharged on 15 Jan 1815.

Curtis, John - Seaman - Company: William Addison.

Curtis, William - Seaman - Company: Simmones Bunbury - Age: 29 - Height: 5' 9 1/4" - Born: Bucktown, Somerset County, MD - Enlistment date: 30 Dec 1813 - Deserted on 2 Jan 1814.

Cushing, Caleb S. - Gunner - Company: John Davis - Age: 25 - Height: 5' 7 1/2" - Born: Hingham, Plymouth County, MA - Trade: Tailor - Enlistment date: 15 Jul 1814 - Place: Portsmouth, NH - Period: 1 Year - Discharged on 29 Mar 1815.

Custis, Watt - Seaman - Company: Lemuel Morris - Age: 26 - Height: 5' 10" - Born: Southberry, MA - Trade: Mariner - Enlistment date: 27 Apr 1814 - Place: New York - Period: 1 Year - Discharged on 25 Mar 1815.

Daily, Henry - Seaman - Company: Noah Terry - Age: 21 - Height: 5' 6 1/2" - Born: Southampton, Suffolk County, NY - Trade: Seaman - Enlistment date: 20 Jul 1814 - Place: Sag Harbor, NY - Period: 1 Year - Discharged at Sag Harbor, NY, on 5 Apr 1815.

Dalton, Edward - Seaman - Company: John Gill - Age: 25 - Height: 5' 8" - Born: Baltimore City - Enlistment date: 11 Jan 1814 - Period: 1 Year.

Dange, Samuel - Seaman - Company: Frederick Brooks - Age: 20 - Height: 5' 8 1/2" - Born: Currituck, NC - Trade: Farmer - Enlistment date: 23 Feb 1814 - Place: Washington, NC - Period: 1 Year.

Daniels, John - Seaman - Company: John Davis - Age: 24 - Height: 5' 6 1/4" - Born: Exeter, Rockingham County, NH - Trade: Farmer - Enlistment date: 5 Aug 1814 - Place: Portsmouth, NH - Period: 1 Year - Discharged on 29 Mar 1815.

Dauel, Simeon - Private.

Daughtry, William - Private - Company: John Nicholson.

David, Turner - Seaman - Company: John Nicholson.

Davis, Caleb - Seaman - Company: John Nicholson - Age: 23 - Height: 5' 10 3/4" - Born: Edgecombe, NC - Trade: Farmer - Enlistment date: 10 Feb 1814 - Place: Elizabeth Town, NC - Period: 1 Year.

Davis, John - Seaman - Company: John Nicholson - Age: 21 - Height: 5' 10 1/2" - Born: Bladen, NC - Trade: Carpenter - Enlistment date: 17 Jan 1814 - Place: Elizabeth Town, NC - Period: 1 Year.

Davis, John S. - Captain - Company: John Davis - Commissioned as a captain on 27 Jun 1814; discharged on 15 Jun 1815.

Davis, Jonathan - Seaman - Company: Noah Terry - Age: 19 - Height: 5' 4" - Born: Southampton, Suffolk County, NY - Trade: Seaman - Enlistment date: 1 Aug 1814 - Place: Sag Harbor, NY - Period: 1 Year - Discharged at Sag Harbor, NY, on 5 Apr 1815.

Davis, Julius - Private - Company: John Nicholson.

Davis, Oliver - Seaman - Company: John Davis - Age: 34 - Height: 5' 6" - Born: City Point, VA - Trade: Mariner - Enlistment date: 24 Jun 1814 - Place: Portsmouth, NH - Period: 1 Year - Discharged on 29 Mar 1815.

Davis, Owen - Seaman - Company: John Davis - Age: 34 - Height: 5' 6" - Born: City Point, VA - Trade: Mariner - Enlistment date: 24 Jun 1814 - Place: Portsmouth, NH - Period: 1 Year.

Davis, Robert - Gunner - Company: John Davis - Age: 21 - Height: 6' 1 3/4" - Born: Cushing, Lincoln County, ME - Trade: Mariner - Enlistment date: 14 Oct 1814 - Place: Portsmouth, NH - Period: 1 Year - Pension: Wife Annie Grafton, SO-504, SC-462; married on 1 Jan 1820 in Friendship, ME; seaman died on 11 May 1877 - BLW 28639-80-50; BLW 48073-80-55 - Discharged on 29 Mar 1815.

Davis, Samuel - Seaman - Company: John Davis - Age: 21 - Height: 5' 9 1/2" - Born: Friendship, Lincoln County, ME - Trade: Mariner - Enlistment date: 14 Oct 1814 - Place: Portsmouth, NH - Period: 1 Year - Pension: Land bounty to Mary Ann Wentworth, former widow of Samuel Davis - BLW 49952-160-55 - Discharged on 29 Mar 1815.

Davis, Turner - Private - Company: John Nicholson.

Davis, William - Seaman - Company: John Nicholson - Age: 43 - Height: 5' 8" - Born: Bladen, NC - Trade: Farmer - Enlistment date: 31 Jan 1814 - Place: Elizabethtown, NC - Period: 1 Year.

Dawson, James - Seaman - Company: John Gill - Age: 24 - Height: 5' 6" - Born: Baltimore or Talbot County, MD - Enlistment date: 2 Jan 1814 - Period: 1 Year.

Day, Cornelius - Seaman - Company: John Gill - Age: 28 - Height: 5' 7 1/2" - Born: Tappan, NY - Enlistment date: 29 Dec 1813.

Dear, Isaac - Seaman - Company: Simmones Bunbury - Age: 27 - Height: 5' 10" - Born: Somerset County, MD - Enlistment date: 23 Dec 1813 - Period: 1 Year - Discharged on 22 Dec 1814.

Dedmont, Edward (Dement) - Seaman - Company: John Gill - Age: 21 - Height: 5' 8" - Born: Charles County, MA - Enlistment date: 13 Jan 1814 - Period: 1 Year.

DeFord, George Washington - Seaman - Company: Benjamin Pearce - Enlistment date: 13 Feb 1815 - Period: 1 Year.

Dellsher, George - Seaman - Company: John Gill - Age: 18 - Height: 5' 6" - Born: Baltimore City - Enlistment date: 9 Jan 1814.

Devon, William J. - Seaman - Company: Simmones Bunbury - Age: 24 - Height: 5' 7 3/4" - Born: New Castle, DE - Enlistment date: 2 Apr 1814 - Period: 1 Year.

Dickerson, James - Seaman - Company: Simmones Bunbury - Age: 50 - Height: 5' 5 1/4" - Born: Philadelphia - Enlistment date: 21 Feb 1814 - Discharged on 7 Mar 1814, unfit for service (over age).

Dickson, James - Gunner - Company: John DuBose - Age: 31 - Height: 5' 10" - Born: Black River, SC - Enlistment date: 12 Dec 1813 - Place: Willow Grove, SC - Period: 1 Year.

Dill, Isaiah - Quarter Gunner - Company: Lemuel Morris - Age: 25 - Height: 5' 7 1/2" - Born: Eastown, MA - Trade: Mariner - Enlistment date: 21 Apr 1814 - Place: New York - Period: 1 Year - Discharged on 25 Mar 1815.

Dillingham, Benjamin - Quarter Gunner - Company: Peleg Barker - Age: 21 - Height: 5' 6" - Born: Fairhaven, Bristol County, MA - Trade: Mariner - Enlistment date: 26 Aug 1814 - Place: Fairhaven, MA - Period: 1 Year.

Dorsey, Henry K. - Seaman - Company: John Gill - Other regiment: 38th US Infantry - Age: 32 - Height: 5' 8 1/2" - Born: Baltimore - Trade: Cabinet maker - Enlistment date: 27 Dec 1813 - Re-enlisted in 38th US Infantry.

Downing, Jonathan - Seaman - Company: John Davis - Other regiment: 21st US Infantry - Age: 26 - Height: 5' 8 3/4" - Born: Greenland, Rockingham County, NH - Trade: Farmer - Enlistment date: 31 Aug 1814 - Place: Portsmouth, NH - Period: 1 Year - Transferred to the 21st US Infantry on 21 Sep 1814; discharged on 20 Mar 1815.

Drear, Joseph - Seaman - Company: Simmones Bunbury - Age: 24 - Height: 5' 10" - Born: Germany - Enlistment date: 7 Jan 1814 - Period: 1 Year - Discharged on 6 Jan 1815.

Drew, Edward - Seaman - Company: Peleg Barker - Age: 32 - Height: 5' 9 1/2" - Born: Kingston, MA - Trade: Mariner - Enlistment date: 10 Dec 1814 - Place: Fairhaven, MA - Period: 1 Year.

Drown, Peter - Gunner - Company: John Davis - Age: 24 - Height: 5' 6" - Born: Pembroke, Rockingham County, NH - Trade: Cabinet maker - Enlistment date: 21 Jul 1814 - Place: Portsmouth, NH - Period: 1 Year - Discharged on 29 Mar 1815.

Drummond, Aaron - Seaman - Company: Lemuel Morris - Enlistment date: 17 Jan 1814 - Period: 1 Year - Discharged on 17 Jan 1815.

DuBose, John - Captain - Company: John DuBose - Born: South Carolina - Commissioned as a captain on 4 Aug 1813; resigned on 20 Sep 1814; recruiting at Willow Grove, SC, from 13 Dec 1813 to 11 Mar 1814.

Duffey, James - Seaman - Company: Lemuel Morris.

Dunlavey, John - Seaman - Company: Lemuel Morris - Age: 28 - Height: 6' 2" - Born: Richmond, VA - Trade: Mariner - Enlistment date: 3 Mar 1814 - Place: New York - Period: 1 Year - Discharged at Sandy Hook, NJ, on 3 Mar 1815.

Dunwell, William - Servant - Company: Lemuel Morris.

Duvall, John - Seaman - Company: Noah Terry - Age: 19 - Height: 5' 10" - Born: Southampton, Suffolk County, NY - Trade: Cordwainer - Enlistment date: 20 Jul 1814 - Place: Sag Harbor, NY - Period: 1 Year - Discharged at Sag Harbor, NY, on 5 Apr 1815.

Easter, James - Private.

Easters, William - Seaman - Company: Frederick Brooks - Age: 19 - Height: 5' 5" - Born: Hyde County, NC - Trade: Seaman - Enlistment date: 2 Mar 1814 - Place: Washington, NC - Period: 1 Year.

Edgecomb, William - Seaman - Company: Lemuel Morris - Age: 27 - Height: 5' 4 1/2" - Born: Marblehead, MA - Enlistment date: 24 Dec 1814 - Period: 1 Year - Discharged at Fort Gates, NJ, on 8 Jan 1815.

Edmonds, Peter - Private.

Edmunds, Abijah - Seaman - Company: Simmones Bunbury - Age: 22 - Height: 5' 8" - Born: Vermont - Enlistment date: 1 Jul 1814 - Period: 1 Year - Deserted on 21 Oct 1814.

Edson, John M. - Seaman - Company: Lemuel Morris - Age: 25 - Height: 5' 8 1/2" - Born: Massachusetts - Enlistment date: 26 Feb 1814 - Deserted on 20 Dec 1814.

Edwards Jr., John - Seaman - Company: Noah Terry - Age: 24 - Height: 5' 7" - Born: Southampton, Suffolk County, NY - Trade: Seaman - Enlistment date: 19 Aug 1814 - Place: Sag Harbor, NY - Period: 1 Year - Discharged at Sag Harbor, NY, on 5 Apr 1815.

Egbert, Daniel - Seaman - Company: Lemuel Morris - Age: 19 - Height: 5' 4 1/4" - Born: New York, NY

- Enlistment date: 22 Dec 1813 - Discharged at Sandy Hook, NY, on 23 Dec 1814; re-enlisted on 17 Jan 1815 for three months in Captain Russell's company, NY Sea Fencibles.

Elden, William - Seaman - Company: Benjamin Pearce - Enlistment date: 9 Dec 1814 - Period: 1 Year - Discharged at Fort Greene, RI, on 27 Mar 1815.

Eldridge, Benjamin G. - Seaman - Company: Noah Terry - Age: 27 - Height: 5' 8" - Born: Southampton, Suffolk County, NY - Trade: Seaman - Enlistment date: 27 Aug 1814 - Place: Sag Harbor, NY - Period: 1 Year - Discharged at Sag Harbor, NY, on 5 Apr 1815.

Elliott, Benjamin - Seaman - Company: John Gill - Enlistment date: 23 Dec 1813.

Elwell, Benjamin - Seaman - Company: John Nicholson - Age: 35 - Height: 5' 10" - Born: Bladen, NC - Trade: Farmer - Enlistment date: 30 Jan 1815 - Place: Elizabeth Town, NC - Period: 1 Year.

Evans, Patrick - Seaman - Company: Simmones Bunbury - Age: 26 - Height: 5' 6" - Born: Dublin, Ireland - Enlistment date: 2 Jun 1814 - Period: 1 Year - Deserted on 5 Nov 1814.

Evins, David - Seaman - Company: William Addison.

Fair, John - Seaman - Company: John Davis - Age: 22 - Height: 5' 4" - Born: Carlow, County Carlow, Ireland - Trade: Farmer - Enlistment date: 24 Jan 1815 - Place: Portsmouth, NH - Period: 1 Year - Discharged on 29 Mar 1815.

Fanning, James - Seaman - Company: Noah Terry - Age: 23 - Height: 5' 8 1/2" - Born: Southampton, Suffolk County, NY - Trade: Joiner - Enlistment date: 30 Aug 1814 - Place: Sag Harbor, NY - Period: 1 Year - Discharged at Sag Harbor, NY, on 5 Apr 1815.

Fargo, Mathew - Seaman - Company: Lemuel Morris - Age: 49 - Height: 5' 6 1/2" - Born: New London, CT.

Farrell, John - Seaman - Company: Lemuel Morris.

Farrell, Peter - Gunner - Company: Lemuel Morris - Age: 37 - Height: 5' 8" - Born: Ireland - Trade: Mariner - Enlistment date: 14 Apr 1814 - Place: New York, NY - Period: 1 Year - Discharged at New York, NY, on 25 Mar 1815.

Farrington, Gilbert - Second Lieutenant - Commissioned as a 2nd lieutenant on 4 Jun 1814; discharged on 15 Jun 1815.

Ferguson, John - Private.

Fernald, Benjamin - Seaman - Company: John Davis - Age: 18 - Height: 5' 8" - Born: Kittery, ME - Trade: Farmer - Enlistment date: 8 Sep 1814 - Place: Portsmouth, NH - Period: 1 Year - Discharged on 29 Mar 1815.

Fernald, Robert - Seaman - Company: John Davis - Age: 18 - Height: 5' 6 3/4" - Born: Kittery, ME - Trade: Sail maker - Enlistment date: 14 Jul 1814 - Place: Portsmouth, NH - Period: 1 Year - BLW 3989-80-55 - Discharged on 29 Mar 1815.

Fernald, William M. - Seaman - Company: John Davis - Age: 18 - Height: 5' 6 1/2" - Born: Kittery, ME - Trade: Cooper - Enlistment date: 12 Jul 1814 - Place: Portsmouth, NH - Period: 1 Year - Pension: Wife Abigail W. Barry, SO-513, SC-553, WO-33197, WC-19446; married on 3 Dec 1820, Boston, MA; seaman died on 6 May 1875, Boston, MA - BLW 40256-80-50, BLW 12880-80-55 - Discharged on 29 Mar 1815.

Fields, Horatio - Private.

Fife, Andrew H. - Gunner - Company: John Gill - Enlistment date: 20 Dec 1813 - Period: 1 Year.

Finch, William - Private.

Fletcher, John - Seaman - Company: Simmones Bunbury - Enlistment date: 2 May 1814 - Period: 1 Year - Discharged at Fort McHenry on 24 Mar 1815.

Flinn, James - Private.

Floyd, Bazil - Seaman - Company: Frederick Brooks - Age: 24 - Height: 5' 8" - Born: Beaufort, Beaufort County, NC - Trade: Farmer - Enlistment date: 6 Feb 1814 - Place: Washington, NC - Period: 1 Year.

Floyd, Miles S. - Seaman - Company: Frederick Brooks - Age: 23 - Height: 5' 11 1/2" - Born: Beaufort County, NC - Trade: Carpenter - Enlistment date: 21 Mar 1814 - Place: Washington, NC - Period: 1 Year.

Forbes, William - Seaman - Company: John Gill - Age: 18 - Height: 5' 2 1/2" - Born: Scotland - Enlistment date: 3 Jan 1814 - Period: 1 Year.

Fordham, Daniel - Gunner - Company: Noah Terry - Age: 24 - Height: 5' 7" - Born: Southampton, Suffolk County, NY - Trade: Hatter - Enlistment date: 20 Jul 1814 - Place: Sag Harbor, NY - Period: 1 Year - BLW 7319-80-55 - Discharged at Sag Harbor, NY, on 5 Apr 1815.

Fordham, James - Gunner - Company: Noah Terry - Age: 21 - Height: 5' 7" - Born: Southampton, Suffolk, County, NY - Trade: Carpenter - Enlistment date: 20 Jul 1814 - Place: Sag Harbor, NY - Period: 1 Year - Pension: Wife Emma N. Harris, SO-10880, SC-6299; married in Apr 1820 in Sag Harbor, NY - BLW 1747-160-50 - Discharged on 3 Apr 1815; also served in Captain John Satterly's Company and Captain David Haynes' Company, NY Militia.

Forsey, Elias P. - Seaman - Company: Simmones Bunbury - Age: 49 - Height: 5' 2 1/2" - Born: Baltimore - Enlistment date: 2 Apr 1814 - Period: 1 Year - Discharged at Fort McHenry on 24 Mar 1815.

Foster, Robert - Seaman - Company: Peleg Barker - Age: 22 - Height: 5' 10" - Born: Kingston, MA - Trade: Mariner - Enlistment date: 13 Oct 1814 - Place: Fairhaven, MA - Period: 1 Year.

Fowler, Nicholas - Seaman - Company: Lemuel Morris - Age: 33 - Height: 5' 5" - Born: Fairfield, CT - Enlistment date: 30 Dec 1814 - Period: 1 Year - Discharged at Fort Gates, NJ, on 8 Jan 1815.

Fowler, William - Gunner - Company: Lemuel Morris - Age: 33 - Height: 5' 7" - Born: Fredericktown, VA - Enlistment date: 9 Nov 1813 - Period: 1 Year - Pension: Navy Minor 1188 - BLW 41218-80-50 - Also served in the U.S. Navy on the US Brig Hornet before enlisting in the US Sea Fencibles and then the US Frigate Guerriere after the war.

Foy, Gregory - First Lieutenant - Company: Simmones Bunbury - Commissioned as a 1st lieutenant on 1 Oct 1813; discharged at Fort McHenry on 15 Jun 1815.

Francis, James - Seaman - Company: Lemuel Morris - Age: 28 - Height: 5' 5 1/4" - Born: Lexington, MA - Enlistment date: 28 Dec 1813 - Period: 1 Year - Deserted on 12 Jun 1814.

Fredericks, Charles - Seaman - Company: Lemuel Morris - Age: 36 - Height: 5' 6 1/2" - Born: Sweden - Enlistment date: 27 Jan 1814 - Period: 1 Year - Discharged on 27 Jan 1815.

Fredericks, George - Private.

Fredericks, Paul - Seaman - Company: Simmones Bunbury - Enlistment date: 23 May 1814 - Period: 1 Year - Discharged at Fort McHenry on 24 Mar 1815.

Freeman, John - Quarter Gunner - Company: Noah Terry - Age: 23 - Height: 6' 1/2" - Born: Philadelphia - Trade: Cordwainer - Enlistment date: 20 Jul 1814 - Place: Sag Harbor, NY - Period: 1 Year - Pension: Wife Martha Strong, SO-30, SC-4511; married in Aug 1826 in Philadelphia, PA; seaman died prior to 12 Mar 1883 - BLW 41813-160-55 - Discharged at Sag Harbor, NY, on 5 Apr 1815.

Freeman, William - Seaman - Company: John Gill - Age: 38 - Height: 5' 3" - Born: Talbot County, MD -

Enlistment date: 7 Jan 1814 - Period: 1 Year.

Fulcher, Francis - Seaman - Company: Frederick Brooks - Age: 25 - Height: 5' 9" - Born: Carver County, NC - Trade: Carpenter - Enlistment date: 12 Mar 1814 - Place: Washington, NC - Period: 1 Year.

Fuller, Solomon - Private.

Gann, John - Seaman - Company: Noah Terry - Age: 18 - Height: 5' 8" - Born: Southampton, Suffolk County, NY - Trade: Seaman - Enlistment date: 30 Jul 1814 - Place: Sag Harbor, NY - Period: 1 Year - Discharged at Sag Harbor, NY, on 5 Apr 1815.

Gardiner, Jeremiah - Quarter Gunner - Company: Noah Terry - Age: 29 - Height: 5' 8" - Born: Southampton, Suffolk County, NY - Trade: Rope maker - Enlistment date: 20 Jul 1814 - Place: Sag Harbor, NY - Period: 1 Year - Discharged at Sag Harbor, NY, on 5 Apr 1815.

Gardiner, Samuel - Seaman - Company: John Gill - Age: 35 - Height: 5' 7 1/2" - Born: Baltimore - Enlistment date: 1 Jan 1814 - Period: 1 Year.

Gardiner, Thomas - Seaman - Company: Lemuel Morris - Enlistment date: 13 Aug 1814.

Gautier, Francis - Seaman - Company: Frederick Brooks - Age: 24 - Height: 5' 6 3/4" - Born: Beaufort, NC - Trade: Farmer - Enlistment date: 7 Feb 1814 - Place: Washington, NC - Period: 1 Year.

Gautier, Joseph B. - Seaman - Company: Frederick Brooks - Age: 22 - Height: 5' 8" - Born: Beaufort County, NC - Trade: Carpenter - Enlistment date: 12 Feb 1814 - Place: Washington, NC - Period: 1 Year - Pension: Wife Frances M., WO-33808.

Gay, Isaac J. - Seaman - Company: John Davis - Age: 21 - Height: 5' 7 1/2" - Born: Cushing, Lincoln County, ME - Trade: Farmer - Enlistment date: 14 Oct 1814 - Place: Portsmouth, NH - Period: 1 Year - Discharged on 29 Mar 1815.

Gazzam, William - Seaman - Company: Lemuel Morris - Age: 24 - Height: 5' 7 1/2" - Born: Pittsburgh, PA - Enlistment date: 9 Nov 1813 - Period: 1 Year - Discharged at Fort Gates, NJ, on 17 Jan 1815.

George, Ezekiel C. - Seaman - Company: John Gill - Age: 22 - Height: 5' 10" - Born: Baltimore - Enlistment date: 10 Jan 1814 - Period: 1 Year.

George, James - Seaman - Company: John Gill - Age: 20 - Height: 5' 5" - Born: Baltimore - Enlistment date: 11 Jan 1814 - Period: 1 Year.

German, Robert - Seaman - Company: Noah Terry - Age: 34 - Height: 5' 1" - Born: New York, NY - Trade: Seaman - Enlistment date: 21 Jul 1814 - Place: Sag Harbor, NY - Period: 1 Year - Discharged at Sag Harbor, NY, on 5 Apr 1815.

Gibbs, Christian - Private.

Gibbs, Joshua - Quarter Gunner - Company: Benjamin Pearce - Enlistment date: 16 Oct 1814 - Period: 1 Year - Discharged on 27 Mar 1815.

Gibbs, Levin - Seaman - Company: John Gill - Age: 25 - Height: 5' 8" - Born: Worcester County, MD - Enlistment date: 8 Jan 1814 - Place: Baltimore.

Gibbs, Pardon - Private.

Gibbs, Seth - Private.

Gibson, Thomas - Seaman - Company: Simmones Bunbury - Age: 27 - Height: 5' 9 1/4" - Born: Baltimore - Enlistment date: 17 Feb 1814 - Period: 1 Year - Discharged at Fort McHenry on 16 Feb 1815.

Gilbert, Martin - Private.

Gill, John - Captain - Company: John Gill - Commissioned as a captain on 25 Nov 1813; negatived by the U.S. Senate 17 Mar 1814.

Gilman, John - Waiter.

Gilman, Nehemiah - Waiter - Company: John Davis - Waiter to Lieutenant Adams.

Gilmore, Stephen - Seaman - Company: Lemuel Morris - Age: 25 - Height: 5' 7 1/2" - Born: New York, NY - Trade: Mariner - Enlistment date: 30 Apr 1814 - Place: New York - Period: 1 Year - Discharged on 25 Mar 1815.

Gladge, Thomas - Private.

Gleason, John - Seaman - Company: John Gill - Enlistment date: 21 Jan 1814 - Pension: Wife Catharine Firsch, WO-21885, WC-20993; married on 10 Sep 1820 in York, PA; seaman died on 30 Nov 1844 in York, PA - BLW 2697-160-50 - Discharged on 28 Feb 1814.

Glenn, James - Seaman - Company: Simmones Bunbury - Age: 42 - Height: 5' 7 1/2" - Born: Ireland - Enlistment date: 9 Jan 1815 - Period: 1 Year - Discharged at Fort McHenry on 24 Mar 1815.

Glover, Charles G. - Gunner - Company: Peleg Barker - Age: 19 - Height: 5' 8" - Born: Nantucket, MA - Trade: Mariner - Enlistment date: 20 Aug 1814 - Place: Fairhaven, MA - Period: 1 Year.

Glover, Joseph - Seaman - Company: John Nicholson - Age: 21 - Height: 5' 11" - Born: Robison, NC - Trade: Cooper - Enlistment date: 2 Mar 1814 - Place: Elizabeth Town, NC - Period: 1 Year.

Goldson, John - Private.

Goodmanson, Peter - Seaman - Company: Simmones Bunbury - Age: 37 - Height: 5' 7 1/2" - Born: Hamburg, Europe - Enlistment date: 23 Dec 1813 - Period: 1 Year - Discharged at Fort McHenry on 24 Mar 1815.

Goodwin, Jesse - Private.

Gordon, George - Seaman - Company: Lemuel Morris - Age: 38 - Height: 5' 5" - Born: New London, CT - Enlistment date: 24 Nov 1813 - Period: 1 Year.

Gordon, John - Seaman - Company: William Addison.

Gorsuch, Gerard - Third Lieutenant - Company: Simmones Bunbury - Commissioned as a 3rd lieutenant on 1 Oct 1813; discharged on 15 Jun 1815.

Gosswel, Anthony - Seaman - Company: John Gill - Age: 20 - Height: 6' - Born: Baltimore - Enlistment date: 12 Jan 1814 - Period: 1 Year - Taken away by civil law on 28 Feb 1814.

Grant, John - Private - Company: John Nicholson.

Gray, Gabriel - Seaman - Company: McQueen McIntosh - BLW 21169-160-50 - Also served in Captain John Nicholson's company.

Gray, James - Seaman - Company: Noah Terry - Age: 28 - Height: 5' 9 1/4" - Born: New York, NY - Trade: Seaman - Enlistment date: 1 Aug 1814 - Place: Sag Harbor, NY - Period: 1 Year - Discharged at Sag Harbor, NY, on 5 Apr 1815.

Green, Anson - Private.

Green, Anthony - Seaman - Company: Simmones Bunbury - Enlistment date: 17 Jan 1814 - Period: 1 Year - Discharged at Baltimore on 16 Jan 1815.

Green, George W. - First Lieutenant - Commissioned as a 1st lieutenant on 17 Mar 1814; discharged on 15 Jun 1815.

Green, John - Seaman - Sentenced to death by General Court-Martial, execution to take place on 4 May 1814 at New Utrecht.

Green, John - Seaman - Company: Simmones Bunbury - Age: 39 - Height: 5' 6" - Born: Ireland - Enlistment date: 16 Apr 1814 - Period: 1 Year - Died at Fort McHenry on 23 Oct 1814.

Green, Joseph H. - Seaman - Company: Frederick Brooks - Age: 23 - Height: 5' 7 1/2" - Born: Craven County, NC - Trade: Carpenter - Enlistment date: 30 May 1814 - Place: Washington, NC - Period: 1 Year - Pension: Wife Agnes Galvin, SO-23646, SC-19187; married on 25 Oct 1821 in Hancock County, GA; died about 1872 - BLW 25372-160-50 - Discharged on 2 Aug 1815.

Green, Robert - Seaman - Company: Simmones Bunbury - Age: 37 - Height: 5' 5" - Born: Charles County, MA - Enlistment date: 13 Jan 1814 - Period: 1 Year - Discharged on 13 Jan 1815.

Greene, Georgia - Private.

Greene, John - Seaman - Company: Lemuel Morris - Age: 25 - Height: 5' 8" - Born: Philipstown, NY - Enlistment date: 30 Dec 1813 - Period: 1 Year.

Greenough, Francis L. - Seaman - Company: John Davis - Age: 19 - Height: 5' 6" - Born: Bedford, MA - Trade: Tobacconist - Enlistment date: 22 Jul 1814 - Place: Portsmouth, NH - Period: 1Year - Discharged on 29 Mar 1815.

Griffin, Henry - Seaman - Company: Frederick Brooks - Age: 18 - Height: 6' - Born: Craven County, NC - Trade: Farmer - Enlistment date: 29 Jul 1814 - Place: Washington, NC - Period: 1 Year.

Griffin, James - Seaman - Company: John DuBose - Age: 34 - Height: 5' 5" - Born: Pitts, NC - Enlistment date: 29 Jan 1814 - Place: Willow Grove, SC - Period: 1 Year - Pension: Wife Sarah Wilkinson, WO-2844, WC-1391; married in 1805 in Chardon, SC; seaman died in 1830 in Charleston, SC - BLW 80742-160-55 - Discharged on 29 Jan 1815.

Griffin, Mrs. - Washerwoman - Company: John DuBose - Recruiting Report, Willow Grove, SC, 11 Jun 1814.

Griffiths, Thomas B. - Seaman - Company: William Addison.

Grimes, Mercer - Seaman - Company: John Nicholson - Age: 26 - Height: 5' 6 1/2" - Born: Norfolk, VA - Trade: Farmer - Enlistment date: 9 Feb 1814 - Place: Elizabeth Town, NC - Period: 1 Year.

Guess, Thomas - Seaman - Company: Simmones Bunbury - Other regiment: 38th US Infantry - Age: 21 - Height: 5' 5" - Born: Calvert County, MD - Trade: Cooper - Enlistment date: 21 Oct 1814 - Period: 1 Year - BLW 234-320-14 - Re-enlisted in 38th US Infantry on 26 Jan 1815 for the war; discharged at Baltimore on 6 Apr 1815.

Guinott, John - Seaman - Company: John DuBose - Age: 28 - Height: 6' 4" - Born: Rochelle, France - Enlistment date: 15 Nov 1813 - Place: Willow Grove, SC - Period: 1 Year.

Hadley, Joseph - Seaman - Company: William Addison.

Hague, Joseph - Servant.

Haley, William - Seaman - Company: John Davis - Age: 22 - Height: 5' 5" - Born: Portsmouth, NH - Trade: Sail maker - Enlistment date: 24 Jun 1814 - Place: Portsmouth, NH - Period: 1 Year - Discharged on 29 Mar 1815.

Hall Jr., Caleb - Seaman - Company: John Gill - Enlistment date: 29 Feb 1814 - Period: 1 Year - Discharged on 6 Jun 1814.

Hall, Caleb - Seaman - Company: Simmones Bunbury - Age: 21 - Height: 5' 11" - Born: Baltimore - Enlistment date: 1 Mar 1814 - Period: 1 Year.

Hall, George - Gunner.

Hall, Joseph - Seaman - Company: Simmones Bunbury - Age: 42 - Height: 5' 5 1/2" - Born: Baltimore - Enlistment date: 17 Feb 1814 - Period: 1 Year - Discharged on 16 Feb 1815.

Hall, Thomas - Seaman - Company: Lemuel Morris - Age: 26 - Height: 5' 6" - Born: New York, NY - Enlistment date: 29 Jan 1814 - Period: 1 Year - Discharged on 25 Mar 1815.

Hallock, Sydney C. - Gunner - Company: Noah Terry - Age: 21 - Height: 5' 9 1/2" - Born: Southold, Suffolk County, NY - Trade: Joiner - Enlistment date: 22 Jul 1814 - Place: Sag Harbor, NY - Period: 1 Year.

Hambley, James - Seaman - Company: John Gill - Age: 24 - Height: 5' 4" - Born: Baltimore City - Enlistment date: 11 Jan 1814 - Period: 1 Year.

Hamilton, Benjamin - Seaman - Company: Noah Terry - Age: 24 - Height: 5' 5 1/2" - Born: Chatham, MA - Trade: Seaman - Enlistment date: 16 Aug 1814 - Place: Sag Harbor, NY - Period: 1 Year - Discharged at Sag Harbor, NY, on 5 Apr 1815.

Hamilton, John - Seaman - Company: William Addison.

Hanalin, Patrick - Gunner - Company: William Addison - Enlistment date: 23 Dec 1813 - Period: 1 Year - Pension: Old War IF-25141.

Hands, Ephraim - Seaman - Company: William Addison.

Hands, Nicholas - Seaman - Company: William Addison.

Hane Jr., Jacob - Seaman - Company: William Addison.

Hanes, James - Seaman - Company: Simmones Bunbury - Enlistment date: 1 Mar 1814 - Period: 1 Year - Discharged on 31 Jan 1815.

Hannis, Thomas - Seaman - Company: Noah Terry - Enlistment date: 29 Sep 1914.

Hanson, William - Quarter Gunner - Company: John Gill - Age: 38 - Height: 5' 6 1/2" - Born: Baltimore - Enlistment date: 28 Dec 1813 - Period: 1 Year.

Harden, Jesse - Private - Pension: Land bounty to Mary Harden, widow of Jesse Harden - BLW 5926-160-55.

Hardison, Henry - Seaman - Company: Frederick Brooks - Age: 19 - Height: 5' 8" - Born: Pitt County, NC - Trade: Farmer - Enlistment date: 17 Mar 1814 - Place: Washington, NC - Period: 1 Year.

Hardwick, John - Third Lieutenant - Commissioned as a 3rd lieutenant on 4 Aug 1813; discharged on 15 Jun 1815.

Hardy, Arthur - Seaman - Company: John Nicholson - Age: 20 - Height: 5' 10" - Born: Marion, SC - Trade: Farmer - Enlistment date: 20 Jan 1814 - Place: Elizabeth Town, NC - Period: 1 Year - Also served in Captain John DuBose's Company.

Hardy, Hitch E. - Gunner.

Hargrove, Britton - Seaman - Company: McQueen McIntosh - Pension: Land bounty to Ann Hargrove, wife of Britton Hargrove - BLW 71897-160-55 - Also served in Captain John Nicholson's company.

Harper, Peter - Gunner - Company: Peleg Barker - Age: 40 - Height: 5' 9 1/2" - Born: Aberdeen, Scotland - Enlistment date: 12 Nov 1814 - Place: Fairhaven, MA - Period: 1 Year.

Harrington, Robert - Gunner - Company: Simmones Bunbury - Enlistment date: 30 Jan 1815 - Period: 1 Year - Discharged at Fort McHenry on 24 Mar 1815.

American Sea Fencibles in the War of 1812

Harris, Elijah - Private.

Harris, John - Seaman - Company: William Addison.

Harris, Thomas R. - Seaman - Company: Noah Terry - Age: 21 - Height: 5' 11 1/4" - Born: Southold, Suffolk County, NY - Trade: Seaman - Enlistment date: 25 Aug 1814 - Place: Sag Harbor, NY - Period: 1 Year - Discharged at Sag Harbor, NY, on 5 Apr 1815.

Hash, Peter - Seaman - Company: Simmones Bunbury.

Haskett, William - Seaman - Company: Lemuel Morris - Age: 24 - Height: 5' 4 3/4" - Born: Harpswell, MA - Enlistment date: 5 Feb 1814 - Period: 1 Year - Discharged at Sandy Hook, NJ, on 5 Feb 1815.

Hastings, Thomas - Seaman - Company: John Davis - Age: 22 - Height: 6' 2" - Born: Dover, NH - Trade: Farmer - Enlistment date: 5 Oct 1814 - Place: Portsmouth, NH - Period: 1 Year - Discharged on 29 Mar 1815.

Hatch, John - Private.

Havens, Jacob - Seaman - Company: Noah Terry - Age: 31 - Height: 5' 10" - Born: Shelter Island, Suffolk County, NY - Trade: Seaman - Enlistment date: 20 Jul 1814 - Place: Sag Harbor, NY - Period: 1 Year - Discharged at Sag Harbor, NY, on 5 Apr 1815.

Havens, Nathaniel T. - Seaman - Company: Noah Terry - Age: 35 - Height: 5' 4" - Born: Shelter Island, Suffolk County, NY - Trade: Tailor - Enlistment date: 1 Aug 1814 - Place: Sag Harbor, NY - Period: 1 Year - Discharged at Sag Harbor, NY, on 5 Apr 1815.

Havens, William H. - Seaman - Company: Noah Terry - Age: 20 - Height: 5' 9" - Born: Shelter Island, Suffolk County, NY - Trade: Seaman - Enlistment date: 20 Jul 1814 - Place: Sag Harbor, NY - Period: 1 Year - Discharged at Sag Harbor, NY, on 5 Apr 1815.

Hawkins, Isaac - Private.

Hayes, Adam - Seaman - Company: Simmones Bunbury - Age: 40 - Height: 5' 10" - Born: Hartford, CT - Enlistment date: 5 Mar 1814 - Period: 1 Year - Discharged at Fort McHenry on 24 Mar 1815.

Haynes, David - Captain - Company: Noah Terry.

Healey, Joseph - Private.

Hedges, Jared - Seaman - Company: Noah Terry - Age: 44 - Height: 5' 10" - Born: Southampton, Suffolk County, NY - Trade: Weaver - Enlistment date: 1 Aug 1814 - Place: Sag Harbor, NY - Period: 1 Year - Discharged at Sag Harbor, NY, on 5 Apr 1815.

Hefers, William (Hofires) - Seaman - Company: John Davis - Age: 22 - Height: 5' 5" - Born: Waldsborough, Lincoln County, NH or ME - Trade: Farmer - Enlistment date: 19 Dec 1814 - Place: Portsmouth, NH - Period: 1 Year - Discharged on 29 Mar 1815.

Henry, John - Seaman - Company: John Gill - Age: 19 - Height: 5' 6" - Born: New York City - Enlistment date: 15 Jan 1814 - Place: Baltimore - Period: 1 Year - BLW 29292-160-55 - Discharged on 14 Jan 1815.

Herd, Samuel - Servant - Company: Simmones Bunbury.

Hewitt, John - Gunner - Company: Thomas Newell - Age: 35 - Height: 4' 8" - Born: Portsmouth, NH - Trade: Sailor - Enlistment date: 27 Jan 1814 - Place: Savannah, GA - Period: 1 Year - Discharged on 9 Feb 1815.

Hicks, William - Seaman - Company: Noah Terry - Age: 19 - Height: 5' 5" - Born: Shelter Island, Suffolk County, NY - Trade: Seaman - Enlistment date: 3 Aug 1814 - Place: Sag Harbor, NY - Period: 1

Year - Discharged at Sag Harbor, NY, on 5 Apr 1815.

Higby, Noah - Gunner - Company: Simmones Bunbury - Age: 42 - Height: 5' 7" - Born: Middletown, MD - Enlistment date: 8 Dec 1813 - Period: 1 Year - Discharged on 13 Oct 1814.

Hill, Daniel - Seaman - Company: Lemuel Morris - Age: 29 - Height: 5' 11 3/4" - Born: Portsmouth, NH - Enlistment date: 28 Dec 1813 - Period: 1 Year.

Hill, Isaiah - Gunner.

Hill, James - Seaman - Company: Thomas Newell - Age: 30 - Height: 6' - Born: Savannah, GA - Trade: Sailor - Enlistment date: 27 Jan 1814 - Place: Savannah, GA - Period: 1 Year - Discharged on 9 Feb 1815.

Hill, John P. - Seaman - Company: John Davis - Age: 22 - Height: 5' 9 1/2" - Born: Epson, Rockingham County, NH - Trade: Blacksmith - Enlistment date: 11 Jul 1814 - Place: Portsmouth, NH - Period: 1 Year - Discharged on 29 Mar 1815.

Hill, John S. - Seaman - Company: John Davis - Age: 40 - Height: 5' 8" - Born: Lee, Rockingham County, NH - Trade: Farmer - Enlistment date: Aug 1814 - Place: Portsmouth, NH - Period: 1 Year - Discharged on 29 Mar 1815.

Hill, John T. - Seaman - Company: John Davis - Age: 23 - Height: 5' 10 1/4" - Born: Portsmouth, NH - Trade: Joiner - Enlistment date: 3 Aug 1814 - Place: Portsmouth, NH - Period: 1 Year - Discharged on 29 Mar 1815.

Hill, Joshua B. - Seaman - Company: John Davis - Age: 21 - Height: 5' 9" - Born: Portsmouth, NH - Trade: Joiner - Enlistment date: 4 Aug 1814 - Place: Portsmouth, NH - Period: 1 Year - Discharged on 29 Mar 1815.

Hitch, Hardy E. - Gunner - Company: Peleg Barker - Age: 39 - Height: 5' 8" - Born: New Bedford, MA - Trade: Sail maker - Enlistment date: 11 Aug 1814 - Place: Fairhaven, MA - Period: 1 Year - Discharged on 5 Apr 1815.

Hogland, Peter - Private.

Hollings, John - Seaman - Company: William Addison.

Holmes, Peter - Seaman - Company: Benjamin Pearce - Enlistment date: 18 Oct 1814 - Period: 1 Year - Discharged on 27 Mar 1815.

Homes, Henry - Seaman - Company: Frederick Brooks - Age: 17 - Height: 5' 4" - Born: Beaufort County, NC - Trade: Farmer - Enlistment date: 4 Jul 1814 - Place: Washington, NC - Period: 1 Year.

Hooper, Erastus - Seaman - Company: Simmones Bunbury - Age: 24 - Height: 5' 8 1/2" - Born: Massachusetts - Enlistment date: 8 Mar 1814 - Period: 1 Year - Deserted on 18 Apr 1814.

Hopkins, Isaac - Seaman - Company: Benjamin Pearce - Enlistment date: 1 Oct 1814 - Period: 1 Year - Discharged at Fort Greene, RI, on 27 Mar 1815.

Horn, John - Seaman - Company: John Davis - Age: 21 - Height: 5' 6 1/2" - Born: Friendship, Lincoln County, ME - Trade: Mariner - Enlistment date: 14 Oct 1814 - Place: Portsmouth, NH - Period: 1 Year - Discharged on 29 Mar 1815.

Horner, Henry - Private.

Hornsby, William - Private.

Horton, Alexander - Private.

Howell, Usher H. - Seaman - Company: Noah Terry - Age: 28 - Height: 5' 5" - Born: Riverhead, Suffolk

County, NY - Trade: Seaman - Enlistment date: 30 Jul 1814 - Place: Sag Harbor, NY - Period: 1 Year - Discharged at Sag Harbor, NY, on 5 Apr 1815.

Howell, William - Seaman - Company: Noah Terry - Age: 35 - Height: 5' 7" - Born: Southampton, Suffolk County, NY - Trade: Cordwainer - Enlistment date: 22 Jul 1814 - Place: Sag Harbor, NY - Period: 1 Year - Discharged at Sag Harbor, NY, on 5 Apr 1815.

Hubbard, Elias - Private.

Hubbard, Joseph - Private.

Hughes, John - Seaman - Company: Lemuel Morris - Age: 18 - Height: 5' 1/4" - Born: England - Trade: Mariner - Enlistment date: 18 Aug 1814 - Place: New York - Period: 1 Year - Discharged on 25 Mar 1815.

Hull, Daniel - Seaman - Company: Benjamin Pearce - Enlistment date: 15 Feb 1815 - Period: 1 Year - Discharged on 27 Mar 1815.

Hunter, William - Seaman - Company: Lemuel Morris - Age: 34 - Height: 5' 8 1/2" - Born: North Castle, NY - Enlistment date: 9 Nov 1813.

Hush, Peter - Seaman - Company: Simmones Bunbury - Enlistment date: 31 Jan 1814 - Period: 1 Year - Discharged at Fort McHenry on 24 Mar 1815.

Hussey, Peter - Quarter Gunner - Company: Peleg Barker - Age: 18 - Height: 5' 7" - Born: Nantucket, MA - Trade: Mariner - Enlistment date: 13 Sep 1814 - Place: Fairhaven, MA - Period: 1 Year.

Hutchings, Samuel - Seaman - Company: John Davis - Age: 24 - Height: 5' 7" - Born: Kittery, ME - Trade: Mariner - Enlistment date: 14 Sep 1814 - Place: Portsmouth, NH - Period: 1 Year - Discharged on 29 Mar 1815.

Hutton, James - Seaman - Company: Lemuel Morris - Age: 36 - Height: 5' 5 1/2" - Born: New York, NY - Trade: Mariner - Enlistment date: 9 Apr 1814 - Period: 1 Year - Discharged on 25 Mar 1815.

Hutton, Samuel - Seaman - Company: John Gill - Enlistment date: 21 Dec 1813.

Hutton, William - Seaman - Company: John Gill - Age: 26 - Height: 5' 10 1/2" - Born: Queen Anne, MD - Enlistment date: 27 Dec 1813 - Period: 1 Year.

Hybert, Augustus - Seaman - Company: Lemuel Morris - Age: 18 - Height: 5' 5" - Born: New York, NY - Trade: Mariner - Enlistment date: 2 May 1814 - Period: 1 Year - Discharged on 25 Mar 1815.

Hyde, Charles - Quarter Gunner - Company: Lemuel Morris - Enlistment date: 22 Jan 1814 - Period: 1 Year - Discharged on 24 Jan 815.

Ing, John - Seaman - Company: William Addison.

Ireland, John - Private.

Irvin, James - Seaman - Company: John Nicholson - Age: 25 - Height: 5' 3 3/4" - Born: Bladen, NC - Trade: Farmer - Enlistment date: 31 Jan 1814 - Place: Elizabeth Town, NC - Period: 1 Year.

Irwin, William - Seaman - Company: Lemuel Morris - Age: 25 - Height: 5' 7 3/4" - Born: Ireland - Trade: Mariner - Enlistment date: 29 Jul 1814 - Place: New York - Period: 1 Year - BLW 19487-80-55 - Discharged at New York on 25 Mar 1815.

Isaacs, John M. - Third Lieutenant - Company: Noah Terry - Commissioned as a 3rd lieutenant on 2 Jul 1814; discharged on 15 Jun 1815.

Ivy, Reuben - Private - Possibly served in the 18th US Infantry for 18 months.

Izer, Joshua - Seaman - Company: John Gill - Age: 20 - Height: 5' 6" - Born: Baltimore City - Enlistment date: 12 Jan 1814.

Jackson, James - Seaman - Company: John Nicholson - Age: 23 - Height: 5' 11" - Born: Bladen, NC - Trade: Shoemaker - Enlistment date: 29 Jan 1814 - Place: Elizabeth Town, NC - Period: 1 Year - Also served in Captain John DuBose's Company.

Jackson, John - Seaman - Company: Simmones Bunbury - Enlistment date: 7 Jun 1814 - Period: 1 Year - Discharged at Fort McHenry on 29 Jan 1815; enlisted as a substitute for Caleb Hall.

James, James - Private.

James, William - Seaman - Company: John Gill - Age: 29 - Height: 5' 6 1/2" - Born: Baltimore - Enlistment date: 1 Jan 1814 - Period: 1 Year.

Jane, John - Seaman - Company: Noah Terry - Deserted at Sag Harbor, NY, on 24 Oct 1814.

Jannett, John - Gunner - Company: John DuBose - Age: 28 - Height: 5' 4" - Born: Rochelle, France - Enlistment date: 15 Nov 1813 - Place: Willow Grove, SC - Period: 1 Year.

Jeffrey, James - Seaman - Company: John Davis - Age: 18 - Height: 5' 10 1/2" - Born: Kittery, ME - Trade: Mariner - Enlistment date: 30 Jul 1814 - Place: Portsmouth, NH - Period: 1 Year - Discharged on 29 Mar 1815.

Jenkins Jr., Thomas - Quarter Gunner - Company: John Davis - Age: 24 - Height: 5' 9" - Born: Kittery, ME - Trade: Mariner - Enlistment date: 30 Jul 1814 - Place: Portsmouth, NH - Period: 1 Year - Discharged on 29 Mar 1815.

Jenkins, Henry - Seaman - Company: John Nicholson.

Jenkins, John - Seaman - Company: John Davis - Age: 22 - Height: 5' 8 1/2" - Born: Kittery, ME - Trade: Mariner - Enlistment date: 17 Oct 1814 - Place: Portsmouth, NH - Period: 1 Year - Pension: Land bounty to Elizabeth Jenkins, widow of John Jenkins - BLW 21373-80-55 - Discharged on 29 Mar 1815.

Jessup, Frederick - Seaman - Company: Noah Terry - Age: 21 - Height: 6' 2" - Born: Shelter Island, Suffolk County, NY - Trade: Rope maker - Enlistment date: 20 Jul 1814 - Place: Sag Harbor, NY - Period: 1 Year - Discharged at Sag Harbor, NY, on 5 Apr 1815.

Jester, Ebenezer - Seaman - Company: Frederick Brooks - Age: 24 - Height: 6' 1/2" - Born: Hyde, Hyde County, NC - Trade: Carpenter - Enlistment date: 5 Feb 1814 - Place: Washington, NC - Period: 1 Year.

Jeter, Jesse - Private.

Johnson, George - Seaman - Company: Thomas Newell - Place: Savannah, GA - Discharged at Savannah, GA, on 12 Feb 1814.

Johnson, Henry - Seaman - Company: Simmones Bunbury - Age: 35 - Height: 5' 8" - Born: Little York, PA - Enlistment date: 6 Jan 1814 - Period: 1 Year.

Johnson, James - Boatswain - Company: Thomas Newell - Age: 30 - Height: 5' 5" - Born: Savannah, GA - Trade: Sailor - Enlistment date: 27 Jan 1814 - Place: Savannah, GA - Period: 1 Year - Discharged on 9 Feb 1815.

Johnson, John - Seaman - Company: Thomas Newell - Age: 27 - Height: 5' 8" - Born: Savannah, GA - Trade: Sailor - Enlistment date: 23 Feb 1814 - Place: Savannah, GA - Period: 1 Year - Died on 7 Nov 1814.

Johnson, John - Seaman - Company: Lemuel Morris - Age: 23 - Height: 5' 8 1/2" - Born: New York, NY - Enlistment date: 19 May 1814 - Period: 1 Year - Pension: Old War IF-28585 - Discharged on 4 Oct or 4 Nov 1814 on Surgeon's Certificate of Disability.

Johnson, John - Seaman - Company: Lemuel Morris - Age: 25 - Height: 5' 7 1/2" - Born: Baltimore - Enlistment date: 16 Jun 1814 - Period: 1 Year - Deserted on 20 Dec 1814.

Johnson, John - Seaman - Company: John Davis - Age: 21 - Height: 5' 6" - Born: Alexandria, DC - Trade: Mariner - Enlistment date: 14 Sep 1814 - Place: Portsmouth, NH - Period: 1 Year - Discharged on 29 Mar 1815.

Johnson, John - Seaman - Company: Lemuel Morris - Age: 27 - Height: 5' 9" - Born: Ireland - Enlistment date: 23 Jan 1814 - Period: 1 Year - Missing since 28 Jan 1814.

Johnson, Michael - Private.

Johnson, Tuhail - Seaman - Company: Thomas Newell - Age: 23 - Height: 6' - Born: Savannah, GA - Trade: Sailor - Enlistment date: 28 Feb 1814 - Place: Savannah, GA - Period: 1 Year.

Jonas, Jones - Seaman - Company: John Nicholson.

Jones, Charles - Seaman - Company: Thomas Newell - Age: 25 - Height: 5' 7" - Born: Newport, RI - Trade: Sailor - Enlistment date: 2 Feb 1814 - Place: Savannah, GA - Period: 1 Year - Died on 11 Sep 1814.

Jones, Henry B. - Third Lieutenant - Company: Thomas Newell - Age: 23 - Height: 6' - Born: Wilms Island, GA - Trade: Sailor - Commissioned as a 3rd lieutenant on 1 Aug 1813; resigned on 1 Jul 1814; recruiting at Savannah, GA, January through March 1814.

Jones, James - Seaman - Company: Lemuel Morris - Age: 19 - Height: 5' 8 1/4" - Born: Baltimore - Enlistment date: 2 Nov 1814 - Discharged on 4 Feb 1815.

Jones, John - Gunner.

Jones, Jonathan - Seaman - Company: John Nicholson - Age: 22 - Height: 5' 8" - Born: Green, NC - Trade: Farmer - Enlistment date: 14 Feb 1814.

Jones, Lewis - Seaman - Company: Noah Terry.

Jones, Samuel - Private.

Jones, Shadrick - Seaman - Company: John Nicholson - Age: 30 - Height: 5' 4" - Born: Green, NC - Trade: Farmer - Enlistment date: 4 Feb 1814 - Place: Elizabeth Town, NC - Period: 1 Year - Also served in Captain John DuBose's Company.

Jones, Thomas - Seaman - Company: Lemuel Morris - Age: 26 - Height: 5' 8 3/4" - Born: New Haven, CT - Enlistment date: 24 Dec 1813 - Period: 1 Year.

Jones, William - Gunner - Company: Lemuel Morris - Enlistment date: 19 Jan 1814 - Period: 1 Year - Discharged on 19 Jan 1815.

Jones, William - Seaman - Company: Simmones Bunbury - Age: 23 - Height: 5' 7" - Born: Norfolk, VA - Enlistment date: 2 Nov 1813 - Period: 1 Year - Discharged on 2 Nov 1814.

Jordan, John - Seaman - Company: John Nicholson - Age: 40 - Height: 5' 7" - Born: Pitt, NC - Trade: Farmer - Enlistment date: 7 Feb 1814 - Place: Elizabeth Town, NC - Period: 1 Year.

Jordan, Samuel - Quarter Gunner - Company: William Addison - Pension: Old War IF-25186.

Kane, John - Gunner - Company: John Davis - Age: 23 - Height: 5' 11 1/2" - Born: Barnstead, Strafford County, NH - Trade: Chair maker - Enlistment date: 4 Jul 1814 - Place: Portsmouth, NH - Period: 1 Year - Discharged on 29 Mar 1815.

Kane Jr., Jacob - Seaman - Company: John Gill - Age: 29 - Height: 6' - Born: Fredericktown, MD -

Enlistment date: 8 Feb 1814 - Period: 1 Year.

Keen, Joseph - Seaman - Company: John Davis - Age: 18 - Height: 5' 2" - Born: Kittery, ME - Trade: Farmer - Enlistment date: 19 Aug 1814 - Place: Portsmouth, NH - Period: 1 Year - Discharged on 29 Mar 1815.

Keeny, John - Private.

Kellyhan, Cornelius - Seaman - Company: John Nicholson - Age: 21 - Height: 5' 6 3/4" - Born: Bladen, NC - Trade: Cooper - Enlistment date: 16 Feb 1814.

Kellyhan, Neil - Private - Company: John Nicholson.

Kenny, John - Seaman - Company: Lemuel Morris - Age: 44 - Height: 5' 7 1/2" - Born: New London, CT - Enlistment date: 24 Dec 1813 - Period: 1 Year.

Keplinger, George - Seaman - Company: John Gill - Age: 19 - Height: 5' 11" - Born: Baltimore City - Enlistment date: 4 Jan 1814 - Period: 1 Year.

Kerswell, Joshua - Seaman - Company: John Davis - Age: 40 - Height: 5' 10" - Born: Kittery, ME - Trade: Mariner - Enlistment date: 30 Jul 1814 - Place: Portsmouth, NH - Period: 1 Year - Discharged on 29 Mar 1815.

Kildue, George M. - Seaman - Company: Simmones Bunbury - Enlistment date: 6 Feb 1815 - Period: 1 Year - Missing at Fort McHenry on 28 Feb 1815.

Kim, John - Seaman - Company: John Gill - Age: 22 - Height: 5' 6" - Born: Baltimore - Enlistment date: 1 Jan 1814 - Period: 1 Year.

Kincaid, Myers - Seaman - Company: Simmones Bunbury - Age: 26 - Height: 5' 5 1/4" - Born: Nottingham, MD - Enlistment date: 12 Feb 1814 - Period: 1 Year - Discharged on 11 Feb 1815.

King, Clark - Seaman - Company: Noah Terry - Age: 19 - Height: 5' 9" - Born: Easthampton, Suffolk County, NY - Trade: Carpenter - Enlistment date: 20 Jul 1814 - Place: Sag Harbor, NY - Period: 1 Year - Discharged at Sag Harbor, NY, on 5 Apr 1815.

King, David - Seaman - Company: Noah Terry - Age: 24 - Height: 5' 8 1/2" - Born: Easthampton, Suffolk County, NY - Trade: Weaver - Enlistment date: 30 Jul 1814 - Place: Sag Harbor, NY - Period: 1 Year - Discharged at Sag Harbor, NY, on 5 Apr 1815.

King, Hubbard - Seaman - Company: Noah Terry - Age: 22 - Height: 5' 7 1/2" - Born: Easthampton, Suffolk County, NY - Trade: Seaman - Enlistment date: 17 Aug 1814 - Place: Sag Harbor, NY - Period: 1 Year - Discharged at Sag Harbor, NY, on 5 Apr 1815.

King, John - Seaman - Company: Noah Terry - Age: 18 - Height: 5' 6 1/2" - Born: Easthampton, Suffolk County, NY - Trade: Seaman - Enlistment date: 20 Jul 1814 - Place: Sag Harbor, NY - Period: 1 Year - Discharged at Sag Harbor, NY, on 5 Apr 1815.

King, Richard - Seaman - Company: Noah Terry - Age: 24 - Height: 5' 6" - Born: Easthampton, Suffolk County, NY - Trade: Seaman - Enlistment date: 20 Jul 1814 - Place: Sag Harbor, NY - Period: 1 Year - Discharged at Sag Harbor, NY, on 5 Apr 1815.

King, Robert R. - Seaman - Company: John Davis - Age: 24 - Height: 5' 6 1/4" - Born: Summerset, Summerset County, NJ - Trade: Currier - Enlistment date: 29 Aug 1814 - Place: Portsmouth, NH - Period: 1 Year - Discharged on 29 Mar 1815; previous served in the 3rd US Artillery in Captain James Romayne's Company for 18 months.

Knower, John - Seaman - Company: Simmones Bunbury - Age: 40 - Height: 5' 8 1/4" - Born: Middletown, MD - Enlistment date: 9 Dec 1813 - Period: 1 Year - Died at Baltimore on 26 Dec 1813.

Knowles, Benjamin - Private.

Koog, Martin - Seaman - Company: Simmones Bunbury - Enlistment date: 27 Jan 1814 - Period: 1 Year - Discharged on 26 Jan 1815.

Kulgars, Dirk - Seaman - Company: Peleg Barker - Age: 25 - Height: 5' 6" - Born: Duxbury, Plymouth County, MA - Trade: Mariner - Enlistment date: 13 Oct 1814 - Place: Fairhaven, MA - Period: 1 Year.

Lacey, William - Seaman - Company: William Addison.

Landsdown, Edward - Seaman - Company: Lemuel Morris - Age: 39 - Height: 5' 3 1/2" - Born: New York City - Trade: Mariner - Enlistment date: 25 Apr 1814 - Place: New York - Period: 1 Year - Discharged at New York on 25 Mar 1815.

Langdon, David - Seaman - Company: Noah Terry - Enlistment date: 9 Apr 1812 - Period: 5 Years - Deserted on 2 Nov 1814.

Lardy, Arthur - Seaman - Company: John Nicholson - Pension: SO-15624, SC-17362 - Also served in 1st Lieutenant Robert Lytles' Detachment, U.S. Sea Fencibles.

Laridon, William - Seaman - Company: Benjamin Pearce - Enlistment date: 9 Sep 1814 - Period: 1 Year - Discharged on 27 Mar 1815.

Lawrence, Elisha - Seaman - Company: Lemuel Morris - Age: 18 - Height: 5' 3 3/4" - Born: Middletown, CT - Enlistment date: 7 Jan 1814 - Period: 1 Year - Discharged on 8 Jan 1815.

Lawrence, James - Boatswain - Company: Simmones Bunbury - Age: 24 - Height: 5' 4 1/2" - Born: New Haven, CT - Enlistment date: 29 Oct 1813 - Period: 1 Year - Discharged at Fort McHenry on 24 Mar 1815.

Leach, B. W. - Seaman - Company: Thomas Newell - Age: 22 - Height: 5' 3" - Born: Savannah, GA - Trade: Sailor - Enlistment date: 27 Jan 1814 - Place: Savannah, GA - Period: 1 Year.

Leach, Benjamin - Quarter Gunner.

Leavitt, Thomas - Seaman - Company: John Davis - Age: 30 - Height: 5' 11" - Born: Exeter, Rockingham County, NH - Trade: Chair maker - Enlistment date: 5 Sep 1814 - Place: Portsmouth, NH - Period: 1 Year - Pension: Land bounty to Sally Leavitt, widow of Thomas Leavitt - BLW 8946-80-55 - Discharged on 29 Mar 1815.

Lee, Joseph - Seaman - Company: McQueen McIntosh - Pension: SO-27080, SC-21067 - Also served in Captain Frederick Brook's Company, NC Militia.

Leek, Abraham - Seaman - Company: Noah Terry - Age: 23 - Height: 5' 1" - Born: Southampton, Suffolk County, NY - Trade: Cordwainer - Enlistment date: 21 Jul 1814 - Place: Sag Harbor, NY - Period: 1 Year - Discharged at Sag Harbor, NY, on 5 Apr 1815.

Leek, Jacob - Gunner - Company: Noah Terry - Age: 29 - Height: 5' 8" - Born: Easthampton, Suffolk County, NY - Trade: Seaman - Enlistment date: 20 Jul 1814 - Place: Sag Harbor, NY - Period: 1 Year - Discharged at Sag Harbor, NY, on 5 Apr 1815.

Leonard, Ichabod - Gunner - Company: Benjamin Pearce - Enlistment date: 8 Dec 1814 - Period: 1 Year - Discharged on 27 Mar 1815.

Lester, Nathaniel - Seaman - Company: Noah Terry - Age: 42 - Height: 5' 8" - Born: Easthampton, Suffolk County, NY - Trade: Seaman - Enlistment date: 1 Aug 1814 - Place: Sag Harbor, NY - Period: 1 Year - Discharged at Sag Harbor, NY, on 5 Apr 1815.

Lester, Platt - Seaman - Company: Lemuel Morris - Age: 25 - Height: 5' 5 3/4" - Born: New York City -

Enlistment date: 30 Dec 1813 - Period: 1 Year - Discharged on 17 Jan 1815.

Lester, Smith - Quarter Gunner - Company: Lemuel Morris - Age: 23 - Height: 5' 6 1/4" - Enlistment date: 4 Nov 1813 - Period: 1 Year - Discharged on 4 Nov 1814.

Letts, Thomas - Seaman - Company: John Gill - Age: 22 - Height: 5' 10" - Born: Perth Amboy, NJ - Enlistment date: 13 Jan 1814 - Place: Maryland - Period: 1 Year - Deserted on 9 Jun 1814.

Lewis, Barall - Seaman - Company: William Addison.

Lewis, Thomas - Seaman - Company: Noah Terry - Age: 19 - Height: 5' 8" - Born: Brookhaven, NY - Trade: Seaman - Enlistment date: 1 Aug 1814 - Place: Sag Harbor, NY - Period: 1 Year - Discharged at Sag Harbor, NY, on 5 Apr 1815.

L'Hommeron, Jabez F. - Seaman - Company: Noah Terry - Age: 21 - Height: 5' 7 1/2" - Born: Southampton, Suffolk County, NY - Trade: Joiner - Enlistment date: 18 Aug 1814 - Place: Sag Harbor, NY - Period: 1 Year - Discharged at Sag Harbor, NY, on 5 Apr 1815.

Liddle, Archibald - Gunner - Company: Lemuel Morris - Age: 23 - Height: 5' 4 1/2" - Born: Portland, MA - Trade: Mariner - Enlistment date: 20 Jun 1814 - Place: New York - Period: 1 Year - Discharged at New York on 25 Mar 1815.

Limmer, Terrance - Seaman - Company: John Gill - Age: 28 - Height: 5' 7" - Born: Nore, County Nore, Ireland - Enlistment date: 4 Jan 1814 - Period: 1 Year.

Linnenburger, John - Seaman - Company: Simmones Bunbury - Age: 21 - Height: 5' 6" - Born: Maryland - Enlistment date: 26 Oct 1814 - Period: 1 Year.

Linsey, Joseph - Seaman - Company: Simmones Bunbury - Age: 34 - Height: 5' 6 1/2" - Born: Ireland - Enlistment date: 31 Aug 1814 - Period: 1 Year - Discharged at Fort McHenry on 24 Mar 1815.

Linton, James - Seaman - Company: Frederick Brooks - Age: 23 - Height: 5' 8" - Born: Hyde County, NC - Trade: Mariner - Enlistment date: 12 Mar 1814 - Place: Washington, NC - Period: 1 Year.

Litig, George - Private.

Livermore, John - Private.

Lives, William G. - Seaman - Company: Simmones Bunbury - Age: 20 - Height: 5' 9" - Born: New York - Enlistment date: 3 Jan 1814 - Period: 1 Year - Died on 16 Jul 1814.

Locey, William - Seaman - Company: John Gill - Age: 27 - Height: 5' 11 1/2" - Born: Hartford, CT - Enlistment date: 11 Feb 1814 - Place: Baltimore - Period: 1 Year.

Loftes, Samuel - Private.

Loper, Abraham - Seaman - Company: Noah Terry - Age: 30 - Height: 5' 6" - Born: Easthampton, Suffolk County, NY - Trade: Carpenter - Enlistment date: 1 Aug 1814 - Place: Sag Harbor, NY - Period: 1 Year - Discharged at Sag Harbor, NY, on 5 Apr 1815.

Loper, Amos - Seaman - Company: Noah Terry - Age: 44 - Height: 5' 9" - Born: Easthampton, Suffolk County, NY - Trade: Seaman - Enlistment date: 22 Aug 1814 - Place: Sag Harbor, NY - Period: 1 Year - Discharged at Sag Harbor, NY, on 5 Apr 1815.

Lough, Michael - Seaman - Company: Simmones Bunbury - Age: 22 - Height: 5' 11" - Born: Ireland - Enlistment date: 25 Oct 1814 - Period: 1 Year - Discharged at Fort McHenry on 24 Mar 1815.

Love, John - Seaman - Company: John Nicholson - Age: 18 - Height: 5' 4" - Born: Columbus, NC - Trade: Farmer - Enlistment date: 14 Feb 1814 - Period: 1 Year.

Lovering, Nathaniel - Seaman - Company: John Davis - Age: 19 - Height: 5' 5" - Born: Exeter,

Rockingham County, NH - Trade: Farmer - Enlistment date: 25 Jul 1814 - Place: Exeter, NH - Period: 1 Year - Discharged on 29 Mar 1815.

Luile, William - Gunner - Company: John DuBose - Age: 38 - Height: 5' 6" - Born: Glasgow, Scotland - Enlistment date: 16 Dec 1813 - Place: Willow Grove, SC - Period: 1 Year.

Luley, Charles - Seaman - Company: Simmones Bunbury - Enlistment date: 18 Jul 1814 - Period: 1 Year.

Lunt, Amos - Seaman - Company: John Davis - Age: 24 - Height: 5' 5" - Born: Kennebec, MA - Enlistment date: 6 Aug 1814 - Period: 1 Year - Deserted on 14 Aug 1814.

Lytle, Robert - First Lieutenant - Company: John Nicholson - Born: North Carolina - Commissioned as a 2nd lieutenant on 1 Aug 1813; promoted to 1st lieutenant on 5 Apr 1815; discharged on 15 Jun 1815.

MacAarel, John - Private.

MacKerall, John - Seaman - Company: Lemuel Morris - Age: 34 - Height: 5' 8 3/4" - Born: Albany, NY - Trade: Mariner - Enlistment date: 11 Apr 1814 - Place: New York - Period: 1 Year - Discharged on 25 Mar 1815.

MacKey, Robert - Seaman - Company: William Addison.

MacLenman, Moran - Seaman - Company: John Nicholson - Age: 23 - Height: 5' 6" - Born: Bladen, NC - Trade: Shoemaker - Enlistment date: 31 Jan 1814 - Period: 1 Year.

MacMillan, Neill - Seaman - Company: John Nicholson - Age: 23 - Height: 5' 7" - Born: Bladen, NC - Trade: Farmer - Enlistment date: 23 Jan 1814 - Period: 1 Year.

Magee, James - Seaman - Company: John Davis - Age: 26 - Height: 5' 5 1/4" - Born: Newton, Ireland - Trade: Mariner - Enlistment date: 24 Jan 1815 - Place: Portsmouth, NH - Period: 1 Year - Discharged on 29 Mar 1815.

Mahoney, Miles - Seaman - Company: Frederick Brooks - Age: 29 - Height: 5' 8" - Born: Philadelphia - Trade: Seaman - Enlistment date: 7 Feb 1814 - Place: Washington, NC - Period: 1 Year.

Maling, Thomas (Mating) - Gunner - Company: John Davis - Age: 39 - Height: 5' 2 1/2" - Born: Portland, DM - Trade: Mariner - Enlistment date: 23 Jun 1814 - Place: Portsmouth, NH - Period: 1 Year - Discharged on 29 Mar 1815.

Manson, Henry - Seaman - Company: Simmones Bunbury - Age: 27 - Height: 5' 6 1/2" - Born: Denmark - Enlistment date: 28 Dec 1813 - Discharged on 22 Dec 1814.

Maples, Charles - Seaman - Company: Lemuel Morris - Age: 32 - Height: 5' 11" - Born: New York City - Trade: Mariner - Enlistment date: 10 Jul 1814 - Place: New York - Period: 1 Year - Discharged on 25 Mar 1815.

Marley, John - Seaman - Company: Lemuel Morris - Age: 35 - Height: 5' 6 3/4" - Born: Ireland - Trade: Mariner - Enlistment date: 4 Mar 1814 - Place: New York - Period: 1 Year - Discharged on 25 Mar 1815.

Marley, John - Captain - Company: John Marley.

Marsh, Phineas - Seaman - Company: Lemuel Morris - Age: 18 - Height: 5' 5 1/2" - Born: Rahway, NY - Enlistment date: 16 Nov 1813 - Period: 1 Year - Discharged at Fort Gates, NJ, on 16 Nov 1814.

Marshall, Elias - Seaman - Company: Simmones Bunbury - Enlistment date: 31 Jan 1814 - Period: 1 Year - Discharged on 30 Jan 1815.

Martin, Martin - Private - Company: John Nicholson.

Mason, Edward S. - Seaman - Company: Frederick Brooks - Age: 23 - Height: 5' 3" - Born: Hyde County, NC - Trade: Farmer - Enlistment date: 3 Mar 1814 - Place: Washington, NC - Period: 1 Year.

Mason, Henry - Seaman - Company: Simmones Bunbury - Pension: Old War IF-25245 - Died on 27 Nov 1832.

Masters, Joseph - Seaman - Company: Frederick Brooks - Age: 22 - Height: 5' 8" - Born: Craven, Craven County, NC - Trade: Carpenter - Enlistment date: 3 Feb 1814 - Place: Washington, NC - Period: 1 Year.

Mathews, Neil - Seaman - Company: John Nicholson - Age: 28 - Height: 5' 8" - Born: Scotland - Trade: Tailor - Enlistment date: 17 Jan 1814 - Place: Elizabeth Town, NC - Period: 1 Year.

Mathis, Jesse - Quarter Gunner.

May, Joseph S. - Seaman - Company: Frederick Brooks - Age: 21 - Height: 5' 8" - Born: Martin County, NC - Trade: Farmer - Enlistment date: 1 Mar 1814 - Place: Washington, NC - Period: 1 Year.

McCally, Neal - Private.

McCasstler, Jacob - Private.

McClanning, Benjamin - Private.

McComas, Charles - Seaman - Company: William Addison.

McCoy, Alexander - Seaman - Company: William Addison.

McCracken, John - Quarter Gunner - Company: William Addison.

McCrackin, James - Seaman - Company: John Gill - Age: 25 - Height: 5' 8" - Born: Baltimore - Enlistment date: 10 Jan 1814 - Place: Baltimore.

McCrumin, Roderick - Seaman - Company: John Nicholson - Age: 30 - Height: 6' - Born: Cumberland, NC - Trade: Brick layer - Enlistment date: 1 Feb 1814 - Place: Elizabeth Town, NC - Period: 1 Year.

McDonald, Daniel - Seaman - Company: John Nicholson - Age: 23 - Height: 5' 2" - Born: Scotland - Trade: Farmer - Enlistment date: 16 Feb 1814 - Place: Elizabeth Town, NC - Period: 1 Year.

McDonald, John - Seaman - Company: John Nicholson - Age: 32 - Height: 5' 5 1/2" - Born: Scotland - Trade: Farmer - Enlistment date: 27 Jan 1814 - Place: Elizabeth Town, NC - Period: 1 Year - Also served in Captain Breath's Company, NY Sea Fencibles, at Convention Blockhouse Number 2, Utrecht, NY, for 3 months before enlisting in the U.S. Sea Fencibles.

McDonald, Samuel - Gunner - Company: John Gill - Enlistment date: 21 Dec 1813 - Period: 1 Year.

McDowell, Thomas - Seaman - Company: John Gill - Age: 21 - Height: 5' 8 3/4" - Born: Baltimore City - Enlistment date: 28 Dec 1813 - Period: 1 Year.

McFatter, Alexander - Seaman - Company: John Nicholson - Age: 21 - Height: 5' 5 1/2" - Born: Robeson, NC - Trade: Farmer - Enlistment date: 5 Feb 1814 - Place: Elizabeth Town, NC - Period: 1 Year.

McFatter, Nivan - Seaman - Company: John Nicholson - Age: 25 - Height: 5' 8" - Born: Bladen, NC - Trade: Farmer - Enlistment date: 29 Jan 1814 - Period: 1 Year.

McGill, Dubao - Private.

McGran, John - Seaman - Company: Noah Terry - Discharged at Sag Harbor, NY, on 20 Oct 1814, unfit for duty.

McIntosh, Lacklan - Second Lieutenant.

McIntosh, McQueen - Captain - Company: McQueen McIntosh - Born: Georgia - Commissioned as a captain on 22 Nov 1814; discharged on 15 Jun 1815.

McIntyre, Daniel - Seaman - Company: John Nicholson - Age: 31 - Height: 5' 5 3/4" - Born: Moore, NC - Trade: Laborer - Enlistment date: 17 Jan 1814 - Place: Elizabeth Town, NC - Period: 1 Year.

McKeal, Richard - Seaman - Company: Frederick Brooks - Age: 18 - Height: 5' 4 1/2" - Born: Beaufort County, NC - Trade: Farmer - Enlistment date: 21 Mar 1814 - Place: Washington, NC - Period: 1 Year.

McKnell, John - Seaman - Company: Lemuel Morris.

McKnight, Lewis - Seaman - Company: Simmones Bunbury - Enlistment date: 31 Jan 1814 - Period: 1 Year - Discharged on 30 Jan 1815.

McLellan, Moran - Seaman - Company: John Nicholson.

McLellan, Samuel - Seaman - Company: John Nicholson - Age: 25 - Height: 5' 6" - Born: Bladen, NC - Trade: Shoemaker - Enlistment date: 23 Jan 1814 - Place: Elizabeth Town, NC - Period: 1 Year.

McMahone, James - Seaman - Company: Frederick Brooks - Age: 22 - Height: 5' 6" - Born: Beaufort, NC - Trade: Printer - Enlistment date: 24 Feb 1814 - Place: Washington, NC - Period: 1 Year.

McMillen, Alexander - Seaman - Company: Lemuel Morris - Age: 33 - Height: 5' 5 1/2" - Born: Scotland - Enlistment date: 28 Dec 1813.

McNeil, Samuel - Seaman - Company: Lemuel Morris - Age: 19 - Height: 5' 5 1/4" - Born: New York City - Trade: Mariner - Enlistment date: 30 Apr 1814 - Place: New York - Period: 1 Year - Discharged on 25 Mar 1815.

McNeill, Neil - Seaman - Company: John Nicholson - Age: 21 - Height: 5' 10" - Born: Cumberland, NC - Trade: Blacksmith - Enlistment date: 24 Feb 1814 - Place: Elizabeth Town, NC - Period: 1 Year - Also served in Captain John DuBose's Company.

McNeir, George - Third Lieutenant - Company: William Addison - Commissioned as a 3rd lieutenant on 17 Mar 1813; resigned on 24 Nov 814.

McPherson, John - Second Lieutenant - Company: Lemuel Morris - Commissioned as a 2nd lieutenant on 9 Jul 1814; discharged on 15 Jun 1815.

McRae, Alexander - Seaman - Company: John Nicholson - Age: 19 - Height: 5' 7" - Born: Cumberland, NC - Trade: Clerk - Enlistment date: 20 Jan 1814 - Place: Elizabeth Town, NC - Period: 1 Year.

Meeks, James P. - Seaman - Company: Simmones Bunbury - Age: 21 - Height: 5' 7" - Born: Baltimore - Enlistment date: 31 Jan 1814 - Period: 1 Year - Discharged at Fort McHenry on 2 Jan 1815.

Merrick, Joseph - Seaman - Company: Lemuel Morris - Age: 18 - Height: 5' 2 3/4" - Born: Newburyport, MA - Enlistment date: 25 Jan 1814 - Period: 1 Year - Discharged on 25 Jan 1815.

Mestler, Coonrod - Seaman - Company: William Addison.

Miles, James - Private.

Miles, John - Seaman - Company: William Addison.

Miller, Abraham - Seaman - Company: Lemuel Morris - Age: 20 - Height: 5' 9" - Born: New York City - Enlistment date: 22 Dec 1813 - Period: 1 Year - Discharged at New York on 22 Dec 1814.

Miller, Eleazer - Seaman - Company: Noah Terry - Age: 27 - Height: 5' 10" - Born: Southampton, Suffolk County, NY - Trade: Cordwainer - Enlistment date: 20 Jul 1814 - Place: Sag Harbor, NY - Period: 1 Year - Discharged at Sag Harbor, NY, on 5 Apr 1815.

Miller, Isaac W. - Seaman - Company: Noah Terry - Died in camp on 12 Oct 1814 of typhus fever.

Miller, Jeremiah - Boatswain.

Miller, Jonathan - Seaman - Company: Noah Terry - Age: 21 - Height: 5' 7" - Born: Easthampton, Suffolk County, NY - Trade: Weaver - Enlistment date: 20 Jul 1814 - Place: Sag Harbor, NY - Period: 1 Year - Discharged at Sag Harbor, NY, on 5 Apr 1815.

Miller, Jonathan J. - Seaman - Company: Noah Terry - Age: 18 - Height: 5' 7" - Born: Easthampton, Suffolk County, NY - Trade: Yeoman - Enlistment date: 8 Nov 1814 - Place: Sag Harbor, NY - Period: 1 Year - Discharged at Sag Harbor, NY, on 5 Apr 1815.

Miller, King - Seaman - Company: Noah Terry - Age: 21 - Height: 5' 10" - Born: Easthampton, Suffolk County, NY - Trade: Cordwainer - Enlistment date: 21 Jul 1814 - Place: Sag Harbor, NY - Period: 1 Year - Discharged at Sag Harbor, NY, on 5 Apr 1815.

Miller, Samuel - Seaman - Company: Noah Terry - Age: 19 - Height: 5' 8" - Born: Easthampton, Suffolk County, NY - Trade: Yeoman - Enlistment date: 25 Aug 1814 - Place: Sag Harbor, NY - Period: 1 Year - Discharged at Sag Harbor, NY, on 5 Apr 1815.

Mills, John B. - Private.

Mitchell, Byrd B. - Second Lieutenant - Company: Frederick Brooks - Commissioned as a 2nd lieutenant on 7 Aug 1813; discharged on 15 Jun 1815.

Molsbay, James - Seaman - Company: John Nicholson - Age: 38 - Height: 5' 6" - Born: Bladen, NC - Trade: Cooper - Enlistment date: 29 Jan 1814.

Montgomery, Archibald - Seaman - Company: Simmones Bunbury - Enlistment date: 18 Jan 1814 - Period: 1 Year - Discharged at Fort McHenry on 17 Jan 1815.

Morgan, John - Seaman - Company: John Gill - Age: 21 - Height: 6' 1/2" - Born: Baltimore City - Enlistment date: 12 Jan 1814 - Period: 1 Year - Deserted.

Morgan, William - Seaman - Company: John Nicholson - Age: 25 - Height: 5' 6" - Born: Pennsylvania - Trade: Farmer - Enlistment date: 2 Feb 1814 - Place: Elizabeth Town, NC - Period: 1 Year.

Morris, George - Seaman - Company: Simmones Bunbury - Enlistment date: 20 Jan 1815 - Period: 1 Year - Discharged at Fort McHenry on 24 Mar 1815.

Morris, George - Seaman - Company: Simmones Bunbury - Enlistment date: 3 Nov 1813 - Period: 1 Year - Discharged on 13 Jan 1815.

Morris, George S. - Seaman - Company: Peleg Barker - Age: 21 - Height: 5' 4" - Born: Nantucket, MA - Trade: Mariner - Enlistment date: 7 Sep 1814 - Place: Fairhaven, MA - Period: 1 Year.

Morris, Lemuel - Captain - Company: Lemuel Morris - Commissioned as a captain on 4 Aug 1813; discharged on 15 Jul 1815.

Morris, Thomas - Seaman - Company: John Davis - Age: 21 - Height: 5' 3/4" - Born: Monmouth, NJ - Enlistment date: 24 Jan 1814 - Discharged on 29 Mar 1815.

Morrison, Joseph - Quarter Gunner - Company: Lemuel Morris - Age: 25 - Height: 5' 5 1/2" - Born: Haverhill, NH - Trade: Mariner - Enlistment date: 20 Jun 1814 - Place: New York - Period: 1 Year - Discharged on 25 Mar 1815.

Morrison, Nathan (Nathaniel) - Seaman - Company: John Davis - Age: 18 - Height: 5' 7 1/2" - Born: Wells, York County, DM - Trade: Sail maker - Enlistment date: 13 Feb 1815 - Place: Portsmouth, NH - Period: 1 Year - Pension: SO-33914 - Discharged on 29 Mar 1815.

Morrow, William - Seaman - Company: Simmones Bunbury - Age: 27 - Height: 5' - Born: Kent County,

MD.

Mott, Young - Seaman - Company: Noah Terry - Age: 20 - Height: 5' 8 1/2" - Born: Brookhaven, NY - Trade: Seaman - Enlistment date: 29 Aug 1814 - Place: Sag Harbor, NY - Period: 1 Year - Discharged at Sag Harbor, NY, on 5 Apr 1815.

Munroe, William - Second Lieutenant - Company: Benjamin Pearce - Commissioned as a 2nd lieutenant on 2 Aug 1814; discharged on 15 Jul 1815.

Myers, Casten - Private.

Myers, George - Seaman - Company: Lemuel Morris - Age: 37 - Height: 5' 5 1/2" - Born: New York - Enlistment date: 24 Jan 1814 - Period: 1 Year - Discharged on 9 Feb 1815.

Myers, John - Seaman - Company: Lemuel Morris - Age: 30 - Height: 5' 9" - Born: New Orleans - Trade: Seaman - Enlistment date: 30 Apr 1814.

Myers, John F. - Seaman - Company: Noah Terry - Age: 40 - Height: 5' 8" - Born: Southampton, Suffolk County, NY - Trade: Seaman - Enlistment date: 23 Aug 1814 - Place: Sag Harbor, NY - Period: 1 Year - Discharged at Sag Harbor, NY, on 5 Apr 1815.

Myers, Richard - Private.

Nary, Michael - Seaman - Company: John Gill - Age: 28 - Height: 5' 3" - Born: Baltimore City - Enlistment date: 10 Jan 1814 - Period: 1 Year.

Neal, William - Private.

Nelson, Benjamin - Seaman - Company: Frederick Brooks - Age: 23 - Height: 5' 9 1/2" - Born: Beaufort County, NC - Trade: Farmer - Enlistment date: 15 Feb 1814 - Place: Washington, NC - Period: 1 Year.

Nesbit, Isaac - Private.

Newby, John - Seaman - Company: Frederick Brooks - Age: 19 - Height: 5' 7" - Born: Perquimmons, NC - Trade: Farmer - Enlistment date: 3 Mar 1814 - Place: Washington, NC - Period: 1 Year.

Newell, Thomas M. - Captain - Company: Thomas Newell - Born: Georgia - Commissioned as a captain on 1 Aug 1813; discharged on 1 Aug 1814.

Newit, Edward - Seaman - Company: William Addison.

Newman, James - Second Lieutenant.

Nichols, Abraham - First Lieutenant - Company: Thomas Newell - Commissioned as a 1st lieutenant on 1 Aug 1813; resigned on 31 Dec 1813.

Nichols, Edward - Seaman - Company: Peleg Barker - Age: 18 - Height: 5' " - Born: Gotland, Sweden - Trade: Mariner - Enlistment date: 21 Sep 1814 - Place: Fairhaven, MA - Period: 1 Year.

Nicholson, John - Captain - Company: John Nicholson - Commissioned as a captain on 1 Aug 1813; died on 5 Apr 1814.

Niles, George - Seaman - Company: Noah Terry - Age: 23 - Height: 5' 8" - Born: Southampton, Suffolk County, NY - Trade: Rope maker - Enlistment date: 20 Jul 1814 - Place: Sag Harbor, NY - Period: 1 Year - Deserted at Sag Harbor, NY, on 5 Apr 1815.

Niles, Peleg - Seaman - Company: Noah Terry - Age: 40 - Height: 6' 1" - Born: Southampton, Suffolk County, NY - Trade: Weaver - Enlistment date: 24 Aug 1814 - Place: Sag Harbor, NY - Period: 1 Year - Discharged at Sag Harbor, NY, on 5 Apr 1815.

Norris, Luke - Private.

Nostrand, John - Seaman - Company: Noah Terry - Deserted at Sag Harbor, NY, on 24 Oct 1814.

Nye, Benjamin - Gunner - Company: Benjamin Pearce - Enlistment date: 8 Sep 1814 - Period: 1 Year - Discharged on 27 Mar 1815.

O'Donnel, John - Private.

Oliver, William - Seaman - Company: Lemuel Morris - Age: 42 - Height: 5' 6 1/4" - Born: Massachusetts - Enlistment date: 24 Dec 1813 - Period: 1 Year - Discharged at Sandy Hook, NJ, on 2 Feb 1815.

O'Neal, Ferdinand Armstrong - Second Lieutenant - Company: Thomas Newell - Commissioned as a 2nd lieutenant on 1 Aug 1813; died on 20 Sep 1814; recruiting at St. Mary's GA, Feb-Mar 1814.

O'Neal, Levy - Private.

Oram, Isaiah - Seaman - Company: Simmones Bunbury - Age: 21 - Height: 5' 6 1/2" - Born: Hookstown, MD - Enlistment date: 3 Jan 1814 - Period: 1 Year.

Oram, John - Seaman - Company: Simmones Bunbury - Age: 22 - Height: 5' 10" - Born: Hookstown, MD - Enlistment date: 18 Nov 1813 - Period: 1 Year - Discharged on 17 Nov 1814.

Oram, Josiah - Private.

Osborn, Samuel - Seaman - Company: Noah Terry - Age: 19 - Height: 5' 5" - Born: Southold, Suffolk County, NY - Trade: Potter - Enlistment date: 1 Aug 1814 - Place: Sag Harbor, NY - Period: 1 Year - Discharged at Sag Harbor, NY, on 5 Apr 1815.

Overton, Mattiah - Seaman - Company: Noah Terry - Age: 38 - Height: 6' 1 3/4" - Born: Southampton, Suffolk County, NY - Trade: Seaman - Enlistment date: 20 Jul 1814 - Place: Sag Harbor, NY - Period: 1 Year - Discharged at Sag Harbor, NY, on 5 Apr 1815.

Owens, James - Seaman - Company: Frederick Brooks - Age: 20 - Height: 5' 7" - Born: Hyde County, NC - Trade: Carpenter - Enlistment date: 1 Mar 1814 - Place: Washington, NC - Period: 1 Year.

Padrick, John - Seaman - Company: McQueen McIntosh - Pension: Wife Hilda, WO-35451, WC-23255 - BLW 4996-160-50.

Page, Jenkin - Seaman - Company: Simmones Bunbury - Age: 27 - Height: 5' 7 1/4" - Born: Dorchester County, MD - Enlistment date: 6 Dec 1813 - Period: 1 Year - Discharged on 5 Dec 1814.

Parham, Matthew - Private - Company: John Nicholson.

Paten, John - Seaman - Company: Thomas Newell - Age: 26 - Height: 5' 9" - Born: Savannah, GA - Trade: Sailor - Enlistment date: 21 Feb 1814 - Place: Savannah, GA - Period: 1 Year.

Patterson, Thomas G. - Seaman - Company: Simmones Bunbury - Age: 24 - Height: 5' 7" - Born: Pennsylvania - Enlistment date: 1 Jul 1814 - Period: 1 Year.

Patterson, William - Seaman - Company: John Gill - Age: 17 - Height: 5' 4" - Born: West Point, MD - Enlistment date: 10 Feb 1814 - Period: 1 Year - Discharged on 9 Feb 1815.

Pattillo, George - Private.

Patton, Robert - Seaman - Company: Lemuel Morris - Age: 33 - Height: 5' 9 1/2" - Born: New York - Trade: Mariner - Enlistment date: 22 Jun 1814 - Place: New York - Period: 1 Year - Discharged on 25 Mar 1815.

Payne, Harry - Private.

Payne, Harvey - Seaman - Company: Noah Terry - Age: 22 - Height: 5' 8" - Born: Southampton, Suffolk County, NY - Trade: Cooper - Enlistment date: 29 Aug 1814 - Place: Sag Harbor, NY - Period: 1 Year - Discharged at Sag Harbor, NY, on 5 Apr 1815.

Payne, Rufus - Seaman - Company: Noah Terry - Age: 37 - Height: 5' 10" - Born: Southampton, Suffolk County, NY - Trade: Cordwainer - Enlistment date: 22 Jul 1814 - Place: Sag Harbor, NY - Period: 1 Year - Pension: Land bounty to Nancy Payne, widow of Rufus Payne - BLW 6774-80-55 - Discharged at Sag Harbor, NY, on 5 Apr 1815.

Pearce, Benjamin - Captain - Company: Benjamin Pearce - Commissioned as a captain on 2 Aug 1814; discharged on 15 Jun 1815.

Pearce, Charles - Gunner - Company: Lemuel Morris - Age: 19 - Height: 5' 6 3/4" - Born: Martinico - Trade: Marine - Enlistment date: 16 Jun 1814 - Place: New York - Period: 1 Year - Discharged on 25 Mar 1815.

Pearce, Thomas - Seaman - Company: Lemuel Morris - Age: 40 - Height: 5' 8 1/2" - Born: New York - Enlistment date: 4 Nov 1813 - Deserted on 12 Jun 1814.

Pell, Thomas - Seaman - Company: Lemuel Morris - Age: 21 - Height: 5' 8" - Born: Hampstead, NY.

Peregoy, William - Gunner - Company: John Gill - Enlistment date: 20 Dec 1813 - Period: 1 Year.

Perry, John - Quarter Gunner - Company: Benjamin Pearce - Enlistment date: 27 Aug 1814 - Period: 1 Year - Discharged at Fort Greene, RI, on 27 Mar 1815.

Perry, John - Seaman - Company: John Nicholson - Age: 24 - Height: 5' 8" - Born: Bladen, NC - Trade: Farmer - Enlistment date: 23 Jan 1814 - Place: Elizabeth Town, NC - Period: 1 Year.

Peters, John - Seaman - Company: Lemuel Morris - Enlistment date: 21 Jan 1814 - Period: 1 Year - Discharged on 17 Mar 1815.

Peters, William - Seaman - Company: William Addison.

Petty, William - Seaman - Company: Noah Terry - Age: 25 - Height: 5' 8 1/2" - Born: Brookhaven, NY - Trade: Seaman - Enlistment date: 27 Aug 1814 - Place: Sag Harbor, NY - Period: 1 Year - Discharged at Sag Harbor, NY, on 5 Apr 1815.

Pierson, John - Seaman - Company: Noah Terry - Age: 20 - Height: 5' 5 1/2" - Born: Southampton, Suffolk County, NY - Trade: Carpenter - Enlistment date: 21 Jul 1814 - Place: Sag Harbor, NY - Period: 1 Year - Died on 23 Feb 1815 from a discharge of a cannon while in the act of ramming a cartridge.

Pinkham, William - Seaman - Company: Frederick Brooks - Age: 24 - Height: 5' 6 1/2" - Born: Beaufort County, NC - Trade: Farmer - Enlistment date: 12 Mar 1814 - Place: Washington, NC - Period: 1 Year.

Pollard, Hiram - Seaman - Company: Frederick Brooks - Age: 20 - Height: 5' 6 1/2" - Born: Craven County, NC - Trade: Farmer - Enlistment date: 25 Jun 1814 - Place: Washington, NC - Period: 1 Year.

Pollard, Jesse - Seaman - Company: Frederick Brooks - Age: 24 - Height: 5' 10 1/2" - Born: Craven County, NC - Trade: Farmer - Enlistment date: 9 Jul 1814 - Place: Washington, NC - Period: 1 Year.

Pongers, Peter - Private.

Pooll, Samuel - Seaman - Company: John Nicholson - Age: 21 - Height: 5' 6 1/2" - Born: Wake, NC - Trade: S. Maker - Enlistment date: 12 Feb 1814.

Potter, Levi - Gunner - Company: John DuBose - Age: 24 - Height: 5' 10 1/4" - Born: Sumter District, SC - Enlistment date: 16 Dec 1813 - Place: Willow Grove, SC - Period: 1 Year.

Potter, Robert - Private.

Potter, Thomas - Servant - Company: William Addison.

Potter, Walter - Gunner - Company: Benjamin Pearce - Enlistment date: 7 Oct 1814 - Period: 1 Year - Pension: Land bounty to Sally L. Potter, widow of Walter Potter - BLW 19390-80-55 - Discharged on 27 Mar 1815.

Priest, Archibald - Gunner - Company: McQueen McIntosh - Pension: Land bounty to Euphamie Priest, widow of Archibald Priest - BLW 11432-160-50.

Priest, Neil - Seaman - Company: John Nicholson - Age: 28 - Height: 5' 8" - Born: Scotland - Trade: Blacksmith - Enlistment date: 17 Jan 1814 - Place: Elizabeth Town, NC - Period: 1 Year - Also served in Captain John DuBose's Company.

Quill, William - Gunner.

Quinton, John F. - Private.

Rabbs, William - Private.

Racket, David - Seaman - Company: Noah Terry - Age: 29 - Height: 5' 8" - Born: Southold, Suffolk County, NY - Trade: Seaman - Enlistment date: 22 Jul 1814 - Place: Sag Harbor, NY - Period: 1 Year - Discharged at Sag Harbor, NY, on 5 Apr 1815.

Ramsdale, James - Seaman - Company: Thomas Newell - Age: 25 - Height: 5' 10" - Born: Savannah, GA - Trade: Sailor - Enlistment date: 23 Feb 1814 - Place: Savannah, GA - Period: 1 Year - Died on 21 Sep 1814.

Rawls, William - Seaman - Company: Frederick Brooks - Age: 27 - Height: 5' 3" - Born: Martin County, NC - Trade: Farmer - Enlistment date: 19 Feb 1814 - Place: Washington, NC - Period: 1 Year.

Raymond, George - Waiter - Company: Noah Terry - Enlistment date: 20 Jul 1814 - Period: 1 Year.

Redman, James - Seaman - Company: John Gill - Age: 18 - Height: 5' 1" - Born: St. Mary's, MD - Enlistment date: 6 Jan 1814 - Period: 1 Year.

Redman, Joshua - Seaman - Company: John Gill - Age: 19 - Height: 5' 4" - Born: Somerset County, MD - Enlistment date: 8 Jan 1814 - Period: 1 Year.

Revells, Henry - Seaman - Company: John Nicholson - Age: 20 - Height: 5' 9" - Born: Bullock, GA - Trade: Farmer - Enlistment date: 24 Feb 1814 - Place: Elizabeth Town, NC - Period: 1 Year - Also served in Captain John DuBose's Company.

Reynolds, Pierce - Servant - Company: Simmones Bunbury - Servant to Lieutenant Foy.

Rhodes, Thomas - Seaman - Company: Thomas Newell - Age: 40 - Height: 6' - Born: Boston, MA - Trade: Sailor - Enlistment date: 2 Feb 1814 - Place: Savannah, GA - Period: 1 Year - Discharged on 9 Feb 1815.

Rice, John - Seaman - Company: Peleg Barker - Age: 21 - Height: 5' 9 1/2" - Born: Nantucket, MA - Trade: Mariner - Enlistment date: 12 Dec 1814 - Place: Fairhaven, MA - Period: 1 Year.

Richards, Samuel - Private.

Richardson, Edward - Seaman - Company: John Davis - Age: 22 - Height: 5' 5" - Born: Chester, NH - Trade: Cooper - Enlistment date: 16 Dec 1814 - Place: Portsmouth, NH - Period: 1 Year - Discharged on 29 Mar 1815.

Richardson, William - Seaman - Company: Simmones Bunbury - Age: 28 - Height: 5' 6" - Born: Bucktown, Somerset County, MD - Enlistment date: 25 Dec 1813 - Period: 1 Year - Discharged on 24 Dec 1814.

Rick, John - Seaman - Company: John Gill - Age: 25 - Height: 5' 8 1/2" - Born: Baltimore - Enlistment date: 7 Jan 1814 - Period: 1 Year.

Ricker, Charles - Seaman - Company: John Davis - Age: 21 - Height: 5' 9 1/2" - Born: Lebanon, MA - Enlistment date: 14 Oct 1814 - Period: 1 Year - Deserted on 22 Oct 1814.

Riddle, Joshua - Gunner - Company: Peleg Barker - Age: 22 - Height: 5' 11" - Born: Nantucket, MA - Trade: Rope maker - Enlistment date: 4 Aug 1814 - Place: Fairhaven, MA - Period: 1 Year.

Riverbank, Frederick - Private - Company: John Nicholson.

Robertson, John - Seaman - Company: Lemuel Morris - Age: 38 - Height: 5' 6" - Born: New York City - Enlistment date: 19 Feb 1814.

Robertson, Robert - Seaman - Company: Thomas Newell - Age: 20 - Height: 5' 5" - Born: New Haven, CT - Trade: Sailor - Enlistment date: 17 Feb 1814 - Place: Savannah, GA - Period: 1 Year - On command on the US Brig Troup, a receiving ship at Savannah, GA.

Robertson, Robert - Seaman - Company: Lemuel Morris - Age: 39 - Height: 5' 5 1/2" - Born: Philadelphia - Trade: Seaman - Enlistment date: 29 Apr 1814.

Robertson, Thomas - Seaman - Company: Simmones Bunbury - Enlistment date: 25 Jan 1814 - Period: 1 Year - Discharged on 26 Jan 1815.

Robinson, Caleb R. - Second Lieutenant - Company: William Addison - Commissioned as a 2nd lieutenant on 17 Mar 1814; died on 28 Jan 1815.

Robinson, James A. - Seaman - Company: Lemuel Morris - Age: 21 - Height: 5' 7 1/2" - Born: New York City - Trade: Mariner - Enlistment date: 3 May 1814 - Place: New York - Period: 1 Year - Pension: SO-20832, SC-18359 - Discharged on 9 Mar 1815; also served in Captain James Breath's Company, Fowler's Detachment, NY Sea Fencibles.

Robinson, Thomas - Seaman - Company: Simmones Bunbury - Died on 25 Apr 1827.

Rodgers, Apollo - Seaman - Company: Noah Terry - Age: 21 - Height: 5' 9" - Born: Southampton, Suffolk County, NY - Trade: Carpenter - Enlistment date: 22 Aug 1814 - Place: Sag Harbor, NY - Period: 1 Year - Discharged at Sag Harbor, NY, on 5 Apr 1815.

Rodgers, David - Seaman - Company: McQueen McIntosh.

Rogers, John - Private.

Rogers, Joseph - Seaman - Company: Simmones Bunbury - Enlistment date: 22 Mar 1814 - Period: 1 Year - Discharged at Fort McHenry on 22 Mar 1815.

Rook, John - Seaman - Company: William Addison.

Rooke, John A. - Gunner - Company: John Gill - Age: 40 - Height: 5' 7 1/2" - Born: Somerset County, MD.

Rose, Horatio - Private.

Rose, Hosea - Seaman - Company: Noah Terry - Age: 34 - Height: 6' 1/2" - Born: Southold, Suffolk County, NY - Trade: Mason - Enlistment date: 1 Aug 1814 - Place: Sag Harbor, NY - Period: 1 Year - Discharged at Sag Harbor, NY, on 5 Apr 1815.

Ross, Samuel S. - Seaman - Company: Simmones Bunbury - Enlistment date: 26 Jan 1814 - Period: 1 Year - Discharged on 25 Jan 1815.

Rowell, John P. - Seaman - Company: John Davis - Age: 18 - Height: 5' 5 3/4" - Born: Bow, NH - Trade: Chair maker - Enlistment date: 18 Aug 1814 - Place: Exeter, NH - Period: 1 Year - Discharged on

29 Mar 1815.

Rue, John J. - Seaman - Company: Frederick Brooks - Age: 20 - Height: 5' 6 3/4" - Born: Hyde County, NC - Trade: Farmer - Enlistment date: 23 Feb 1814 - Place: Washington, NC - Period: 1 Year.

Ruland, Israel - Seaman - Company: Noah Terry - Age: 24 - Height: 5' 7" - Born: Brookhaven, NY - Trade: Cordwainer - Enlistment date: 6 Aug 1814 - Place: Sag Harbor, NY - Period: 1 Year - Discharged at Sag Harbor, NY, on 5 Apr 1815.

Runalds, Danny (Drury) - Seaman - Company: McQueen McIntosh - Also served in Captain John Nicholson's company.

Russ, James - Seaman - Company: McQueen McIntosh - BLW 7353-160-50.

Russ, John M. - Seaman - Company: John Nicholson - Age: 22 - Height: 5' 4" - Born: Bladen, NC - Trade: Sail maker - Enlistment date: 29 Jan 1814 - Place: Elizabeth Town, NC - Period: 1 Year - Also served in Captain John DuBose's Company.

Russ, Josiah - Seaman - Company: John Nicholson - Age: 20 - Height: 5' 10" - Born: Bladen, NC - Trade: Shoemaker - Enlistment date: 29 Jan 1814 - Place: Elizabeth Town, NC - Period: 1 Year - Also served in Captain John DuBose's Company.

Russ, Thomas - Seaman - Company: John Nicholson - Age: 21 - Height: 5' 11" - Born: Bladen, NC - Trade: Shoemaker - Enlistment date: 27 Jan 1814 - Place: Elizabeth Town, NC - Period: 1 Year - Also served in Captain John DuBose's Company.

Russell, George J. - Private.

Russell, James - Seaman - Company: Benjamin Pearce - Enlistment date: 18 Oct 1814 - Period: 1 Year - Discharged at Fort Greene, RI, on 27 Mar 1815.

Russell, William H. - First Lieutenant - Commissioned as a 1st lieutenant on 4 Jun 1814; discharged on 15 Jun 1815.

Rymes, George - Seaman - Company: John Davis - Age: 28 - Height: 5' 7 3/4" - Born: Portsmouth, NH - Trade: Sail maker - Enlistment date: 22 Jun 1814 - Place: Portsmouth, NH - Period: 1 Year - Discharged on 29 Mar 1815.

Sadler, Augustus - Seaman - Company: William Addison.

Sales, John B. - Seaman - Company: John Gill - Age: 21 - Height: 5' 8" - Born: Baltimore - Enlistment date: 14 Jan 1814 - Period: 1 Year - BLW 405-120-55.

Sammis, Daniel - Seaman - Company: Noah Terry - Age: 19 - Height: 5' 5" - Born: Shelter Island, Suffolk County, NY - Trade: Yeoman - Enlistment date: 20 Jul 1814 - Place: Sag Harbor, NY - Period: 1 Year - Discharged at Sag Harbor, NY, on 5 Apr 1815.

Sandford, Jesse - Seaman - Company: Noah Terry - Age: 18 - Height: 5' 10" - Born: Southampton, Suffolk County, NY - Enlistment date: 6 Aug 1814 - Place: Sag Harbor, NY - Period: 1 Year - Discharged at Sag Harbor, NY, on 5 Apr 1815.

Saunders, Charles - Seaman - Company: John Davis - Age: 21 - Height: 5' 4 1/2" - Born: Gloucester, Essex County, MA - Trade: Schoolmaster - Enlistment date: 15 Oct 1814 - Place: Portsmouth, NH - Period: 1 Year - Discharged on 29 Mar 1815.

Scarborough, Jacob - Seaman - Company: Frederick Brooks - Age: 18 - Height: 5' 5" - Born: Currituck County, NC - Trade: Seaman - Enlistment date: 12 Feb 1814 - Place: Washington, NC - Period: 1 Year.

Scissell, Joseph - Seaman - Company: Lemuel Morris - Age: 35 - Height: 5' 7 3/4" - Born: St. Mary's,

MD - Trade: Mariner - Enlistment date: 6 May 1814 - Place: New York - Period: 1 Year - Discharged on 25 Mar 1815.

Scott, Elijah - Private.

Scott, Henry - Private.

Scott, Joseph - Seaman - Company: William Addison.

Scott, Richard - Seaman - Company: John Gill - Age: 27 - Height: 5' 9" - Born: Baltimore - Enlistment date: 4 Jan 1814 - Period: 1 Year.

Scracklin, Lewis - Seaman - Company: Simmones Bunbury.

Scurlock, Eli - Private.

Searles, Edward - Seaman - Company: McQueen McIntosh - Pension: Wife Sidney, WO-29761, WC-17810 - BLW 17357-160-50 - Also served in the North Carolina Militia.

Shartle, Henry - Seaman - Company: William Addison.

Shaw, Daniel - Seaman - Company: McQueen McIntosh.

Shaw, Donald - Seaman - Company: John Nicholson - Age: 31 - Height: 6' - Born: Cumberland, NC - Trade: Shoemaker - Enlistment date: 27 Jan 1814 - Place: Elizabeth Town, NC - Period: 1 Year.

Shaw, Thomas - Private.

Shay, Thomas - Seaman - Company: Lemuel Morris - Age: 19 - Height: 5' 6 1/2" - Born: New York City - Enlistment date: 1 Feb 1814 - Period: 1 Year.

Shayack, Samuel - Seaman - Company: John Gill - Age: 25 - Height: 6' 2 1/2" - Born: Baltimore - Enlistment date: 3 Jan 1814 - Period: 1 Year.

Shearman, John - Seaman - Company: Noah Terry - Age: 40 - Height: 5' 10" - Born: Southampton, Suffolk County, NY - Trade: Seaman - Enlistment date: 6 Aug 1814 - Place: Sag Harbor, NY - Period: 1 Year - Discharged at Sag Harbor, NY, on 5 Apr 1815.

Shehey, Michael - Seaman - Company: William Addison.

Sheriff, Henry A. - Seaman - Company: John Davis - Age: 21 - Height: 5' 6 1/2" - Born: Exeter, NH - Trade: Sadler - Enlistment date: 21 Sep 1814 - Place: Portsmouth, NH - Period: 1 Year - Discharged on 29 Mar 1815.

Sherman, John - Seaman - Company: Noah Terry.

Sherman, Lewis J. - Seaman - Company: Simmones Bunbury - Age: 20 - Height: 5' 3" - Born: Baltimore - Enlistment date: 15 Dec 1813 - Period: 1 Year - Discharged on 16 Jan 1815.

Sherry, William - Servant - Company: Noah Terry - Enlistment date: 3 Aug 1814 - Period: 1 Year.

Shipper, David - Seaman - Company: John Gill - Age: 20 - Height: 5' 6" - Born: Baltimore City - Enlistment date: 5 Jan 1814 - Period: 1 Year.

Shorben, John - Seaman - Company: John Gill - Age: 26 - Height: 5' 10" - Born: Baltimore - Enlistment date: 3 Jan 1814 - Period: 1 Year.

Sibbels, John - Private.

Silverthorn, Derison - Seaman - Company: Frederick Brooks - Age: 21 - Height: 5' 7 1/2" - Born: Hyde County, NC - Trade: Farmer - Enlistment date: 15 Feb 1814 - Place: Washington, NC - Period: 1 Year.

Silverthorn, Guilford - Seaman - Company: Frederick Brooks - Age: 18 - Height: 5' 4" - Born: Hyde County, NC - Trade: Farmer - Enlistment date: 2 Mar 1814 - Place: Washington, NC - Period: 1 Year.

Simons, James - Seaman - Company: John Gill - Age: 28 - Height: 5' 5 1/4" - Born: Norwich, CT - Enlistment date: 12 Feb 1814 - Period: 1 Year - Pension: Land bounty to Sary Day, former widow of James Simons - BLW 25066-80-55.

Simpson, Robert - Seaman - Company: John Davis - Age: 40 - Height: 5' 3" - Born: Newbury, MA - Trade: Marine - Enlistment date: 24 Jan 1814 - Place: Portsmouth, NH - Period: 1 Year - Discharged on 29 Mar 1815.

Sinton, Francis - Seaman - Company: John Gill - Age: 24 - Height: 5' 5" - Born: Baltimore - Enlistment date: 9 Jan 1814 - Period: 1 Year.

Skelton, Abel - Private.

Slade, Benjamin - Private.

Slaker, Zacheus - Gunner - Company: John Gill - Enlistment date: 22 Dec 1813 - Period: 1 Year.

Smith, Alexander - Seaman - Company: Simmones Bunbury - Age: 18 - Height: 5' 7" - Born: Baltimore - Enlistment date: 15 Jan 1814 - Period: 1 Year - Discharged at Fort McHenry on 14 Jan 1815.

Smith, Benjamin - Seaman - Company: Noah Terry - Age: 18 - Height: 5' 7 1/2" - Born: Cape Cod, Suffolk County MA - Trade: Seaman - Enlistment date: 27 Aug 1814 - Place: Sag Harbor, NY - Period: 1 Year - Discharged at Sag Harbor, NY, on 5 Apr 1815.

Smith, Charles - Seaman - Company: Lemuel Morris - Deserted on 12 Jun 1814.

Smith, Eldridge - Seaman - Company: Noah Terry - Age: 28 - Height: 5' 8" - Born: Southampton, Suffolk County, NY - Trade: Carpenter - Enlistment date: 30 Aug 1814 - Place: Sag Harbor, NY - Period: 1 Year - Discharged at Sag Harbor, NY, on 5 Apr 1815.

Smith, James - Seaman - Company: Lemuel Morris - Age: 20 - Height: 5' 5 1/4" - Born: Liverpool, England - Enlistment date: 29 Dec 1813.

Smith, John - Seaman - Company: John Nicholson - Age: 28 - Height: 5' 7" - Born: Johnson County, NC - Trade: Farmer - Enlistment date: 8 Feb 1814 - Place: Elizabeth Town, NC - Period: 1 Year.

Smith, John - Seaman - Company: Lemuel Morris - Age: 30 - Height: 5' 6 1/2" - Born: Ireland - Enlistment date: 4 Nov 1812.

Smith, John - Seaman - Company: Lemuel Morris - Age: 18 - Height: 5' 2 3/4" - Born: Sowharbor, Long Island, NY - Enlistment date: 14 Jan 1814.

Smith, Judah - Seaman - Company: Noah Terry - Age: 19 - Height: 5' 8" - Born: Southampton, Suffolk County, NY - Trade: Seaman - Enlistment date: 21 Jul 1814 - Place: Sag Harbor, NY - Period: 1 Year - Discharged at Sag Harbor, NY, on 5 Apr 1815.

Smith, Lewis - Seaman - Company: Noah Terry - Age: 44 - Height: 6' 1" - Born: Southampton, Suffolk County, NY - Trade: Seaman - Enlistment date: 6 Aug 1814 - Place: Sag Harbor, NY - Period: 1 Year - Discharged at Sag Harbor, NY, on 5 Apr 1815.

Smith, Martin - Seaman - Company: Benjamin Pearce - Enlistment date: 10 Oct 1814 - Period: 1 Year - Discharged at Fort Greene, RI, on 27 Mar 1815.

Smith, Neil - Seaman - Company: John Nicholson - Age: 19 - Height: 5' 9" - Born: Cumberland, NC - Trade: Chair maker - Enlistment date: 25 Feb 1814 - Place: Elizabeth Town, NC - Period: 1 Year.

Smith, Peter - Seaman - Company: Simmones Bunbury - Enlistment date: 29 Jan 1814 - Period: 1 Year -

Pension: Navy Widow File 1413 Rejected - Died at Baltimore on 27 Feb 1814.

Smith, Samuel - Seaman - Company: Frederick Brooks - Age: 25 - Height: 5' 10 1/2" - Born: Beaufort County, NC - Trade: Farmer - Enlistment date: 12 Mar 1814 - Place: Washington, NC - Period: 1 Year.

Smith, Thomas - Seaman - Company: John Nicholson - Age: 22 - Height: 5' 5 3/4" - Born: North Carolina - Trade: Saddler - Enlistment date: 17 Jan 1814 - Place: Elizabeth Town, NC - Period: 1 Year.

Smith, Whellen - Quarter Gunner - Company: Benjamin Pearce - Enlistment date: 8 Sep 1814 - Period: 1 Year - Discharged at Fort Greene, RI, on 27 Mar 1815.

Smith, William - Seaman - Company: John Gill - Age: 20 - Height: 5' 8" - Born: Baltimore - Enlistment date: 16 Jan 1814 - Period: 1 Year.

Smithson, Luther - Seaman - Company: John Gill - Age: 22 - Height: 6' - Born: Harford County, MD - Enlistment date: 6 Jan 1814 - Period: 1 Year.

Smother, Aderick - Servant - Company: Simmones Bunbury - Servant to Captain Bunbury.

Smothers, John - Servant - Company: Simmones Bunbury - Discharged at Fort McHenry on 24 Mar 1815.

Snale, Robert - Gunner - Company: Lemuel Morris - Enlistment date: 17 Jan 1814 - Period: 1 Year - Discharged at Fort Gates, NJ, on 17 Jan 1815.

Snow, Nathaniel - Seaman - Company: Peleg Barker - Age: 34 - Height: 5' 9" - Born: Rochester, MA - Trade: Mariner - Enlistment date: 12 Sep 1814 - Place: Fairhaven, MA - Period: 1 Year.

Sorter, John - Private.

Southerland, Thomas - Seaman - Company: Lemuel Morris - Age: 20 - Height: 5' 4 1/2" - Born: New Castle, DE - Enlistment date: 9 Nov 1813 - Period: 1 Year - Discharged on 14 Feb 1815.

Spangler, George - Private.

Sparks, William - Seaman - Company: Simmones Bunbury - Enlistment date: 21 Feb 1814 - Period: 1 Year - Pension: Wife Jane, SO-2037, SC-10334, WO-24846, WC-15462 - Discharged on 20 Feb 1815.

Spence, John - Seaman - Company: Lemuel Morris - Age: 29 - Height: 5' 5 1/2" - Born: Baltimore - Trade: Mariner - Enlistment date: 10 Jun 1814 - Place: New York - Period: 1 Year - Deserted at Sandy Hook, NJ, on 8 Feb 1815.

Spencer, Henry - Private.

Spencer, Thomas L. - Seaman - Company: John Nicholson - Age: 22 - Height: 6' - Born: Rhode Island - Trade: Bricklayer - Enlistment date: 17 Jan 1814 - Place: Elizabeth Town, NC - Period: 1 Year - May have served for 18 months in the 18th US Infantry as a sergeant, enlisted on 20 Jun 1812.

Stansborough, David - Seaman - Company: Noah Terry - Age: 37 - Height: 5' 6" - Born: Southampton, Suffolk County, NY - Trade: Weaver - Enlistment date: 31 Aug 1814 - Place: Sag Harbor, NY - Period: 1 Year - Discharged at Sag Harbor, NY, on 5 Apr 1815.

Stansborough, Isaac - Seaman - Company: Noah Terry - Age: 33 - Height: 5' 5" - Born: Southampton, Suffolk County, NY - Trade: Seaman - Enlistment date: 30 Aug 1814 - Place: Sag Harbor, NY - Period: 1 Year - Discharged at Sag Harbor, NY, on 5 Apr 1815.

Stephens, George B. - Seaman - Company: Lemuel Morris - Age: 32 - Height: 5' 3 3/4" - Born: Philadelphia - Trade: Mariner - Enlistment date: 19 Apr 1814 - Place: New York - Period: 1 Year - Discharged on 25 Mar 1815.

Stephens, James L. - Gunner - Company: William Addison - Pension: Old War IF-25852.

Stephens, Levi - Seaman - Company: John Nicholson - Age: 23 - Height: 5' 5 1/2" - Born: Bladen, NC - Trade: Farmer - Enlistment date: 8 Feb 1814 - Place: Elizabeth Town, NC - Period: 1 Year.

Stephens, Timothy - Seaman - Company: Simmones Bunbury - Age: 22 - Height: 5' 7 1/2" - Born: New Bedford, MA - Enlistment date: 25 Jul 1814 - Period: 1 Year - Deserted on 17 Mar 1815.

Sterrett, Robert - Seaman - Company: Simmones Bunbury - Age: 34 - Height: 5' 10" - Born: Norfolk, VA - Enlistment date: 6 Jan 1814 - Period: 1 Year - Discharged on 5 Jan 1815.

Stevens, James L. - Gunner - Company: John Gill - Age: 31 - Height: 5' 7" - Born: Charleston, SC - Enlistment date: 29 Dec 1813 - Period: 1 Year.

Stevens, Thomas - Seaman - Company: Peleg Barker - Age: 18 - Height: 5' 8" - Born: Rochester, MA - Trade: Mariner - Enlistment date: 15 Nov 1814 - Place: Fairhaven, MA - Period: 1 Year.

Steward, Charles - Seaman - Company: Lemuel Morris - Age: 20 - Height: 5' 9 1/2" - Born: New York City - Enlistment date: 29 Dec 1813.

Stewart, John - Gunner.

Stewart, John - Seaman - Company: John DuBose - Age: 30 - Height: 5' 7" - Born: Mecklenburg, NC - Enlistment date: 1 Nov 1813 - Place: Willow Grove, SC - Period: 1 Year - Pension: SO-28786, SC-20763 - Re-enlisted on 16 Feb 1814 for one year.

Stewart, Silas - Gunner - Company: Noah Terry - Age: 38 - Height: 5' 9 1/2" - Born: Southampton, Suffolk County, NY - Trade: Sail maker - Enlistment date: 20 Jul 1814 - Place: Sag Harbor, NY - Period: 1 Year - Discharged at Sag Harbor, NY, on 5 Apr 1815.

Stiner, Joseph - Private - Company: John Nicholson.

Stinson, Stephen - Seaman - Company: John Gill - Age: 28 - Height: 5' 10" - Born: Berwick, MA - Enlistment date: 12 Jan 1814 - Period: 1 Year.

Stiron, Wallis - Private.

Stiverson, Allen - Seaman - Company: Noah Terry - Age: 20 - Height: 5' 6" - Born: South Hempstead, Suffolk County, NY - Trade: Weaver - Enlistment date: 21 Aug 1814 - Place: Sag Harbor, NY - Period: 1 Year - Discharged at Sag Harbor, NY, on 5 Apr 1815.

Stiverson, John - Private.

Stoke, Zacheous - Gunner - Company: William Addison.

Stout, John - Seaman - Company: John Gill - Age: 21 - Height: 5' 6 1/2" - Born: Philadelphia - Enlistment date: 29 Dec 1812 - Period: 1 Year.

Stringham, John - Seaman - Company: Noah Terry - Age: 42 - Height: 5' 10" - Born: Northumpsted, Queens County, NY - Trade: Carpenter - Enlistment date: 6 Aug 1814 - Place: Sag Harbor, NY - Period: 1 Year - Discharged at Sag Harbor, NY, on 5 Apr 1815.

Stuart, John - Seaman - Company: John Nicholson - Age: 19 - Height: 5' 6" - Born: Scotland - Trade: Carpenter - Enlistment date: 16 Feb 1814.

Swain, Benjamin - Boatswain - Company: Peleg Barker - Age: 31 - Height: 5' 6" - Born: Nantucket, MA - Trade: Mariner - Enlistment date: 4 Aug 1814 - Place: Fairhaven, MA - Period: 1 Year.

Sweezy, Nathan B. - Seaman - Company: Noah Terry - Age: 23 - Height: 5' 6 1/4" - Born: Southampton, Suffolk County, NY - Trade: Seaman - Enlistment date: 21 Aug 1814 - Place: Sag Harbor, NY - Period: 1 Year - Discharged at Sag Harbor, NY, on 5 Apr 1815.

Swift, John - Seaman - Company: John Gill - Age: 21 - Height: 5' 11 1/2" - Born: Philadelphia - Enlistment date: 15 Jan 1814 - Period: 1 Year.

Swinson, Nicholas - Private.

Symmes, Isaac - Seaman - Company: Peleg Barker - Age: 44 - Height: 5' - Born: Plymouth, MA - Trade: Mariner - Enlistment date: 10 Dec 1814 - Place: Fairhaven, MA - Period: 1 Year.

Taber, Charles - Waiter.

Taber, Joseph - Waiter.

Tabor, Pardon T. - Second Lieutenant - Born: New York - Commissioned as a 2nd lieutenant on 18 Jun 1814; discharged on 15 Jul 1815.

Tabu, William - Waiter - Company: Peleg Barker - Age: 15 - Height: 5' - Born: Fairhaven, MA - Trade: Waiter - Enlistment date: 4 Aug 1814.

Taggart, James - Seaman - Company: Lemuel Morris - Age: 22 - Height: 5' 9 3/4" - Born: Philadelphia - Enlistment date: 3 Jan 1814 - Period: 1 Year - Discharged on 17 Jan 1814.

Talbot, Joseph - Seaman - Company: Simmones Bunbury - Age: 33 - Height: 5' 5" - Born: Massachusetts - Enlistment date: 2 Nov 1814 - Period: 1 Year - Discharged at Fort McHenry on 24 Mar 1815.

Tarbox, Thomas - Seaman - Company: Thomas Newell - Age: 23 - Height: 6' - Born: St. Marys, GA - Trade: Sailor - Enlistment date: 21 Feb 1814 - Place: Savannah, GA - Period: 1 Year - Died on 19 Jan 1815.

Tarlton, William S. - Seaman - Company: John Davis - Age: 18 - Height: 5' 8 1/2" - Born: Portsmouth, NH - Trade: Mariner - Enlistment date: 8 Aug 1814 - Place: Portsmouth, NH - Period: 1 Year - Discharged on 29 Mar 1815.

Taylor, John - Gunner - Company: John DuBose - Age: 37 - Height: 5' 7 3/4" - Born: Philadelphia, PA - Enlistment date: 3 Jan 1814 - Place: Willow Grove, SC - Period: 1 Year.

Taylor, William - Gunner - Company: Lemuel Morris - Age: 38 - Height: 5' 2 3/4" - Born: New York City - Enlistment date: 13 Jan 1814 - Period: 1 Year - Discharged on 12 Jan 1815.

Terry, Amon - Servant - Company: Noah Terry - Enlistment date: 3 Aug 1814 - Period: 1 Year.

Terry, Noah - Captain - Company: Noah Terry - Commissioned as a captain on 18 Jun 1814; discharged on 15 Jun 1815.

Terry, Shadrach - Seaman - Company: Noah Terry - Age: 20 - Height: 5' 8" - Born: Riverhead, Suffolk County, NY - Trade: Seaman - Enlistment date: 20 Jul 1814 - Place: Sag Harbor, NY - Period: 1 Year - Discharged at Sag Harbor, NY, on 5 Apr 1815.

Thomas, John - Seaman - Company: Peleg Barker - Age: 21 - Height: 5' 8" - Born: Duxbury, MA - Trade: Mariner - Enlistment date: 11 Nov 1814 - Place: Fairhaven, MA - Period: 1 Year - Pension: SO-754, SC-152 - BLW 25403-80-55.

Thomas, Peter - Sergeant.

Thompson, Elisha - Seaman - Company: Simmones Bunbury - Enlistment date: 13 Feb 1815 - Period: 1 Year - Discharged at Fort McHenry on 24 Mar 1815.

Thompson, John - Private.

Thompson, Joseph - Seaman - Company: Lemuel Morris - Age: 18 - Height: 5' 3 1/2" - Born: Lewistown, DE - Enlistment date: 3 Jan 1814 - Period: 1 Year.

Thompson, Richard - Seaman - Company: Simmones Bunbury - Age: 27 - Height: 5' 9 1/2" - Born:

Ireland - Enlistment date: 16 Mar 1812 - Period: 1 Year - Discharged on 16 Mar 1815.

Thompson, William - Seaman - Company: John Nicholson.

Tillotson, David - Seaman - Company: Noah Terry.

Tilton, John - Seaman - Company: John Davis - Age: 40 - Height: 5' - Born: Hampton Falls, NH - Trade: Laborer - Enlistment date: 24 Aug 1814 - Place: Exeter, NH - Period: 1 Year - Discharged on 29 Mar 1815.

Tilton, Winthrop - Waiter - Company: John Davis - Discharged on 29 Mar 1815.

Tison, Aaron - Seaman - Company: John Nicholson - Age: 23 - Height: 5' 5" - Born: Pitt, NC - Trade: Farmer - Enlistment date: 4 Feb 1814 - Place: Elizabeth Town, NC - Period: 1 Year - Also served in Captain John DuBose's Company.

Tod, Rebecca - Washerwoman - Company: John Davis - Absent on 28 Feb 1815.

Todd, George - Seaman - Company: Simmones Bunbury - Age: 35 - Height: 5' 5" - Born: Ireland - Enlistment date: 2 Sep 1814 - Period: 1 Year - Discharged at Fort McHenry on 24 Mar 1815.

Tonison, Jones - Private.

Tooley, Anson - Seaman - Company: Frederick Brooks - Age: 22 - Height: 5' 8 1/2" - Born: Hyde County, NC - Trade: Farmer - Enlistment date: 3 Mar 1814 - Place: Washington, NC - Period: 1 Year.

Tooley, Atkins - Seaman - Company: Frederick Brooks - Age: 20 - Height: 5' 11" - Born: Hyde County, NC - Trade: Farmer - Enlistment date: 1 Mar 1814 - Place: Washington, NC - Period: 1 Year.

Tooley, Jonathan - Seaman - Company: Frederick Brooks - Age: 26 - Height: 5' 8" - Born: Hyde County, NC - Trade: Carpenter - Enlistment date: 3 May 1814 - Place: Washington, NC - Period: 1 Year.

Tooley, Laban - Seaman - Company: Frederick Brooks - Age: 32 - Height: 6' 3 1/2" - Born: Hyde County, NC - Trade: Farmer - Enlistment date: 21 Feb 1814 - Place: Washington, NC - Period: 1 Year.

Townsend, John - Seaman - Company: Frederick Brooks - Age: 25 - Height: 5' 7 3/4" - Born: Baltimore - Trade: Mariner - Enlistment date: 5 Mar 1814 - Place: Washington, NC - Period: 1 Year.

Tranquille, Lewis - Seaman - Company: Simmones Bunbury - Age: 24 - Height: 5' 7" - Born: St. Domingo (Haiti) - Enlistment date: 3 Aug 1814 - Period: 1 Year - Discharged at Fort McHenry on 24 Mar 1815.

Travelles, John - Seaman - Company: Simmones Bunbury - Age: 29 - Height: 5' 7 1/2" - Born: Hookstown, MD - Enlistment date: 3 Jan 1814 - Period: 1 Year - Discharged on 2 Jan 1814.

Travlot, John - Seaman - Company: Simmones Bunbury.

Trimble, John - Quarter Gunner - Company: John Gill - Age: 33 - Height: 5' 6 1/2" - Born: Baltimore - Enlistment date: 1 Jan 1814 - Period: 1 Year.

Tuck, Josiah - Seaman - Company: John Davis - Age: 40 - Height: 6' 2 1/2" - Born: Hampton, NH - Trade: Farmer - Enlistment date: 24 Aug 1814 - Place: Portsmouth, NH - Period: 1 Year - Discharged on 29 Mar 1815.

Tucker, Henry - Seaman - Company: John Davis - Age: 40 - Height: 5' 8" - Born: New Castle, NH - Trade: Mariner - Enlistment date: 13 Jul 1814 - Place: Portsmouth, NH - Period: 1 Year - Discharged on 29 Mar 1815.

Tucker, Joshua - Seaman - Company: John Gill - Age: 20 - Height: 5' 2" - Born: Baltimore - Enlistment date: 4 Jan 1814 - Period: 1 Year.

Tucker, Mary - Washerwoman.

Tupper, Peleg - Gunner - Company: Peleg Barker - Age: 21 - Height: 5' 9" - Born: Kingston, MA - Trade: Mariner - Enlistment date: 13 Oct 1814 - Place: Fairhaven, MA - Period: 1 Year.

Turner, John - Seaman - Company: Benjamin Pearce - Enlistment date: 17 Nov 1814 - Period: 1 Year - Discharged at Fort Greene, RI, on 27 Mar 1815.

Turner, Thomas - Seaman - Company: Lemuel Morris - Enlistment date: 23 Jan 1814 - Period: 1 Year - Discharged on 22 Jan 1815.

Tuthill, Joshua - Seaman - Company: Noah Terry - Age: 39 - Height: 6' 1 1/2" - Born: Southampton, Suffolk County, NY - Trade: Cordwainer - Enlistment date: 20 Jul 1814 - Place: Sag Harbor, NY - Period: 1 Year - Discharged at Sag Harbor, NY, on 5 Apr 1815.

Tyler, Cornelius - Seaman - Company: Benjamin Pearce - Enlistment date: 16 Nov 1814 - Period: 1 Year - Discharged at Fort Greene, RI, on 27 Mar 1815.

Tyler, John - Seaman - Company: Simmones Bunbury - Age: 28 - Height: 5' 10" - Born: Dorchester County, MD - Enlistment date: 6 Jan 1814 - Period: 1 Year - Discharged at Fort McHenry on 24 Mar 1815.

Tyson, John William - Gunner.

Tyson, William - Seaman - Company: Frederick Brooks - Age: 20 - Height: 5' 11" - Born: Hyde County, NC - Trade: Farmer - Enlistment date: 3 Mar 1814 - Place: Washington, NC - Period: 1 Year.

Umphris, William - Private.

Underhill, David - Seaman - Company: John Davis - Age: 28 - Height: 5' 9 1/2" - Born: Chester, Rockingham County, NH - Trade: Farmer - Enlistment date: 29 Jul 1814 - Place: Portsmouth, NH - Period: 1 Year - Discharged on 29 Mar 1815.

Valiant, John - Gunner - Company: Simmones Bunbury - Age: 30 - Height: 5' 4 1/2" - Born: Talbot County, MD - Enlistment date: 18 Nov 1813 - Period: 1 Year - Discharged on 17 Nov 1814.

Vanalstine, Christopher - Seaman - Company: Lemuel Morris - Age: 21 - Height: 5' 5 3/4" - Born: New York City - Enlistment date: 28 Dec 1813 - Period: 1 Year - Discharged on 17 Jan 1815.

Vaughn, Francis - Private.

Venters, Francis - Private - Company: John Nicholson.

Vinning, Shaderick - Private.

Vinyard, James - Seaman - Company: William Addison - Enlistment date: 7 Feb 1814 - Period: 1 Year - Discharged at Baltimore on 7 Jan 1815.

Wadsworth, John - Seaman - Company: Peleg Barker - Age: 21 - Height: 5' 7" - Born: Duxbury, MA - Trade: Mariner - Enlistment date: 28 Nov 1814 - Place: Fairhaven, MA - Period: 1 Year.

Wadsworth, Seth - Seaman - Company: Peleg Barker - Age: 23 - Height: 5' 8 1/2" - Born: Duxbury, MA - Trade: Mariner - Enlistment date: 28 Nov 1814 - Place: Fairhaven, MA - Period: 1 Year - BLW 16348-80-55.

Walker, John - Seaman - Company: Lemuel Morris - Age: 16 - Height: 5' - Born: New York City - Enlistment date: 1 Feb 1814 - Period: 1 Year - Discharged on 1 Feb 1815.

Walker, Thomas - Seaman - Company: Lemuel Morris - Age: 39 - Height: 5' 6" - Born: Boston - Trade: Mariner - Enlistment date: 20 Jun 1814 - Place: New York - Period: 1 Year - Discharged on 25 Mar 1815.

Wallace, James - Seaman - Company: William Addison.

Wallace, Simon - Seaman - Company: John Davis - Age: 26 - Height: 5' 1 1/2" - Born: Deerfield, NH - Trade: Farmer - Enlistment date: 3 Aug 1814 - Place: Portsmouth, NH - Period: 1 Year - BLW 18780-80-55 - Discharged on 29 Mar 1815.

Wallis, John - Seaman - Company: Peleg Barker - Age: 45 - Height: 6' - Born: Vienna, VA - Trade: Mariner - Enlistment date: 12 Sep 1814 - Place: Fairhaven, MA - Period: 1 Year.

Walmsby, James - Seaman - Company: Lemuel Morris - Age: 39 - Height: 5' 2" - Born: New York, NY - Enlistment date: 8 Jan 1814 - Period: 1 Year - Discharged at Fort Gates, NJ, on 17 Jan 1815.

Walsh, Moses - Seaman - Company: William Addison.

Walters, William - Seaman - Company: Lemuel Morris - Age: 24 - Height: 5' 6" - Born: West Indies - Enlistment date: 10 Jan 1814 - Period: 1 Year - Transferred to the U.S. Navy on 26 Jan 1814.

Wane, John - Seaman - Company: John Nicholson - Age: 33 - Height: 5' 6" - Born: Philadelphia - Trade: Farmer - Enlistment date: 24 Feb 1814.

Ward Jr., John - Seaman - Company: Lemuel Morris - Age: 33 - Height: 5' 5 1/2" - Born: Ireland - Enlistment date: 3 Jan 1814 - Period: 1 Year - Also served in Captain Silliman's Company, NY Sea Fencibles, at Hurl Gate, NY.

Warfield, George - Seaman - Company: Simmones Bunbury - Age: 22 - Height: 5' 10 1/4" - Born: Anne Arundel County, MD - Enlistment date: 8 Jan 1814 - Period: 1 Year - Discharged on 7 Jan 1815.

Warrick, John - Seaman - Company: John Gill - Age: 20 - Height: 5' 7 1/2" - Born: Harford County, MD - Enlistment date: 9 Jan 1814 - Period: 1 Year.

Waters, William - Seaman - Company: Peleg Barker - Age: 28 - Height: 5' 6" - Born: Holland - Trade: Mariner - Enlistment date: 3 Oct 1814 - Place: Fairhaven, MA - Period: 1 Year.

Watts, John - Seaman - Company: Noah Terry - Deserted on 24 Oct 1814.

Welch, Mathew - Seaman - Company: Frederick Brooks - Age: 22 - Height: 5' 8 1/4" - Born: Beaufort County, NC - Trade: Farmer - Enlistment date: 15 Feb 1814 - Place: Washington, NC - Period: 1 Year.

Welch, Moses - Seaman - Company: John Gill - Enlistment date: 20 Dec 1813 - Period: 1 Year.

Welch, Samuel - Seaman - Company: John Davis - Age: 18 - Height: 5' 9" - Born: Rochester, NH - Trade: Farmer - Enlistment date: 19 Sep 1814 - Place: Portsmouth, NH - Period: 1 Year - Discharged on 29 Mar 1815.

Welsh, John - Seaman - Company: Simmones Bunbury - Age: 19 - Height: 5' 7 1/2" - Born: Baltimore City - Enlistment date: 3 Jan 1814 - Period: 1 Year - Died on 24 Nov 1814.

Welsh, Pierce - Seaman - Company: Simmones Bunbury - Age: 25 - Height: 5' 6" - Born: Baltimore - Enlistment date: 18 Jan 1814 - Period: 1 Year - Discharged on 24 Mar 1815.

West, Edward B. - Gunner - Company: Peleg Barker - Age: 26 - Height: 5' 11" - Born: New Bedford, MA - Trade: Mariner - Enlistment date: 16 Aug 1814 - Place: Fairhaven, MA - Period: 1 Year.

West, Gibson - Seaman - Company: McQueen McIntosh - Born: Bladen County, NC - BLW 91977-160-55 - Also served in Captain John DuBose's Company.

West, Samuel - Private - Company: John Nicholson.

West, Thomas - Quarter Gunner - Company: Peleg Barker - Age: 32 - Height: 5' 10" - Born: Fairhaven, MA - Trade: Mariner - Enlistment date: 30 Aug 1814 - Place: Fairhaven, MA - Period: 1 Year.

Westwood, Thomas - Seaman - Company: John Gill - Age: 21 - Height: 5' 1" - Born: Baltimore - Enlistment date: 3 Jan 1814 - Period: 1 Year.

Whailing, Timothy - Servant - Company: Simmones Bunbury.

Wheaton, Henry - Seaman - Company: Lemuel Morris - Age: 19 - Height: 5' 7 3/4" - Born: Boston - Enlistment date: 25 Jan 1814 - Period: 1 Year - Discharged on 25 Jan 1815.

Whetson, George - Seaman - Company: William Addison - Discharged at Baltimore on 7 Jan 1815.

Whitaker, John - Private.

White, Benjamin - Quarter Gunner - Company: Simmones Bunbury - Age: 32 - Height: 5' 8" - Born: Talbot County, MD - Enlistment date: 2 Dec 1813 - Period: 1 Year - Discharged on 28 Jul 1814.

White, Charles - Seaman - Company: Simmones Bunbury - Enlistment date: 19 Jan 1814 - Period: 1 Year - Discharged on 18 Jan 1815.

White, David J. - Seaman - Company: John Nicholson - Age: 21 - Height: 5' 6" - Born: North Carolina - Trade: Merchant - Enlistment date: 17 Jan 1814 - Place: Elizabeth Town, NC - Period: 1 Year - Also served in Captain John DuBose's Company.

White, Ebenezer - First Lieutenant - Company: Benjamin Pearce - Born: Massachusetts - Commissioned as a 1st lieutenant on 2 Aug 1814; discharged on 15 Jun 1815.

White, Elias - Seaman - Company: Noah Terry - Age: 19 - Height: 5' 5" - Born: Rochester, Suffolk County, NY - Trade: Seaman - Enlistment date: 19 Aug 1814 - Place: Sag Harbor, NY - Period: 1 Year - Discharged at Sag Harbor, NY, on 5 Apr 1815.

White, George - Seaman - Company: Frederick Brooks - Age: 24 - Height: 5' 7" - Born: Pitt County, NC - Trade: Farmer - Enlistment date: 12 Feb 1814 - Place: Washington, NC - Period: 1 Year.

White, John - Gunner - Company: Lemuel Morris - Age: 32 - Height: 5' 6 1/4" - Born: New York City - Enlistment date: 15 Jan 1814 - Period: 1 Year - Discharged in Jan 1815.

White, Joseph P. - Gunner - Company: Simmones Bunbury - Age: 45 - Height: 5' 6" - Born: Saybrook, CT - Enlistment date: 8 Nov 1813 - Period: 1 Year - Discharged on 8 Nov 1814.

White, William - Seaman - Company: John Nicholson - Age: 21 - Height: 5' 3" - Born: Bladen, NC - Trade: Hatter - Enlistment date: 10 Feb 1814 - Place: Elizabeth Town, NC - Period: 1 Year - Also served in Captain John DuBose's Company.

White, William N. - Seaman - Company: John Gill - Age: 18 - Height: 6' - Born: Rockingham, VT - Enlistment date: 10 Feb 1814 - Period: 1 Year.

Wiggins, Elijah - Seaman - Company: John Nicholson - Age: 32 - Height: 5' 6" - Born: Bladen, NC - Trade: Farmer - Enlistment date: 4 Feb 1814 - Place: Elizabeth Town, NC - Period: 1 Year - Also served in Captain John DuBose's Company.

Wilkerson, Edward - Private.

Wilkerson, John - Private.

Wilkinson, James - Seaman - Company: John Nicholson - Age: 38 - Height: 5' 6 1/2" - Born: Verile, Scotland - Trade: Seaman - Enlistment date: 1 Feb 1814 - Place: Elizabeth Town, NC - Period: 1 Year - Also served in Captain John DuBose's Company.

Wilkison, Thomas - Seaman - Company: John Nicholson - Age: 21 - Height: 5' 5" - Born: Bladen, NC - Trade: Saddler - Enlistment date: 7 Jan 1814 - Place: Elizabeth Town, NC - Period: 1 Year - Also served in Captain John DuBose's Company.

Willey, Robert - Seaman - Company: John Davis - Age: 25 - Height: 5' 9 1/2" - Born: New Durham, NH - Trade: Farmer - Enlistment date: 15 Jul 1814 - Place: Portsmouth, NH - Period: 1 Year - Discharged in New Hampshire on 20 Mar 1815.

Williams, George - Private.

Williams, James - Seaman - Company: John DuBose - Age: 21 - Height: 6' - Born: Pee Dee, SC - Enlistment date: 13 May 1814 - Place: Willow Grove, SC - Period: 1 Year.

Williams, James - Seaman - Company: Simmones Bunbury - Age: 22 - Height: 5' 4 1/2" - Born: Stonington, CT - Enlistment date: 12 Feb 1814 - Period: 1 Year.

Williams, James - Seaman - Company: Simmones Bunbury - Enlistment date: 11 Mar 1814 - Period: 1 Year - Discharged on 10 Mar 1815.

Williams, Job - Servant - Company: William Addison.

Williams, John - Private.

Williams, Mathew - Seaman - Company: Frederick Brooks - Age: 23 - Height: 5' 8 3/4" - Born: Craven County, NC - Trade: Sail maker - Enlistment date: 28 Jun 1814 - Place: Washington, NC - Period: 1 Year.

Williams, Richard - Seaman - Company: William Addison.

Williams, Stephen - First Lieutenant.

Williams, William - Seaman - Company: William Addison.

Williamson, John M. - First Lieutenant - Company: Noah Terry - Born: New York - Commissioned as a 1st lieutenant on 18 Jun 1814; discharged on 15 Jun 1815.

Willis, John - Private.

Willey, John E. - Waiter.

Wilmot, Henry - Seaman - Company: Noah Terry - Age: 28 - Height: 5' 5" - Born: New Haven, CT - Trade: Seaman - Enlistment date: 30 Aug 1814 - Place: Sag Harbor, NY - Period: 1 Year - Discharged at Sag Harbor, NY, on 5 Apr 1815.

Wilson, Aaron - Seaman - Company: John Davis - Age: 27 - Height: 5' 7" - Born: Kittery, ME - Trade: Mariner - Enlistment date: 9 Jan 1815 - Place: Portsmouth, NH - Period: 1 Year - Discharged on 29 Mar 1815.

Wilson, Charles - Seaman - Company: William Addison.

Wilson, George C. - Gunner - Company: Simmones Bunbury - Age: 28 - Height: 5' 11 3/4" - Born: King & Queen County, VA - Enlistment date: 7 Dec 1813 - Period: 1 Year - Pension: Old War IF-25953 - Re-enlisted on 7 Dec 1814 for one year; discharged at Fort McHenry on 24 Mar 1815.

Wilson, William - Gunner - Company: Simmones Bunbury - Enlistment date: 24 Jan 1814 - Period: 1 Year - Discharged on 23 Jan 1815.

Winstraw, Charles - Private.

Winters, Isaac - Private.

Wood, John - Seaman - Company: Simmones Bunbury - Age: 26 - Height: 5' 9 3/4" - Born: Essex, MA - Enlistment date: 1 Nov 1813 - Period: 1 Year - Re-enlisted on 25 Nov 1814 for one year; discharged on 24 Mar 1815.

Woods, Lewis - Seaman - Company: Simmones Bunbury - Age: 20 - Height: 5' 7" - Born: Havre de

Grace, MD - Enlistment date: 30 Dec 1813 - Period: 1 Year.

Wormesdorff, John - Private.

Worner, Joseph - Seaman - Company: Frederick Brooks - Age: 26 - Height: 5' 4" - Born: Beaufort County, NC - Trade: Farmer - Enlistment date: 6 Jun 1814 - Place: Washington, NC - Period: 1 Year.

Wright, Jonathan - Seaman - Company: John DuBose - Age: 22 - Height: 6' 3" - Born: St. Stephens, SC - Enlistment date: 13 May 1814 - Place: Willow Grove, SC - Period: 1 Year.

Wright, Thomas - Seaman - Company: John Nicholson - Age: 47 - Height: 5' 6" - Born: Charleston, SC - Trade: Seaman - Enlistment date: 1 Feb 1814 - Place: Elizabeth Town, NC - Period: 1 Year - Also served in Captain John DuBose's Company.

Yates, Ignatius - Private - Company: John Nicholson.

Yates, Uriah G. - Seaman - Company: John Nicholson - Age: 22 - Height: 5' 10" - Born: Columbus, NC - Enlistment date: 14 Feb 1814 - Place: Elizabeth Town, NC - Period: 1 Year - Also served in Captain John DuBose's Company.

Yeomans Jr., John - Third Lieutenant - Company: Benjamin Pearce - Commissioned as a 3rd lieutenant on 2 Aug 1814; discharged on 15 Jun 1815.

Young, John - Seaman - Company: Benjamin Pearce - Enlistment date: 9 Sep 1814 - Period: 1 Year - Discharged at Fort Greene, RI, on 27 Mar 1815.

Young, Peter - Quarter Gunner - Company: Simmones Bunbury - Age: 38 - Height: 5' 9 1/2" - Born: Lancaster, PA - Enlistment date: 30 Dec 1813 - Period: 1 Year - Re-enlisted on 29 Nov 1814 for one year; discharged at Fort McHenry on 24 Mar 1815.

Young, Samuel - Seaman - Company: Noah Terry - Age: 36 - Height: 5' 6" - Born: Southold, Suffolk County, NY - Trade: Seaman - Enlistment date: 25 Jul 1814 - Place: Sag Harbor, NY - Period: 1 Year - Discharged at Sag Harbor, NY, on 5 Apr 1815.

American Sea Fencibles in the War of 1812

State Sea Fencibles Roster

Abdel, John - Ordinary Seaman - Major Leonard's Battalion, NY Sea Fencibles.

Abrams, William - Private - Major Leonard's Battalion, NY Sea Fencibles - Company: Alexander Robinson.

Acker, Abraham - Seaman - Major Wooster's Battalion, NY Sea Fencibles.

Ackerley, Frederick - Ordinary Seaman - NY Sea Fencibles - Company: Josiah Ingersoll.

Ackley, John - Private - Major Wooster's Battalion, NY Sea Fencibles - Company: John Randlet - Enlistment date: 16 Sep 1814 - Pension: Wife Phebe Morgan, WO-44597, WC-34946; married on 7 Jul 1821 in New York City; seaman died on 14 Aug 1857 in Brooklyn, NY - BLW 16733-120-55 & 25130-40-50 - Discharged on 1 Dec 1814.

Ackley, Stephen - Boy - Major Fowler's Detachment, NY Sea Fencibles - Company: James Breath.

Adams, Atkins - Private - MA Sea Fencibles - Company: Nehemiah Skillings.

Adams, John - First Lieutenant - Major Wooster's Battalion, NY Sea Fencibles.

Adams, John - Servant - Major Wooster's Battalion, NY Sea Fencibles.

Adams, John - Ordinary Seaman - NY Sea Fencibles - Company: Josiah Ingersoll.

Adams, Rufus - Seaman - Major Wooster's Battalion, NY Sea Fencibles - BLW 57630-120-55.

Adams, Thomas - Private - MA Sea Fencibles - Company: Jeremiah Stickney.

Adams, Thomas D. - Seaman - Major Fowler's Detachment, NY Sea Fencibles.

Adams, Thomas S. - Gunner - Major Fowler's Detachment, NY Sea Fencibles.

Adams, William - Servant - Major Leonard's Battalion, NY Sea Fencibles - Company: William Russell.

Adamson, John - Private - MA Sea Fencibles - Company: Nehemiah Skillings.

Adlington, Thomas - Seaman - Major Leonard's Battalion, NY Sea Fencibles.

Aherly, Frederick - Ordinary Seaman - NY Sea Fencibles - Company: Josiah Ingersoll.

Aires, Frederick W. - Private - MA Sea Fencibles - Company: Nehemiah Skillings.

Airhart, James - Seaman - NY Sea Fencibles - Company: Josiah Ingersoll.

Albert, Sebastian - Quarter Gunner - Major Wooster's Battalion, NY Sea Fencibles.

Allen Jr., William - Seaman - Major Fowler's Detachment, NY Sea Fencibles.

Allen, James - Seaman - Major Wooster's Battalion, NY Sea Fencibles.

Allen, James A. - Private - MA Sea Fencibles - Company: Nehemiah Skillings.

Allen, William - Quarter Gunner - Major Leonard's Battalion, NY Sea Fencibles - Company: William Russell - Enlistment date: 23 Jan 1815 - Period: 3 Months.

Allen, William - Private - Major Fowler's Detachment, NY Sea Fencibles - Company: James Breath - Pension: Land bounty to Charlotte Allen, widow of William Allen - BLW 1714-80-55.

Alley, James - Quarter Gunner - NY Sea Fencibles - Company: Paul Burrows - Enlistment date: 8 Oct 1814 - Period: 3 Months - BLW 5086-120-55.

Alpheus, John - Seaman - NY Sea Fencibles - Company: Josiah Ingersoll.

American Sea Fencibles in the War of 1812

Alveridge, Sylvester - Seaman - Major Wooster's Battalion, NY Sea Fencibles.

Ames, James - Private - Major Fowler's Detachment, NY Sea Fencibles - Company: James Breath.

Ames, Thomas - Private - NY Sea Fencibles - Company: Paul Burrows - Enlistment date: 10 Oct 1814 - Period: 3 Months.

Anderan, Aaron - Seaman - Major Leonard's Battalion, NY Sea Fencibles.

Anderson, Hans J. - Gunner - Major Leonard's Battalion, NY Sea Fencibles - Company: William Russell - Enlistment date: 14 Jan 1815 - Period: 3 Months - Deserted.

Anderson, James - Seaman - Major Leonard's Battalion, NY Sea Fencibles.

Anderson, John - Quarter Gunner - NY Sea Fencibles - Company: Paul Burrows - Enlistment date: 23 Sep 1814 - Period: 3 Months.

Anderson, John - Boatswain - NY Sea Fencibles - Company: Paul Burrows - Enlistment date: 20 Sep 1814 - Period: 3 Months.

Anderson, William - Quarter Gunner - Major Leonard's Battalion, NY Sea Fencibles.

Anderson, William - Third Lieutenant - Major Leonard's Battalion, NY Sea Fencibles - Company: Alexander Robinson.

Andra, John - Private - Major Fowler's Detachment, NY Sea Fencibles - Company: James Breath.

Andrews, David - Seaman - Major Wooster's Battalion, NY Sea Fencibles.

Andrews, John - Seaman - Major Fowler's Detachment, NY Sea Fencibles.

Andrews, William - Seaman - Major Leonard's Battalion, NY Sea Fencibles.

Angles, Lewis D. - Seaman - Major Leonard's Battalion, NY Sea Fencibles - Company: William Russell - Enlistment date: 30 Dec 1814 - Period: 3 Months.

Anthony, Robert - Seaman - Major Wooster's Battalion, NY Sea Fencibles - Company: Isaac Silliman - Enlistment date: 5 Jan 1815 - Period: 12 Months.

Antonie, Mark - Seaman - Major Leonard's Battalion, NY Sea Fencibles.

Antons, Robert - Seaman - Major Leonard's Battalion, NY Sea Fencibles.

Archer, Charles - Sergeant - Major Fowler's Detachment, NY Sea Fencibles.

Armstrong, Archibald - Seaman - NY Sea Fencibles - Company: Josiah Ingersoll.

Armstrong, James - Ordinary Seaman - Major Leonard's Battalion, NY Sea Fencibles.

Arnet, John - Third Lieutenant - Major Wooster's Battalion, NY Sea Fencibles.

Arnet, Joseph - Third Lieutenant - Major Wooster's Battalion, NY Sea Fencibles - Company: Isaac Silliman.

Arnold, Effingham W. - Ordinary Seaman - Major Leonard's Battalion, NY Sea Fencibles.

Arnott, Shelby - Seaman - Major Leonard's Battalion, NY Sea Fencibles.

Arthur, John - Private - Major Leonard's Battalion, NY Sea Fencibles - Company: Alexander Robinson - Enlistment date: 15 Sep 1814 - Period: 3 Months - Discharged at Sandy Hook, NY, on 15 Dec 1814.

Arthur, John - Private - NY Sea Fencibles - Company: Josiah Ingersoll - Enlistment date: 30 Dec 1814.

Ashby, Henry - Waiter - NY Sea Fencibles - Company: Paul Burrows - Enlistment date: 1 Oct 1814 -

Period: 3 Months.

Ashley, Denison - Private - NY Sea Fencibles - Company: Paul Burrows - Enlistment date: 10 Oct 1814 - Period: 3 Months.

Astran, John - Seaman - Major Fowler's Detachment, NY Sea Fencibles.

Astreen, John - Private - Major Fowler's Detachment, NY Sea Fencibles - Company: Benjamin Muzzy.

Atkins, Isaac - Private - MA Sea Fencibles - Company: Nehemiah Skillings.

Atkinson, Anthony H. - Seaman - Major Leonard's Battalion, NY Sea Fencibles.

Atkinson, John - Seaman - Major Wooster's Battalion, NY Sea Fencibles.

Atkinson, John H. - Seaman - Major Leonard's Battalion, NY Sea Fencibles.

Aubin, Joseph - Corporal - MA Sea Fencibles - Company: Jeremiah Stickney.

Augustus, Peter - Private - Major Fowler's Detachment, NY Sea Fencibles - Company: James Breath.

Austin, James - Seaman - Major Wooster's Battalion, NY Sea Fencibles.

Austin, William - Private - MA Sea Fencibles - Company: Nehemiah Skillings.

Aykins, William - Seaman - NY Sea Fencibles - Company: John Cunningham.

Aymar, Benjamin - Quartermaster - Major Fowler's Detachment, NY Sea Fencibles - Company: Staff.

Bacon, Benjamin - Seaman - Major Leonard's Battalion, NY Sea Fencibles.

Bailey Jr., Benjamin - Private - Major Leonard's Battalion, NY Sea Fencibles - Company: Alexander Robinson - Enlistment date: 24 Oct 1814 - Discharged on 24 Jan 1815.

Bailey Sr., Benjamin - Seaman - Major Leonard's Battalion, NY Sea Fencibles.

Bailey, Henry - Private - NY Sea Fencibles - Company: Paul Burrows.

Bailey, Richard - Seaman - NY Sea Fencibles - Company: John Cunningham.

Bain, Daniel - Gunner - Major Leonard's Battalion, NY Sea Fencibles.

Bain, John - Ordinary Seaman - Major Wooster's Battalion, NY Sea Fencibles.

Bakeman, John - Seaman - NY Sea Fencibles - Company: John Cunningham.

Baker, Ephraim - Seaman - NY Sea Fencibles - Company: Josiah Ingersoll.

Baker, Francis - Seaman - NY Sea Fencibles - Company: John Cunningham.

Baker, James McLaughlin - Private - Major Leonard's Battalion, NY Sea Fencibles - Company: Francis Costigan - Pension: SO-33466, 27168, 25645, 30554 - BLW 71459-40-50; BLW 93316-120-55 - Also served in Captain Elijah Dean's Company, GA Militia, in the Seminole War of 1818.

Baker, John - Ordinary Seaman - Major Wooster's Battalion, NY Sea Fencibles.

Baker, Paul - Private - NY Sea Fencibles - Company: Paul Burrows.

Baker, William - Seaman - Major Wooster's Battalion, NY Sea Fencibles.

Baker, William - Servant - NY Sea Fencibles - Company: Josiah Ingersoll.

Balls, William - Gunner - Major Leonard's Battalion, NY Sea Fencibles.

Bankoff, James - Quarter Gunner - Major Fowler's Detachment, NY Sea Fencibles.

Bantan, John - Ordinary Seaman - Major Leonard's Battalion, NY Sea Fencibles.

American Sea Fencibles in the War of 1812

Bantz, John T. - Ordinary Seaman - Major Leonard's Battalion, NY Sea Fencibles.

Bany, Nicholas C. - Private - MA Sea Fencibles - Company: Nehemiah Skillings.

Baptist, John - Cook - Major Wooster's Battalion, NY Sea Fencibles - Company: Lieutenant Benjamin Dayton - Enlistment date: 31 Dec 1814 - Period: 3 Months - Discharged on 11 Mar 1815.

Barbier, Joseph - Quarter Gunner - Major Wooster's Battalion, NY Sea Fencibles.

Barker, James - Seaman - Major Leonard's Battalion, NY Sea Fencibles.

Barker, James - Private - NY Sea Fencibles - Company: Paul Burrows.

Barkley, William - Seaman - NY Sea Fencibles - Company: Josiah Ingersoll.

Barlow, Edward - Seaman - NY Sea Fencibles - Company: Josiah Ingersoll.

Barnard, George - Ordinary Seaman - Major Wooster's Battalion, NY Sea Fencibles.

Barnes, Henry - Seaman - Major Fowler's Detachment, NY Sea Fencibles.

Barnes, John - Sergeant - Major Wooster's Battalion, NY Sea Fencibles.

Barnes, John - Seaman - NY Sea Fencibles - Company: John Cunningham.

Barnet, George - Ordinary Seaman - Major Wooster's Battalion, NY Sea Fencibles.

Barrell, John - Seaman - Major Leonard's Battalion, NY Sea Fencibles.

Barrett, John - Seaman - Major Leonard's Battalion, NY Sea Fencibles.

Barry, John - Quarter Gunner - NY Sea Fencibles - Company: John Cunningham.

Barry, John - Seaman - NY Sea Fencibles - Company: Josiah Ingersoll.

Bartlett Jr., William - Sergeant - MA Sea Fencibles - Company: Jeremiah Stickney.

Barton, Peter - Seaman - Major Wooster's Battalion, NY Sea Fencibles.

Bass, George - Gunner - NY Sea Fencibles - Company: Josiah Ingersoll - Pension: Land bounty to Eliza Bass, widow of George Bass - BLW 69078-160-55.

Bassett, Christopher - Private - MA Sea Fencibles - Company: Jeremiah Stickney.

Bates, Andrew - Gunner - Major Leonard's Battalion, NY Sea Fencibles.

Bates, Ashel C. - Seaman - Major Leonard's Battalion, NY Sea Fencibles.

Bates, Benjamin - Private - NY Sea Fencibles - Company: Paul Burrows - Enlistment date: 23 Sep 1814 - Period: 3 Months.

Bates, Thomas F. - Seaman - Major Wooster's Battalion, NY Sea Fencibles.

Batricks, John - Ordinary Seaman - Major Leonard's Battalion, NY Sea Fencibles.

Batricks, Robert - Seaman - Major Leonard's Battalion, NY Sea Fencibles.

Battis, John - Seaman - Major Wooster's Battalion, NY Sea Fencibles.

Bayley, Moses - Musician - MA Sea Fencibles - Company: Jeremiah Stickney.

Beatty, Thomas - Seaman - Major Wooster's Battalion, NY Sea Fencibles.

Beck, Frederick - Seaman - Major Fowler's Detachment, NY Sea Fencibles.

Beckman, Charles - Seaman - Major Wooster's Battalion, NY Sea Fencibles.

Beekman, John - Seaman - NY Sea Fencibles - Company: John Cunningham.

American Sea Fencibles in the War of 1812

Bell, John - Seaman - Major Fowler's Detachment, NY Sea Fencibles.

Bell, Meshack - Private - NH Sea Fencibles - Company: William Marshall - Enlistment date: 27 May 1813 - Discharged on 27 Nov 1813.

Bellancy, William - Private - Major Leonard's Battalion, NY Sea Fencibles.

Bellands, Paul - Treasurer - Major Leonard's Battalion, NY Sea Fencibles.

Belmount, Charlie - Seaman - Major Leonard's Battalion, NY Sea Fencibles.

Benian, William - Seaman - NY Sea Fencibles - Company: Josiah Ingersoll.

Benjamin, Parchal - Seaman - Major Leonard's Battalion, NY Sea Fencibles.

Bennett, James - Seaman - Major Fowler's Detachment, NY Sea Fencibles.

Benstead, Richard - Seaman - Major Wooster's Battalion, NY Sea Fencibles.

Bergen, Hugh - Seaman - Major Leonard's Battalion, NY Sea Fencibles.

Bergenny, Renny - Quarter Gunner - NY Sea Fencibles - Company: Josiah Ingersoll.

Berger, Hugh - Seaman - Major Wooster's Battalion, NY Sea Fencibles.

Bergmar, Frederick A. - Gunner - Major Wooster's Battalion, NY Sea Fencibles.

Berry, George - Seaman - Major Wooster's Battalion, NY Sea Fencibles.

Bertody, Charles - Private - MA Sea Fencibles - Company: Nehemiah Skillings.

Bice, Joseph - Drummer - Major Leonard's Battalion, NY Sea Fencibles.

Biles, Joseph - Seaman - Major Wooster's Battalion, NY Sea Fencibles.

Billard, William - Seaman - Major Leonard's Battalion, NY Sea Fencibles.

Billings, Harry - Seaman - Major Wooster's Battalion, NY Sea Fencibles.

Billings, Henry - Seaman - Major Leonard's Battalion, NY Sea Fencibles.

Bilson, John - Seaman - Major Wooster's Battalion, NY Sea Fencibles.

Birch, John I. - Seaman - Major Fowler's Detachment, NY Sea Fencibles.

Bird, Robertson - Seaman - Major Leonard's Battalion, NY Sea Fencibles.

Bishop, Reuben - Seaman - Major Fowler's Detachment, NY Sea Fencibles.

Bisset, Isaac - Seaman - Major Fowler's Detachment, NY Sea Fencibles.

Black, Bristol - Servant - Major Fowler's Detachment, NY Sea Fencibles.

Black, Joseph - Seaman - Major Leonard's Battalion, NY Sea Fencibles.

Blackley, William - Gunner - Major Wooster's Battalion, NY Sea Fencibles.

Blair, Victor - Private - MA Sea Fencibles - Company: Nehemiah Skillings.

Blaisdell, David - Private - MA Sea Fencibles - Company: Isaac Lyman - Enlistment date: 26 Jul 1814 - Discharged on 23 Sep 1814.

Blanchard Jr., Jeremiah - Private - MA Sea Fencibles - Company: Jeremiah Stickney.

Blanchard, Andrew - Private - MA Sea Fencibles - Company: Nehemiah Skillings.

Blanchard, Charles - Private - MA Sea Fencibles - Company: Nehemiah Skillings.

American Sea Fencibles in the War of 1812

Blanchard, David - Seaman - Major Leonard's Battalion, NY Sea Fencibles.

Blanche, Anthony - Quarter Gunner - Major Fowler's Detachment, NY Sea Fencibles.

Blank, Jacob - Seaman - Major Wooster's Battalion, NY Sea Fencibles.

Bliss, John - Private - NY Sea Fencibles - Company: John Cunningham - Pension: Land bounty to Nancy Bliss, widow of John Bliss - BLW 7299-120-55.

Bloome, Joseph - Seaman - Major Leonard's Battalion, NY Sea Fencibles.

Blow, Samuel - Seaman - Major Wooster's Battalion, NY Sea Fencibles.

Blume, Joseph - Seaman - Major Leonard's Battalion, NY Sea Fencibles.

Boardman, Thomas - Private - MA Sea Fencibles - Company: Jeremiah Stickney.

Boddery, John - Private - MA Sea Fencibles - Company: Jeremiah Stickney.

Bogardus, Abraham - Boatswain - Major Leonard's Battalion, NY Sea Fencibles.

Bogardus, Richard - Seaman - Major Fowler's Detachment, NY Sea Fencibles.

Bogart, Daniel - Seaman - Major Leonard's Battalion, NY Sea Fencibles.

Bogert, John - Seaman - Major Leonard's Battalion, NY Sea Fencibles.

Bomer, William - Seaman - Major Leonard's Battalion, NY Sea Fencibles.

Bond, Nathaniel J. - Seaman - NY Sea Fencibles - Company: Josiah Ingersoll.

Bool, Joseph - Seaman - NY Sea Fencibles - Company: Josiah Ingersoll.

Booth, Joseph - Seaman - Major Leonard's Battalion, NY Sea Fencibles.

Bopp, Baptist - Gunner - Major Wooster's Battalion, NY Sea Fencibles.

Borchard, John B. - Quarter Gunner - Major Wooster's Battalion, NY Sea Fencibles.

Borches, Jenny - Seaman - NY Sea Fencibles - Company: John Cunningham.

Boston, Isaac - Seaman - Major Wooster's Battalion, NY Sea Fencibles.

Botchford, Richard - Seaman - Major Wooster's Battalion, NY Sea Fencibles.

Bounds, William - Seaman - Major Leonard's Battalion, NY Sea Fencibles.

Bowen, Benjamin G. - Seaman - Major Fowler's Detachment, NY Sea Fencibles.

Bower, Benjamin - Seaman - Major Fowler's Detachment, NY Sea Fencibles.

Bowers, George - Seaman - Major Fowler's Detachment, NY Sea Fencibles.

Bowers, John - Seaman - Major Leonard's Battalion, NY Sea Fencibles.

Bowley, Jay - Seaman - Major Leonard's Battalion, NY Sea Fencibles.

Bowman, John - Drummer - Major Wooster's Battalion, NY Sea Fencibles - Company: Lieutenant Benjamin Dayton.

Bowne, Benjamin J. - Seaman - Major Fowler's Detachment, NY Sea Fencibles.

Boyd, William - Private - NY Sea Fencibles - Company: John Cunningham - Enlistment date: 3 Sep 1814 - Period: 3 Months.

Boyer, Daniel - Private - MA Sea Fencibles - Company: Nehemiah Skillings.

Bradford, John - Ordinary Seaman - Major Wooster's Battalion, NY Sea Fencibles.

American Sea Fencibles in the War of 1812

Bradstreet, Samuel H. - Private - MA Sea Fencibles - Company: Nehemiah Skillings.

Brady, Francis - Seaman - Major Leonard's Battalion, NY Sea Fencibles.

Brady, John - Seaman - Major Leonard's Battalion, NY Sea Fencibles.

Bramer, John - Seaman - NY Sea Fencibles - Company: Josiah Ingersoll.

Brant, Christopher - Seaman - NY Sea Fencibles - Company: Josiah Ingersoll.

Bray, George - Seaman - Major Leonard's Battalion, NY Sea Fencibles.

Breath, James - Captain - Major Fowler's Detachment, NY Sea Fencibles - Company: James Breath.

Brewer, Edward - Seaman - Major Wooster's Battalion, NY Sea Fencibles.

Briggs, John - Quarter gunner - Major Wooster's Battalion, NY Sea Fencibles.

Brigham, Dexter - Seaman - Major Leonard's Battalion, NY Sea Fencibles.

Brimont, Charles - Seaman - Major Leonard's Battalion, NY Sea Fencibles.

Broderick, John - Seaman - Major Leonard's Battalion, NY Sea Fencibles.

Bronson, Shubael G. - Private - MA Sea Fencibles - Company: Nehemiah Skillings.

Brooks, Thomas - Seaman - Major Leonard's Battalion, NY Sea Fencibles.

Brothers, Siah - Seaman - Major Fowler's Detachment, NY Sea Fencibles - Company: James Breath.

Brower, Jeremiah - Gunner - Major Wooster's Battalion, NY Sea Fencibles - Company: Lieutenant Benjamin Dayton.

Brown, Ackman - Seaman - Major Leonard's Battalion, NY Sea Fencibles.

Brown, Andrew - Private - Major Leonard's Battalion, NY Sea Fencibles - Company: Alexander Robinson - Enlistment date: 16 Sep 1814 - Discharged on 16 Dec 1814.

Brown, Charles - Seaman - Major Fowler's Detachment, NY Sea Fencibles.

Brown, Francis - Boatswain - Major Wooster's Battalion, NY Sea Fencibles.

Brown, George - Seaman - Major Leonard's Battalion, NY Sea Fencibles.

Brown, Gilbert - First Lieutenant - NY Sea Fencibles - Company: John Cunningham.

Brown, James - Private - NY Sea Fencibles - Company: Paul Burrows.

Brown, John - Second Lieutenant - Major Fowler's Detachment, NY Sea Fencibles.

Brown, John - Waiter - Major Leonard's Battalion, NY Sea Fencibles.

Brown, John - Private - Major Leonard's Battalion, NY Sea Fencibles - Company: William Russell - Enlistment date: 27 Jan 1815 - Period: 3 Months.

Brown, Lewis - Ordinary Seaman - Major Wooster's Battalion, NY Sea Fencibles.

Brown, Nathan - Private - MA Sea Fencibles - Company: Jeremiah Stickney.

Brown, Peter - Quarter Gunner - NY Sea Fencibles - Company: Paul Burrows - Enlistment date: 1 Oct 1814 - Period: 3 Months.

Brown, Samuel - Second Lieutenant - NY Sea Fencibles - Company: John Cunningham.

Brown, Thomas - Seaman - Major Leonard's Battalion, NY Sea Fencibles.

Brown, Walter S. - Third Lieutenant - NY Sea Fencibles - Company: John Cunningham.

American Sea Fencibles in the War of 1812

Brown, William - Waiter - Major Wooster's Battalion, NY Sea Fencibles.

Brown, William - Private - Major Fowler's Detachment, NY Sea Fencibles - Company: James Breath.

Brown, William - Servant - Major Leonard's Battalion, NY Sea Fencibles.

Browning, Isaac - Gunner - Major Wooster's Battalion, NY Sea Fencibles.

Bruce, Henry - Quarter Gunner - NY Sea Fencibles - Company: Josiah Ingersoll.

Bruce, John - Seaman - Major Fowler's Detachment, NY Sea Fencibles.

Brunow, Barnett J. - First Lieutenant - Major Wooster's Battalion, NY Sea Fencibles.

Bruorson, Elisha - Servant - Major Leonard's Battalion, NY Sea Fencibles - Company: William Russell.

Brush, James - Seaman - Major Wooster's Battalion, NY Sea Fencibles.

Brush, William - Private - NY Sea Fencibles - Company: John Cunningham - Enlistment date: 3 Sep 1814 - Period: 3 Months.

Brushel, Moses - Private - NY Sea Fencibles - Company: Paul Burrows.

Bryan, John - Seaman - Major Fowler's Detachment, NY Sea Fencibles.

Bull, Thomas - Gunner - Major Wooster's Battalion, NY Sea Fencibles.

Bull, Thomas - Seaman - Major Leonard's Battalion, NY Sea Fencibles.

Bunker, John - Seaman - Major Leonard's Battalion, NY Sea Fencibles.

Bunshane, Francis - Boatswain - Major Fowler's Detachment, NY Sea Fencibles.

Bunt, William - Private - NY Sea Fencibles - Company: Paul Burrows.

Buntin, Joseph - Sergeant - MA Sea Fencibles - Company: Jeremiah Stickney.

Burgess, Thomas - Gunner - Major Wooster's Battalion, NY Sea Fencibles.

Burnham, F. A. - Private - MA Sea Fencibles - Company: Nehemiah Skillings.

Burns, James - Quarter Gunner - Major Leonard's Battalion, NY Sea Fencibles.

Burns, Thomas - Seaman - Major Leonard's Battalion, NY Sea Fencibles.

Burr, David - Ordinary Seaman - Major Wooster's Battalion, NY Sea Fencibles.

Burrows Jr., Paul - Captain - NY Sea Fencibles - Company: Paul Burrows.

Burrows, Benjamin - Gunner - NY Sea Fencibles - Company: Paul Burrows.

Burrows, Berndt J. - Lieutenant - NY Sea Fencibles.

Burrows, Ebenezer - Seaman - NY Sea Fencibles - Company: John Cunningham.

Burrows, Frederick - Waiter - NY Sea Fencibles - Company: Paul Burrows - Enlistment date: 1 Oct 1814 - Period: 3 Months.

Burrows, George - Quarter Gunner - NY Sea Fencibles - Company: Paul Burrows.

Burrows, James - Musician - NY Sea Fencibles - Company: Paul Burrows.

Burrows, William - Private - MA Sea Fencibles - Company: Nehemiah Skillings.

Burt, William - Private - NY Sea Fencibles - Company: Paul Burrows - Enlistment date: 6 Oct 1814 - Period: 3 Months.

Butler, Fortune - Seaman - Major Wooster's Battalion, NY Sea Fencibles.

Butler, Francis C. - Private - MA Sea Fencibles - Company: Nehemiah Skillings.

Butler, John - Seaman - Major Wooster's Battalion, NY Sea Fencibles.

Butody, Chs. - Private - MA Sea Fencibles - Company: Nehemiah Skillings.

Byrns, George - Seaman - Major Fowler's Detachment, NY Sea Fencibles.

Cady, Arnold - Seaman - Major Wooster's Battalion, NY Sea Fencibles.

Caffrey, Francis - Seaman - Major Wooster's Battalion, NY Sea Fencibles.

Cahill, Thomas - Ordinary Seaman - NY Sea Fencibles - Company: Josiah Ingersoll.

Califlower, Edward - Seaman - Major Leonard's Battalion, NY Sea Fencibles.

Call, Charles - Private - MA Sea Fencibles - Company: Jeremiah Stickney.

Call, John - Seaman - Major Wooster's Battalion, NY Sea Fencibles.

Callender, Joseph - Sergeant - MA Sea Fencibles - Company: Nehemiah Skillings.

Calligan, John - Second Lieutenant - Major Leonard's Battalion, NY Sea Fencibles.

Calmell, Paul - Seaman - Major Wooster's Battalion, NY Sea Fencibles.

Camp, Alexander - Gunner - Major Fowler's Detachment, NY Sea Fencibles.

Campbell, John - Seaman - Major Leonard's Battalion, NY Sea Fencibles.

Campbell, John - Seaman - Major Wooster's Battalion, NY Sea Fencibles.

Campbell, John - Private - NY Sea Fencibles - Company: John Cunningham - Enlistment date: 7 Sep 1814 - Period: 3 Months.

Campbell, John - Boatswain - Major Fowler's Detachment, NY Sea Fencibles.

Candle, Thomas - Seaman - Major Wooster's Battalion, NY Sea Fencibles - Company: Isaac Silliman - Enlistment date: 10 Jan 1815 - Period: 1 Yr.

Cannel, John - Seaman - Major Wooster's Battalion, NY Sea Fencibles.

Cannon, David - Private - Major Fowler's Detachment, NY Sea Fencibles - Company: Benjamin Muzzy.

Cannon, Jacob - Seaman - Major Leonard's Battalion, NY Sea Fencibles.

Cannon, Robert - Seaman - NY Sea Fencibles - Company: Josiah Ingersoll.

Caragher, Patrick - Seaman - Major Wooster's Battalion, NY Sea Fencibles - Company: Isaac Silliman - Enlistment date: 7 Feb 1815 - Period: 1 Yr.

Card, John - Private - NH Sea Fencibles - Company: William Marshall - Enlistment date: 27 May 1813 - Discharged on 27 Nov 1813.

Carlock, John - Seaman - Major Wooster's Battalion, NY Sea Fencibles - Company: John Roorbach - Enlistment date: 12 Sep 1814 - Discharged on 12 Dec 1814.

Carlock, William - Seaman - Major Wooster's Battalion, NY Sea Fencibles - Company: John Randlet - Enlistment date: 20 Sep 1814 - Discharged on 20 Dec 1814.

Carlow, William - Seaman - NY Sea Fencibles - Company: Josiah Ingersoll.

Carman, John B. - Ward master - Major Wooster's Battalion, NY Sea Fencibles.

Carman, John B. - Hospital Ward Master - NY Sea Fencibles - Company: Josiah Ingersoll - Enlistment date: 21 Dec 1814.

American Sea Fencibles in the War of 1812

Carman, Robert - Seaman - NY Sea Fencibles - Company: Josiah Ingersoll.

Carpenter, John - Surgeon - NY Sea Fencibles - Company: John Cunningham - Enlistment date: 15 Oct 1814 - BLW 46815-80-55.

Carpenter, Samuel - Ordinary Seaman - Major Wooster's Battalion, NY Sea Fencibles.

Carpenter, Walter - Seaman - Major Leonard's Battalion, NY Sea Fencibles - Company: Alexander Robinson.

Carr, Richard - Private - NY Sea Fencibles - Company: Paul Burrows - Enlistment date: 10 Oct 1814 - Period: 3 Months.

Carragan, Haugh - Seaman - Major Wooster's Battalion, NY Sea Fencibles.

Carragan, Patrick - Seaman - Major Wooster's Battalion, NY Sea Fencibles.

Carragher, Hugh - Seaman - Major Wooster's Battalion, NY Sea Fencibles - Company: Isaac Silliman - Enlistment date: 1 Feb 1815 - Period: 1 Yr.

Carroll, Charles - Private - Major Leonard's Battalion, NY Sea Fencibles - Company: Alexander Robinson - Enlistment date: 15 Sep 1814 - Discharged on 15 Dec 1814.

Carroll, James - Private - Major Leonard's Battalion, NY Sea Fencibles - Company: Alexander Robinson - Enlistment date: 19 Sep 1814 - Discharged on 19 Dec 1814.

Carroll, William - Seaman - NY Sea Fencibles - Company: Josiah Ingersoll.

Carso, Daniel - Gunner - Major Wooster's Battalion, NY Sea Fencibles.

Carson, Andrew - Seaman - Major Fowler's Detachment, NY Sea Fencibles.

Cartange, James - Ordinary Seaman - NY Sea Fencibles - Company: Josiah Ingersoll.

Carter, George - Seaman - Major Leonard's Battalion, NY Sea Fencibles.

Carter, Robert - Private - MA Sea Fencibles - Company: Nehemiah Skillings.

Carver, William - Seaman - Major Leonard's Battalion, NY Sea Fencibles - Company: William Russell - Enlistment date: 4 Jan 1815 - Period: 3 Months.

Cary, Nathan - Private - Major Wooster's Battalion, NY Sea Fencibles - Company: Isaac Silliman - Enlistment date: 31 Jan 1815 - Period: 1 Yr.

Cary, Nathaniel - Private - NY Sea Fencibles - Company: Paul Burrows - Enlistment date: 17 Oct 1814 - Period: 3 Months.

Case, Joseph - Private - Major Leonard's Battalion, NY Sea Fencibles - Company: Alexander Robinson - Deserted.

Case, Peter - Gunner - Major Fowler's Detachment, NY Sea Fencibles.

Case, Thomas - Seaman - Major Leonard's Battalion, NY Sea Fencibles - Company: Alexander Robinson - Enlistment date: 27 Oct 1814 - Period: 3 Months - Discharged on 27 Jan 1815.

Caswell, Lewin - Quarter Gunner - NY Sea Fencibles - Company: Paul Burrows - Enlistment date: 30 Sep 1814 - Period: 3 Months.

Caudle, Wilkes - Seaman - Major Fowler's Detachment, NY Sea Fencibles.

Cavannah, Stephen - Seaman - Major Leonard's Battalion, NY Sea Fencibles - Company: Alexander Robinson - Enlistment date: 23 Sep 1814 - Period: 3 Months - Discharged on 23 Dec 1814.

Ceaser, Friend - Seaman - Major Wooster's Battalion, NY Sea Fencibles.

American Sea Fencibles in the War of 1812

Chambers, Andrew - Quarter Gunner - Major Leonard's Battalion, NY Sea Fencibles.

Chapman, Edward - Private - MA Sea Fencibles - Company: Nehemiah Skillings.

Chapman, Nathaniel - Private - MA Sea Fencibles - Company: Nehemiah Skillings.

Chase, Samuel - Private - Major Leonard's Battalion, NY Sea Fencibles - Company: Alexander Robinson - Missing since 12 Oct 1814 at New York.

Cheeny Jr., Abiel - Seaman - NY Sea Fencibles - Company: Josiah Ingersoll.

Cheney, Abiel - Seaman - NY Sea Fencibles - Company: Josiah Ingersoll.

Chessey, John Francis - Seaman - Major Leonard's Battalion, NY Sea Fencibles.

Choat, Ebenezer - Private - NY Sea Fencibles - Company: Paul Burrows.

Chubb, David - Seaman - Major Leonard's Battalion, NY Sea Fencibles.

Churchill, John - Seaman - Major Wooster's Battalion, NY Sea Fencibles.

Cinefield, Edward - Gunner - NY Sea Fencibles - Company: Josiah Ingersoll.

Clap, Edward - Private - MA Sea Fencibles - Company: Nehemiah Skillings.

Clark, Chester - Seaman - NY Sea Fencibles - Company: Josiah Ingersoll.

Clark, James - Private - NY Sea Fencibles - Company: Paul Burrows - Enlistment date: 28 Sep 1814 - Period: 3 Months.

Clark, James - Private - NY Sea Fencibles - Company: John Cunningham.

Clark, James A. - Seaman - Major Leonard's Battalion, NY Sea Fencibles.

Clark, John - Quarter Gunner - Major Leonard's Battalion, NY Sea Fencibles - Company: William Russell - Enlistment date: 16 Jan 1815.

Clark, John - Seaman - Major Fowler's Detachment, NY Sea Fencibles.

Clark, Moses - Waiter - Major Wooster's Battalion, NY Sea Fencibles - Company: Isaac Silliman.

Clark, Peter G. - Seaman - Major Leonard's Battalion, NY Sea Fencibles - Company: Alexander Robinson - Enlistment date: 15 Sep 1814 - Period: 3 Months - Discharged on 15 Dec 1814.

Clark, William - Private - NY Sea Fencibles - Company: John Cunningham - Enlistment date: 5 Sep 1814 - Period: 3 Months.

Clarke, Henry - Seaman - Major Leonard's Battalion, NY Sea Fencibles.

Clarke, John A. - Seaman - Major Leonard's Battalion, NY Sea Fencibles.

Clason, Henry - Private - NY Sea Fencibles - Company: Josiah Ingersoll - Enlistment date: 5 Jan 1815.

Clawson, Henry - Seaman - Major Fowler's Detachment, NY Sea Fencibles.

Cleves, Charles - Seaman - Major Leonard's Battalion, NY Sea Fencibles.

Clifton, Thomas - Seaman - Major Wooster's Battalion, NY Sea Fencibles.

Cline, Frederick - Seaman - Major Leonard's Battalion, NY Sea Fencibles.

Cline, Jacob - Seaman - NY Sea Fencibles - Company: Josiah Ingersoll.

Clough, Nathaniel - Second Lieutenant - Major Wooster's Battalion, NY Sea Fencibles - Company: Isaac Silliman.

American Sea Fencibles in the War of 1812

Coats, John - Captain's servant - Major Wooster's Battalion, NY Sea Fencibles.

Cobb, Lom - Private - MA Sea Fencibles - Company: Nehemiah Skillings.

Cobbs, Ebenezer - Sergeant - Major Wooster's Battalion, NY Sea Fencibles.

Cock, Robert - Private - NY Sea Fencibles - Company: John Cunningham - Enlistment date: 6 Sep 1814 - Period: 3 Months.

Coffin Jr., David - Private - MA Sea Fencibles - Company: Jeremiah Stickney.

Coffin, Hector - Second Lieutenant - MA Sea Fencibles - Company: Jeremiah Stickney.

Colberth, John - Private - Major Leonard's Battalion, NY Sea Fencibles - Company: Alexander Robinson - Enlistment date: 16 Oct 1814 - Period: 3 Months - Discharged on 16 Jan 1815.

Colburn, Hugh - Seaman - Major Wooster's Battalion, NY Sea Fencibles.

Coleman, Silas - Seaman - NY Sea Fencibles - Company: Josiah Ingersoll - Enlistment date: 2 Jan 1815.

Coles, John - Gunner - Major Leonard's Battalion, NY Sea Fencibles - Company: William Russell - Enlistment date: 5 Dec 1814 - Period: 3 Months - Pension: Old War IF-28440 - BLW 2287-80-55.

Collens, Thomas - Seaman - Major Fowler's Detachment, NY Sea Fencibles.

Colles, Christopher - Captain - NY Sea Fencibles - Company: Christopher Colles - Enlistment date: 1 Nov 1814.

Colles, David - Private - Major Leonard's Battalion, NY Sea Fencibles - Company: Alexander Robinson - Enlistment date: 26 Oct 1814 - Discharged on 26 Jan 1814.

Collier, Hezekiah - First Lieutenant - Major Leonard's Battalion, NY Sea Fencibles - Company: William Russell - Enlistment date: 6 Dec 1814.

Colligan, Edward - Seaman - Major Leonard's Battalion, NY Sea Fencibles - Company: William Russell - Enlistment date: 14 Jan 1815 - Period: 3 Months.

Collins, Michael - Seaman - Major Fowler's Detachment, NY Sea Fencibles.

Collins, Thomas - Private - Major Fowler's Detachment, NY Sea Fencibles - Company: James Breath - Deserted on 9 Nov 1814.

Colton, William - Private - Major Leonard's Battalion, NY Sea Fencibles.

Colwell, Thomas D. - Gunner - Major Leonard's Battalion, NY Sea Fencibles - Company: William Russell - Enlistment date: 6 Dec 1814 - Period: 3 Months.

Concklin, John - Private - NY Sea Fencibles - Company: Paul Burrows.

Concklin, Samuel - Private - NY Sea Fencibles - Company: Paul Burrows - Enlistment date: 7 Nov 1814 - Period: 3 Months.

Conklin, Jacob - Seaman - Major Fowler's Detachment, NY Sea Fencibles - Company: James Breath.

Connelly, Francis - Seaman - Major Wooster's Battalion, NY Sea Fencibles.

Connelly, Thomas - Seaman - Major Fowler's Detachment, NY Sea Fencibles.

Conner, John - Seaman - Major Fowler's Detachment, NY Sea Fencibles - Company: James Breath.

Conner, Thomas - Gunner - NY Sea Fencibles - Company: John Cunningham.

Connor, Thomas - Gunner - Major Leonard's Battalion, NY Sea Fencibles - Company: Alexander Robinson - Enlistment date: 5 Oct 1814.

Connurl, John - Seaman - NY Sea Fencibles - Company: John Cunningham.

Conover, Joseph I. - Seaman - Major Leonard's Battalion, NY Sea Fencibles.

Conover, Joseph J. - Seaman - Major Wooster's Battalion, NY Sea Fencibles - Company: Isaac Silliman - Enlistment date: 25 Jan 1815 - Period: 1 Yr.

Cook, Charles - Corporal - MA Sea Fencibles - Company: Jeremiah Stickney.

Cook, Patrick - Waiter - NY Sea Fencibles - Company: John Cunningham.

Cook, Richard A. - Private - NY Sea Fencibles - BLW 13127-80-55.

Cooper, James - Private - NY Sea Fencibles - Company: Paul Burrows.

Cooper, James - Private - Major Fowler's Detachment, NY Sea Fencibles - Company: James Breath - Enlistment date: 22 Sep 1814 - Period: 3 Months.

Copper, Elisha - Private - Major Fowler's Detachment, NY Sea Fencibles - Company: James Breath - Deserted at Blockhouse Constitution on 7 Nov 1814.

Corbett, Charles - Seaman - Major Leonard's Battalion, NY Sea Fencibles.

Corbey, Joseph - Boatswain - Major Leonard's Battalion, NY Sea Fencibles - Company: Alexander Robinson - Enlistment date: 13 Oct 1814 - Discharged on 13 Jan 1815.

Corbil, Charles - Seaman - Major Leonard's Battalion, NY Sea Fencibles.

Corby, Seph - Boatswain - Major Leonard's Battalion, NY Sea Fencibles.

Corley, Joseph - Private - Major Leonard's Battalion, NY Sea Fencibles.

Cornish, Isaac - Seaman - Major Fowler's Detachment, NY Sea Fencibles - Company: James Breath.

Corry, William - Seaman - Major Leonard's Battalion, NY Sea Fencibles.

Cosse, Peter - Quarter Gunner - Major Fowler's Detachment, NY Sea Fencibles - Company: James Breath.

Costigan, Francis - Captain - Major Leonard's Battalion, NY Sea Fencibles - Company: Francis Costigan.

Costigan, Samuel Fisker - Ordinary Seaman - Major Leonard's Battalion, NY Sea Fencibles.

Cotton Jr., William M. - Seaman - Major Leonard's Battalion, NY Sea Fencibles.

Cotton, William - Seaman - Major Leonard's Battalion, NY Sea Fencibles - Company: William Russell - Enlistment date: 18 Jan 1815 - Period: 3 Months - Deserted, a boy.

Cottrell, Shephard - Private - NY Sea Fencibles - Company: Paul Burrows - Enlistment date: 1 Oct 1814 - Period: 3 Months.

Couch, John - Private - MA Sea Fencibles - Company: Jeremiah Stickney.

Cowan, Andrew - Gunner - Major Fowler's Detachment, NY Sea Fencibles.

Cox, Miles - Seaman - Major Leonard's Battalion, NY Sea Fencibles.

Cox, Samuel G. - Boatswain - Major Leonard's Battalion, NY Sea Fencibles - Company: Alexander Robinson.

Craig, Matthew - Seaman - NY Sea Fencibles - Company: Josiah Ingersoll - Enlistment date: 30 Dec 1814.

Craig, Robert - Ordinary Seaman - Major Wooster's Battalion, NY Sea Fencibles.

American Sea Fencibles in the War of 1812

Crandle, Silas - Seaman - Major Wooster's Battalion, NY Sea Fencibles - Company: Isaac Silliman - Enlistment date: 25 Jan 1815 - Period: 1 Yr.

Crane, James - Seaman - Major Leonard's Battalion, NY Sea Fencibles.

Crane, Philip - Seaman - Major Wooster's Battalion, NY Sea Fencibles.

Cranston, William - First Lieutenant - Major Leonard's Battalion, NY Sea Fencibles - Company: Alexander Robinson.

Crawford, Peter - Seaman - Major Leonard's Battalion, NY Sea Fencibles.

Creeley, Nicholas - Seaman - Major Wooster's Battalion, NY Sea Fencibles.

Crery, Samuel - Sergeant - Major Fowler's Detachment, NY Sea Fencibles.

Crocker, Ichabod - Private - NY Sea Fencibles - Company: Paul Burrows - Enlistment date: 27 Oct 1814 - Period: 3 Months.

Crocker, Joseph - Private - NY Sea Fencibles - Company: Paul Burrows - Enlistment date: 10 Oct 1814 - Period: 3 Months.

Cromwell, Ephraim - Musician - Major Wooster's Battalion, NY Sea Fencibles.

Crone, Thomas - Seaman - Major Leonard's Battalion, NY Sea Fencibles - Company: William Russell - Enlistment date: 12 Jan 1815 - Period: 3 Months.

Crooker, Tilden - Private - MA Sea Fencibles - Company: Nehemiah Skillings.

Crosby, James M. - Seaman - NY Sea Fencibles - Company: Josiah Ingersoll.

Crosdale, William Henry - Second Lieutenant - Major Wooster's Battalion, NY Sea Fencibles.

Cuffee, Amos - Seaman - Major Wooster's Battalion, NY Sea Fencibles - Company: Isaac Silliman - Enlistment date: 7 Jan 1815 - Period: 1 Yr.

Cuffee, Amos - Seaman - Major Leonard's Battalion, NY Sea Fencibles.

Culbert, John - Seaman - Major Wooster's Battalion, NY Sea Fencibles - Company: Isaac Silliman - Enlistment date: 21 Jan 1815 - Period: 1 Yr.

Culleday, James - Private - NY Sea Fencibles - Company: John Cunningham - Enlistment date: 5 Sep 1814 - Period: 3 Months.

Culler, James - Seaman - NY Sea Fencibles - Company: John Cunningham.

Culoris, Charles - Ordinary Seaman - Major Wooster's Battalion, NY Sea Fencibles.

Culver, William - Gunner - Major Fowler's Detachment, NY Sea Fencibles - Company: James Breath.

Cummings, George - Seaman - Major Leonard's Battalion, NY Sea Fencibles.

Cummings, James - Private - MA Sea Fencibles - Company: Jeremiah Stickney.

Cunningham, James - Gunner - Major Leonard's Battalion, NY Sea Fencibles.

Cunningham, James - Seaman - Major Wooster's Battalion, NY Sea Fencibles - Company: Isaac Silliman - Enlistment date: 25 Jan 1815 - Period: 1 Yr.

Cunningham, John - Captain - NY Sea Fencibles - Company: John Cunningham.

Cunningham, Owen - Private - NY Sea Fencibles - Company: Paul Burrows - Enlistment date: 4 Nov 1814 - Period: 3 Months.

Cure, Robert - Seaman - Major Fowler's Detachment, NY Sea Fencibles.

American Sea Fencibles in the War of 1812

Curran, James - Seaman - Major Leonard's Battalion, NY Sea Fencibles - Company: William Russell - Enlistment date: 5 Jan 1815 - Period: 3 Months.

Curran, Nicholas - Seaman - Major Fowler's Detachment, NY Sea Fencibles.

Curren, John - Seaman - Major Leonard's Battalion, NY Sea Fencibles.

Currier, William - Seaman - Major Leonard's Battalion, NY Sea Fencibles - Company: Alexander Robinson - Enlistment date: 29 Sep 1814 - Period: 3 Months - Discharged on 29 Dec 1814.

Curry, James - Seaman - Major Wooster's Battalion, NY Sea Fencibles.

Curry, William - Seaman - Major Wooster's Battalion, NY Sea Fencibles.

Curtis, Benjamin - Gunner - Major Fowler's Detachment, NY Sea Fencibles - Company: James Breath.

Curtis, Caleb - Corporal - MA Sea Fencibles - Company: Nehemiah Skillings.

Curtis, Joseph - Private - NY Sea Fencibles - Company: Paul Burrows.

Curtis, Josiah - Private - NY Sea Fencibles - Company: Paul Burrows - Enlistment date: 4 Nov 1814 - Period: 3 Months.

Curtis, Theodore - Private - MA Sea Fencibles - Company: Nehemiah Skillings.

Dailey, John - Private - NY Sea Fencibles - Company: Paul Burrows - Enlistment date: 2 Nov 1814 - Period: 3 Months.

Dall, James L. - Quarter gunner - Major Wooster's Battalion, NY Sea Fencibles - Company: Isaac Silliman - Enlistment date: 2 Dec 1814 - Period: 6 Months.

Daniels, James - Seaman - Major Wooster's Battalion, NY Sea Fencibles - Company: Isaac Silliman - Enlistment date: 2 Feb 1815 - Period: 1 Yr.

Daniels, James - Private - NY Sea Fencibles - Company: Paul Burrows - Enlistment date: 24 Oct 1814 - Period: 3 Months.

Daniels, John - Seaman - Major Wooster's Battalion, NY Sea Fencibles - Company: Isaac Silliman - Enlistment date: 8 Feb 1815 - Period: 1 Yr.

Daniels, William - Boy - Major Leonard's Battalion, NY Sea Fencibles - Company: William Russell - Enlistment date: 20 Jan 1815 - Period: 3 Months.

Dansh, John - Seaman - Major Leonard's Battalion, NY Sea Fencibles - Company: Alexander Robinson - Enlistment date: 24 Oct 1814 - Discharged on 2 Jan 1815.

Dark, Nicholas A. - Seaman - Major Wooster's Battalion, NY Sea Fencibles.

Darrah, John - Seaman - Major Wooster's Battalion, NY Sea Fencibles - Company: Isaac Silliman - Enlistment date: 4 Feb 1815 - Period: 1 Yr.

Dauson, Robert - Seaman - Major Leonard's Battalion, NY Sea Fencibles.

Davis, Aaron - Seaman - Major Wooster's Battalion, NY Sea Fencibles.

Davis, David - Seaman - Major Wooster's Battalion, NY Sea Fencibles.

Davis, George - Seaman - Major Wooster's Battalion, NY Sea Fencibles - Company: John Randlet.

Davis, James - Seaman - Major Wooster's Battalion, NY Sea Fencibles.

Davis, John - Quarter Gunner - Major Leonard's Battalion, NY Sea Fencibles - Company: William Russell - Enlistment date: 16 Jan 1815 - Period: 3 Months.

American Sea Fencibles in the War of 1812

Davis, John - Seaman - Major Wooster's Battalion, NY Sea Fencibles.

Davis, John - Seaman - Major Fowler's Detachment, NY Sea Fencibles - Company: Benjamin Muzzy.

Davis, Joseph - Private - MA Sea Fencibles - Company: Nehemiah Skillings.

Davis, Lewis - Seaman - NY Sea Fencibles - Company: Josiah Ingersoll.

Davis, Samuel P. - Private - NH Sea Fencibles - Company: William Marshall - Enlistment date: 2 Nov 1813 - Pension: Wife Rachel Edwards, Old War CF-994, Old War IF-20334, WO-254, WC-1288; married on 7 Jan 1812 in Lewistown, DE; seaman died on 15 (or 17) Feb 1824 in Lewistown, DE - BLW 9096-160-50 - Discharged on 2 Sep 1814; also served in Captain James Holland's Company, DE Militia, from 4 Sep 1814 to 13 Mar 1815.

Davis, William - Seaman - Major Fowler's Detachment, NY Sea Fencibles.

Davis, William - Seaman - Major Leonard's Battalion, NY Sea Fencibles.

Dawson, John - Seaman - Major Wooster's Battalion, NY Sea Fencibles.

Dayton, Benjamin G. - Lieutenant - Major Wooster's Battalion, NY Sea Fencibles - Company: Lieutenant Benjamin Dayton - Enlistment date: 9 Dec 1814 - In charge of British POWs on a prison ship near North Battery.

DeForrest, William T. - Private - Major Wooster's Battalion, NY Sea Fencibles - Company: John Roorbach - BLW 20558-120-55.

Delafield, Edward - Surgeon - Major Leonard's Battalion, NY Sea Fencibles - Company: William Russell.

Delany, Peter - Private - NY Sea Fencibles - Company: Paul Burrows - Enlistment date: 28 Sep 1814 - Period: 3 Months.

Delaplain, William B. - Seaman - Major Leonard's Battalion, NY Sea Fencibles - Company: Alexander Robinson - Enlistment date: 30 Sep 1814 - Period: 3 Months.

Delaware, Thomas - Seaman - Major Leonard's Battalion, NY Sea Fencibles.

Dempsey, Charles D. - Seaman - Major Fowler's Detachment, NY Sea Fencibles.

Dennis, Amos - Private - MA Sea Fencibles - Company: Jeremiah Stickney.

Dennis, John - Private - NY Sea Fencibles - Company: John Cunningham - Enlistment date: 5 Sep 1814 - Period: 3 Months.

Dennis, Thomas - Private - MA Sea Fencibles - Company: Nehemiah Skillings.

Denny, William - Gunner - NY Sea Fencibles - Company: Josiah Ingersoll.

Derrick, Cornelius - Gunner - Major Wooster's Battalion, NY Sea Fencibles - Company: Isaac Silliman.

Devorix, Robert - Private - NY Sea Fencibles - Company: Paul Burrows - Enlistment date: 5 Nov 1814 - Period: 3 Months.

Deweize, John - Seaman - Major Fowler's Detachment, NY Sea Fencibles.

Dewey, John - Private - NY Sea Fencibles - Company: Paul Burrows - Enlistment date: 10 Oct 1814 - Period: 3 Months - Pension: Wife Rebecca Brown, WO-18516, WC-16532; married on 15 Jan 1815, Groton, CT; seaman died on 6 May 1861, Preston, CT - BLW 34203-40-50 Cancelled, BLW 3483-40-50, BLW 102260-40-50, BLW 1174-80-55 - Discharged on 10 Jan 1815; also served in Captain Stephen Billings' Company, CT Militia, from 9 Aug 1814 to 20 Sep 1814.

Dewint, Henry - Seaman - Major Wooster's Battalion, NY Sea Fencibles - Company: Isaac Silliman - Enlistment date: 8 Feb 1815 - Period: 12 Months.

American Sea Fencibles in the War of 1812

Dewson, Francis - Private - MA Sea Fencibles - Company: Nehemiah Skillings.

Dickinson, John - Seaman - Major Fowler's Detachment, NY Sea Fencibles - Company: James Breath - Deserted at Blockhouse Constitution on 14 Nov 1814.

Dickson, John - Seaman - Major Wooster's Battalion, NY Sea Fencibles.

Dickson, Joshua D. - Private - MA Sea Fencibles - Company: Nehemiah Skillings.

Dickson, William - Seaman - Major Leonard's Battalion, NY Sea Fencibles.

Dimorest, Daniel - Seaman - NY Sea Fencibles - Company: Josiah Ingersoll.

Dix, West - Seaman - Major Leonard's Battalion, NY Sea Fencibles - Company: William Russell - Enlistment date: 16 Jan 1815 - Period: 3 Months.

Dixon, Richards - Seaman - Major Leonard's Battalion, NY Sea Fencibles.

Dixon, Thomas - Seaman - NY Sea Fencibles - Company: John Cunningham - Enlistment date: 5 Sep 1814 - Period: 3 Months.

Dixon, Thomas - First Lieutenant - Major Leonard's Battalion, NY Sea Fencibles.

Dixon, William - Seaman - NY Sea Fencibles - Company: Josiah Ingersoll - Enlistment date: 2 Jan 1815.

Doak, John - Private - MA Sea Fencibles - Company: Nehemiah Skillings.

Dobbing, Samuel - Seaman - Major Fowler's Detachment, NY Sea Fencibles.

Dobbins, Samuel - Seaman - Major Wooster's Battalion, NY Sea Fencibles - Company: Lieutenant Benjamin Dayton - Enlistment date: 29 Dec 1814 - Served on board a prison ship; discharged on 11 Mar 1815.

Dole, John - Private - MA Sea Fencibles - Company: Jeremiah Stickney.

Dominick, John W. - Gunner - Major Leonard's Battalion, NY Sea Fencibles.

Donnell, Henry - Private - MA Sea Fencibles - Company: Isaac Lyman - Enlistment date: 25 Jul 1814 - Discharged on 24 Aug 1814.

Donnell, Nathaniel - Private - MA Sea Fencibles - Company: Isaac Lyman - Enlistment date: 25 Jul 1814 - Discharged on 23 Sep 1814.

Donnelly, Owen - Seaman - Major Leonard's Battalion, NY Sea Fencibles - Company: William Russell - Enlistment date: 19 Jan 1815 - Period: 3 Months - Deserted.

Donohue, John - Ordinary Seaman - Major Leonard's Battalion, NY Sea Fencibles.

Doran, Patrick - Seaman - Major Leonard's Battalion, NY Sea Fencibles - Company: William Russell - Period: 3 Months.

Dorimus, George G. - Seaman - Major Leonard's Battalion, NY Sea Fencibles.

Dorsey, James - Seaman - Major Fowler's Detachment, NY Sea Fencibles - Company: James Breath.

Dougherty, Philip - Ordinary Seaman - Major Leonard's Battalion, NY Sea Fencibles.

Dougherty, William - Seaman - Major Leonard's Battalion, NY Sea Fencibles - Company: William Russell - Enlistment date: 16 Jan 1815 - Period: 3 Months.

Douglass, William - Drummer - Major Fowler's Detachment, NY Sea Fencibles.

Dow, Joseph - Seaman - Major Wooster's Battalion, NY Sea Fencibles.

Downing, Elisha - Private - NY Sea Fencibles - Company: Paul Burrows - Enlistment date: 10 Oct 1814 -

Period: 3 Months.

Downing, William - Quarter Gunner - Major Wooster's Battalion, NY Sea Fencibles.

Downs, Francis - Seaman - Major Fowler's Detachment, NY Sea Fencibles - Company: James Breath.

Drake, William - Seaman - Major Wooster's Battalion, NY Sea Fencibles.

Driver, Samuel - Seaman - Major Wooster's Battalion, NY Sea Fencibles.

Dubois, Cato - Seaman - Major Fowler's Detachment, NY Sea Fencibles - Company: James Breath.

Dugan, James - Seaman - Major Leonard's Battalion, NY Sea Fencibles - Company: William Russell - Enlistment date: 4 Jan 1815 - Period: 3 Months - Deserted.

Duggin, James - Seaman - Major Wooster's Battalion, NY Sea Fencibles.

Duke, James - Gunner - NY Sea Fencibles - Company: John Cunningham - Enlistment date: 3 Sep 1814 - Period: 3 Months.

Dumm, Edward - Seaman - Major Wooster's Battalion, NY Sea Fencibles.

Dunham, John - Private - NY Sea Fencibles - Company: Paul Burrows - Enlistment date: 10 Oct 1814 - Period: 3 Months.

Dunking, Samuel - Private - NH Sea Fencibles - Company: William Marshall - Enlistment date: 27 Nov 1813 - Discharged on 16 Nov 1813.

Dunlap, James - Seaman - Major Wooster's Battalion, NY Sea Fencibles.

Dunn, E. - Seaman - Major Wooster's Battalion, NY Sea Fencibles - Company: John Roorbach.

Dunn, Samuel - Seaman - Major Wooster's Battalion, NY Sea Fencibles.

Dunnica, Edward - Seaman - NY Sea Fencibles - Company: Josiah Ingersoll.

Duryee, George - Seaman - Major Leonard's Battalion, NY Sea Fencibles.

Duvault, Jacob - Seaman - Major Leonard's Battalion, NY Sea Fencibles.

Dwart, Nicholas - Seaman - Major Wooster's Battalion, NY Sea Fencibles - Company: Isaac Silliman - Enlistment date: 5 Jan 1815 - Period: 1 Yr.

Earles, Cornelius - Seaman - Major Leonard's Battalion, NY Sea Fencibles.

Earles, James - Seaman - Major Leonard's Battalion, NY Sea Fencibles.

Edes, Robert B. - Private - MA Sea Fencibles - Company: Nehemiah Skillings.

Edwards, John - Seaman - Major Wooster's Battalion, NY Sea Fencibles.

Edwards, Shelby - Seaman - Major Leonard's Battalion, NY Sea Fencibles.

Eeason, James - Seaman - Major Fowler's Detachment, NY Sea Fencibles - Company: James Breath - Deserted at Blockhouse Constitution on 10 Oct 1814.

Egbert, Frederick - Seaman - NY Sea Fencibles - Company: John Cunningham - Enlistment date: 2 Sep 1814 - Period: 3 Months.

Egburt, Daniel - Seaman - Major Leonard's Battalion, NY Sea Fencibles.

Elder, Jacob - Seaman - Major Leonard's Battalion, NY Sea Fencibles.

Ellingham, John - Seaman - NY Sea Fencibles - Company: Paul Burrows - Enlistment date: 11 Nov 1814 - Period: 3 Months - Deserted.

American Sea Fencibles in the War of 1812

Elliott, Charles - Quarter Gunner - Major Leonard's Battalion, NY Sea Fencibles.

Elliott, Nicholas - Seaman - Major Leonard's Battalion, NY Sea Fencibles.

Ellis, Samuel - Private - NY Sea Fencibles - Company: Paul Burrows - Enlistment date: 7 Nov 1814.

Ellis, Thomas - Ordinary Seaman - Major Leonard's Battalion, NY Sea Fencibles.

Elliston, William - Seaman - Major Wooster's Battalion, NY Sea Fencibles.

Ellit, Thomas - Seaman - Major Wooster's Battalion, NY Sea Fencibles.

Ellston, William - Seaman - Major Wooster's Battalion, NY Sea Fencibles.

Elsworth, Arthur - Ordinary Seaman - Major Leonard's Battalion, NY Sea Fencibles.

Elsworth, Francis - Seaman - Major Leonard's Battalion, NY Sea Fencibles.

Elwill, George P. - Ordinary Seaman - NY Sea Fencibles - Company: John Cunningham.

Ely, Charles - Seaman - Major Fowler's Detachment, NY Sea Fencibles.

Endicott Jr., William - Private - MA Sea Fencibles - Company: Nehemiah Skillings.

England, William - Quarter Gunner - Major Leonard's Battalion, NY Sea Fencibles.

Enney, Jacob - Seaman - Major Leonard's Battalion, NY Sea Fencibles.

Ennis, Benjamin - Private - NY Sea Fencibles - Company: John Cunningham - Enlistment date: 2 Sep 1814 - Period: 3 Months.

Ephraim, Stephen - Private - Major Fowler's Detachment, NY Sea Fencibles - Company: James Breath.

Etsell, Richard - Seaman - Major Wooster's Battalion, NY Sea Fencibles.

Eustace, Ames - Seaman - Major Fowler's Detachment, NY Sea Fencibles.

Evans, John - Seaman - Major Wooster's Battalion, NY Sea Fencibles.

Evans, Robert - Ordinary Seaman - Major Leonard's Battalion, NY Sea Fencibles.

Evans, William - Gunner - NY Sea Fencibles - Company: John Cunningham - Enlistment date: 2 Sep 1814 - Period: 3 Months.

Evas, Henry - Seaman - Major Wooster's Battalion, NY Sea Fencibles.

Evertson, Alexander - Seaman - Major Wooster's Battalion, NY Sea Fencibles - Company: John Randlet.

Ewen, George W. - Seaman - Major Leonard's Battalion, NY Sea Fencibles - Company: Alexander Robinson - Enlistment date: 8 Oct 1814 - Period: 3 Months - BLW 55377-158-55.

Ewing, Thomas - Gunner - Major Wooster's Battalion, NY Sea Fencibles.

Fanqeret, Nicholas - Band - Major Wooster's Battalion, NY Sea Fencibles - Company: Isaac Silliman.

Farneil, Ebing - Private - NH Sea Fencibles - Company: William Marshall - Enlistment date: 27 Nov 1813 - Discharged on 31 Dec 1813.

Farniel, Samuel - Private - NH Sea Fencibles - Company: William Marshall - Enlistment date: 17 Nov 1813 - Discharged on 31 Dec 1813.

Fellows, George - First Lieutenant - NY Sea Fencibles - Company: Paul Burrows - Enlistment date: 16 Sep 1814 - Discharged on 8 Nov 1814.

Fennell, James - Gunner - Major Leonard's Battalion, NY Sea Fencibles.

Ferguson, George - Seaman - Major Wooster's Battalion, NY Sea Fencibles.

Field, Josiah - Private - MA Sea Fencibles - Company: Nehemiah Skillings.

Fields, Samuel - Ordinary Seaman - Major Leonard's Battalion, NY Sea Fencibles.

Finch, John - Ordinary Seaman - Major Leonard's Battalion, NY Sea Fencibles.

Finnegan, John - Seaman - NY Sea Fencibles - Company: Josiah Ingersoll - Enlistment date: 2 Jan 1815.

Fish, Coddington B. - Seaman - NY Sea Fencibles - Company: Paul Burrows - Enlistment date: 1 Oct 1814 - Period: 3 Months.

Fish, James G. - Seaman - NY Sea Fencibles - Company: Josiah Ingersoll.

Fish, Sprague - Gunner - NY Sea Fencibles - Company: Paul Burrows - Enlistment date: 7 Oct 1814 - Period: 3 Months.

Fisher, John - Seaman - NY Sea Fencibles - Company: John Cunningham - Enlistment date: 5 Sep 1814 - Period: 3 Months.

Fisley, Richard - Seaman - NY Sea Fencibles - Company: John Cunningham - Enlistment date: 3 Sep 1814 - Period: 3 Months.

Fitch, Richard - Waiter - Major Wooster's Battalion, NY Sea Fencibles.

Fitzsimmons, William - Seaman - Major Wooster's Battalion, NY Sea Fencibles - Company: John Randlet.

Flanagan, Hugh - Seaman - Major Leonard's Battalion, NY Sea Fencibles.

Flinn, Edwards - Seaman - Major Leonard's Battalion, NY Sea Fencibles.

Flinn, Henry - Seaman - NY Sea Fencibles - Company: Josiah Ingersoll.

Flocker, John - Seaman - Major Leonard's Battalion, NY Sea Fencibles.

Fortune, Julius - Seaman - Major Wooster's Battalion, NY Sea Fencibles.

Foss, Benjamin - Private - NH Sea Fencibles - Company: William Marshall - Enlistment date: 5 Sep 1813 - Discharged on 27 Nov 1813.

Foss, Samuel - Musician - NH Sea Fencibles - Company: William Marshall - Enlistment date: 27 May 1813 - Discharged on 27 Nov 1813.

Foster, Nathan - Gunner - Major Leonard's Battalion, NY Sea Fencibles - Company: Alexander Robinson - Enlistment date: 21 Sep 1814.

Fougerat, Fitz - Boy - Major Wooster's Battalion, NY Sea Fencibles - Company: Staff - Governor's Band.

Fougeret, Fils - Musician - Major Wooster's Battalion, NY Sea Fencibles.

Fowler, Abraham - Waiter - NY Sea Fencibles - Company: Josiah Ingersoll.

Fowler, Adam - Seaman - Major Fowler's Detachment, NY Sea Fencibles.

Fowler, James H. - Seaman - Major Wooster's Battalion, NY Sea Fencibles.

Fowler, Levi - Seaman - Major Wooster's Battalion, NY Sea Fencibles.

Fowler, Nicholas - Seaman - Major Wooster's Battalion, NY Sea Fencibles.

Fowler, Noah - Seaman - Major Wooster's Battalion, NY Sea Fencibles - Company: Isaac Silliman - Enlistment date: 19 Jan 1815 - Period: 1 Yr.

Fowler, Pexcel - Major - Major Fowler's Detachment, NY Sea Fencibles.

Foy, John - Ensign - NH Sea Fencibles - Company: William Marshall - Enlistment date: 27 May 1813 - Discharged on 27 Nov 1813.

Francis, James - Corporal - MA Sea Fencibles - Company: Jeremiah Stickney.

Francis, John - Seaman - Major Fowler's Detachment, NY Sea Fencibles.

Francis, John - Seaman - NY Sea Fencibles - Company: Josiah Ingersoll - Enlistment date: 2 Jan 1815.

Francis, John - Waiter - Major Wooster's Battalion, NY Sea Fencibles.

Francis, John - Gunner - NY Sea Fencibles - Company: John Cunningham - Enlistment date: 6 Sep 1814 - Period: 3 Months.

Francis, Peter - Seaman - Major Leonard's Battalion, NY Sea Fencibles.

Franklin, William - Private - NY Sea Fencibles - Company: John Cunningham - Enlistment date: 2 Sep 1814 - Period: 3 Months - Pension: Land bounty to Mary Franklin, widow of William Franklin - BLW 39252-120-55.

Frazier, James - Quarter Gunner - Major Leonard's Battalion, NY Sea Fencibles.

Frazier, James - Seaman - NY Sea Fencibles - Company: John Cunningham - Enlistment date: 3 Sep 1814 - Period: 3 Months.

Fredericks, Andrew - Seaman - Major Leonard's Battalion, NY Sea Fencibles.

Freeman, John - Private - NY Sea Fencibles - Company: John Cunningham - Enlistment date: 5 Sep 1814.

Freeman, William - Seaman - Major Wooster's Battalion, NY Sea Fencibles.

Frennon, Harvey - Seaman - Major Fowler's Detachment, NY Sea Fencibles.

Frennon, Henry - Seaman - Major Fowler's Detachment, NY Sea Fencibles.

Fricks, Richard - Quarter Gunner - Major Leonard's Battalion, NY Sea Fencibles.

Friend, William - Private - MA Sea Fencibles - Company: Jeremiah Stickney.

Frisby, Richard - Seaman - NY Sea Fencibles - Company: John Cunningham.

Fritzh, John - Seaman - Major Wooster's Battalion, NY Sea Fencibles.

Frogwell, Edward - Private - NY Sea Fencibles - Company: John Cunningham - Enlistment date: 3 Sep 1814.

Front, Andrew - Seaman - Major Wooster's Battalion, NY Sea Fencibles.

Fuller, Zachers R. - Quarter Gunner - Major Wooster's Battalion, NY Sea Fencibles.

Fullum, Thomas - Seaman - Major Leonard's Battalion, NY Sea Fencibles - Company: Alexander Robinson - Enlistment date: 14 Sep 1814 - Period: 3 Months.

Fulton, Eliakim - Ordinary Seaman - Major Leonard's Battalion, NY Sea Fencibles.

Funk, Nathaniel - Seaman - Major Fowler's Detachment, NY Sea Fencibles.

Furgusson, George - Seaman - Major Wooster's Battalion, NY Sea Fencibles - Company: Isaac Silliman - Enlistment date: 4 Jan 1815 - Period: 1 Yr.

Furlong, Henry - Private - MA Sea Fencibles - Company: Jeremiah Stickney.

Furman, Daniel - Seaman - Major Wooster's Battalion, NY Sea Fencibles.

American Sea Fencibles in the War of 1812

Furrill, Caleb C. - Seaman - Major Wooster's Battalion, NY Sea Fencibles.

Gabriel, Ross - Seaman - NY Sea Fencibles - Company: John Cunningham - Enlistment date: 5 Sep 1814.

Gale, Joseph - Seaman - NY Sea Fencibles - Company: Josiah Ingersoll - Enlistment date: 6 Jan 1815.

Gallagher, James - Seaman - Major Leonard's Battalion, NY Sea Fencibles.

Gallagher, Thomas - Seaman - Major Leonard's Battalion, NY Sea Fencibles.

Gammon, Ralph - Seaman - Major Leonard's Battalion, NY Sea Fencibles.

Gammon, William - Seaman - Major Fowler's Detachment, NY Sea Fencibles.

Gantz, Francis - Seaman - Major Wooster's Battalion, NY Sea Fencibles.

Gantz, Gabriel - Seaman - Major Wooster's Battalion, NY Sea Fencibles - Company: Lieutenant Benjamin Dayton - Enlistment date: 29 Dec 1814 - Period: 3 Months - Served on board a prison ship.

Gardinier, Thomas - Quarter Gunner - Major Wooster's Battalion, NY Sea Fencibles.

Gardner, Benjamin - Private - MA Sea Fencibles - Company: Nehemiah Skillings.

Gardner, Gilbert C. - Seaman - Major Leonard's Battalion, NY Sea Fencibles - Company: Alexander Robinson - Discharged on 6 Oct 1814.

Gardner, Henry - Seaman - Major Leonard's Battalion, NY Sea Fencibles.

Garrett, John - Seaman - Major Wooster's Battalion, NY Sea Fencibles.

Garrisher, Charles - Seaman - Major Leonard's Battalion, NY Sea Fencibles - Company: William Russell - Enlistment date: 15 Jan 1815 - Period: 3 Months.

Garrison, Peter - Seaman - Major Leonard's Battalion, NY Sea Fencibles - Company: Alexander Robinson - Enlistment date: 12 Oct 1814 - Period: 1 Yr.

Garrison, William - Seaman - Major Wooster's Battalion, NY Sea Fencibles - Company: John Roorbach.

Gazzam, William - Seaman - Major Wooster's Battalion, NY Sea Fencibles.

Gedney, John - Seaman - Major Leonard's Battalion, NY Sea Fencibles - Company: William Russell - Enlistment date: 10 Dec 1814 - Period: 3 Months.

Gellis, Marshall - Seaman - NY Sea Fencibles - Company: Josiah Ingersoll.

Genn, William - Gunner - Major Wooster's Battalion, NY Sea Fencibles.

George, William - Seaman - Major Leonard's Battalion, NY Sea Fencibles - Company: Alexander Robinson.

Gerisher, Charles - Ordinary Seaman - Major Leonard's Battalion, NY Sea Fencibles.

Gerrish, Enoch - Private - MA Sea Fencibles - Company: Jeremiah Stickney.

Gerrish, Mays - Private - MA Sea Fencibles - Company: Jeremiah Stickney.

Getty, Francis - Private - MA Sea Fencibles - Company: Nehemiah Skillings.

Gham, Daniel M. - Seaman - Major Leonard's Battalion, NY Sea Fencibles - Company: Alexander Robinson - Enlistment date: 2 Nov 1814 - Period: 3 Months.

Gibbons, Andrew - Seaman - Major Wooster's Battalion, NY Sea Fencibles.

Gibbs, Thomas - Seaman - Major Wooster's Battalion, NY Sea Fencibles - Company: Isaac Silliman -

Enlistment date: 4 Jan 1815 - Period: 1 Yr.

Gibson, James - Private - NY Sea Fencibles - Company: John Cunningham - Enlistment date: 3 Sep 1814 - Period: 3 Months.

Gilbert, Henry - Seaman - Major Fowler's Detachment, NY Sea Fencibles.

Gilbert, Peter - Seaman - Major Leonard's Battalion, NY Sea Fencibles - Company: William Russell - Enlistment date: 16 Jan 1815 - Period: 3 Months - Deserted.

Giles, John - Seaman - Major Wooster's Battalion, NY Sea Fencibles.

Giles, William - Ordinary Seaman - Major Wooster's Battalion, NY Sea Fencibles.

Gilligan, Martin - Seaman - Major Leonard's Battalion, NY Sea Fencibles - Company: William Russell - Enlistment date: 5 Jan 1815 - Period: 3 Months.

Gillis, John - Quarter Gunner - Major Fowler's Detachment, NY Sea Fencibles.

Gilman, George - Private - MA Sea Fencibles - Company: Isaac Lyman - Enlistment date: 25 Jul 1814 - Discharged on 24 Aug 1814.

Glantein, Thomas - Seaman - Major Wooster's Battalion, NY Sea Fencibles.

Glanter, Thomas - Seaman - Major Wooster's Battalion, NY Sea Fencibles.

Glauseau, John - Seaman - NY Sea Fencibles - Company: Josiah Ingersoll.

Glover, Edward - Seaman - Major Leonard's Battalion, NY Sea Fencibles.

Glover, Russell - Sergeant - MA Sea Fencibles - Company: Nehemiah Skillings.

Glover, Stephen - Private - MA Sea Fencibles - Company: Nehemiah Skillings.

Godwin, Thomas - Ordinary Seaman - Major Leonard's Battalion, NY Sea Fencibles.

Goldsmith, Silas H. - Seaman - Major Leonard's Battalion, NY Sea Fencibles.

Golett, John - Private - NY Sea Fencibles - Company: Paul Burrows - Enlistment date: 7 Nov 1814 - Period: 3 Months - Deserted on 25 Nov 1814.

Golly, James - Seaman - Major Fowler's Detachment, NY Sea Fencibles - Company: James Breath.

Goodman, Thomas - Seaman - NY Sea Fencibles - Company: John Cunningham.

Goodwin, Abiel - Private - MA Sea Fencibles - Company: Isaac Lyman - Born: 26 Jul 1814 - Discharged on 23 Sep 1814.

Goodwin, Thomas - Private - Major Leonard's Battalion, NY Sea Fencibles.

Goodwin, Timothy - Private - MA Sea Fencibles - Company: Nehemiah Skillings.

Gordon, James - Seaman - Major Fowler's Detachment, NY Sea Fencibles - Company: James Breath.

Gorham, Benjamin - Private - MA Sea Fencibles - Company: Nehemiah Skillings.

Gould, George - Seaman - NY Sea Fencibles - Company: Paul Burrows - Enlistment date: 13 Oct 1814 - Period: 3 Months.

Gould, John - Seaman - NY Sea Fencibles - Company: Josiah Ingersoll - Enlistment date: 30 Dec 1814.

Gould, John - Seaman - Major Fowler's Detachment, NY Sea Fencibles.

Gould, Robert - Ordinary Seaman - Major Leonard's Battalion, NY Sea Fencibles.

Gracie, Edward G. - Third Lieutenant - Major Wooster's Battalion, NY Sea Fencibles - Company: John

American Sea Fencibles in the War of 1812

Roorbach.

Grally, Nicholas - Seaman - Major Leonard's Battalion, NY Sea Fencibles.

Grant, George - Seaman - Major Fowler's Detachment, NY Sea Fencibles - Company: Benjamin Muzzy.

Gray, John - Seaman - Major Fowler's Detachment, NY Sea Fencibles - Company: James Breath.

Greenfield, William - Seaman - Major Leonard's Battalion, NY Sea Fencibles.

Green, John - Third Lieutenant - Major Leonard's Battalion, NY Sea Fencibles - Company: Alexander Robinson - Enlistment date: 13 Oct 1814.

Greene, John - Seaman - Major Wooster's Battalion, NY Sea Fencibles.

Greene, William - Gunner - Major Wooster's Battalion, NY Sea Fencibles.

Greenfield, William - Seaman - Major Leonard's Battalion, NY Sea Fencibles - Company: Alexander Robinson - Enlistment date: 18 Oct 1814 - Period: 3 Months - Re-enlisted on 23 Jan 1815 for three months.

Greenleaf, Charles - Ordinary Seaman - Major Wooster's Battalion, NY Sea Fencibles.

Greenwich, John - Seaman - Major Wooster's Battalion, NY Sea Fencibles.

Gregory, Prince - Seaman - Major Fowler's Detachment, NY Sea Fencibles - Company: James Breath.

Grennell, Jordan - Seaman - Major Leonard's Battalion, NY Sea Fencibles.

Griffin, William - Private - MA Sea Fencibles - Company: Nehemiah Skillings.

Griffith, George - Gunner - Major Leonard's Battalion, NY Sea Fencibles.

Griffith, Henry - Private - NY Sea Fencibles - Company: John Cunningham - Enlistment date: 6 Sep 1814 - Period: 3 Months.

Grim, Peter - Seaman - Major Wooster's Battalion, NY Sea Fencibles.

Grimes, William - Boy - Major Leonard's Battalion, NY Sea Fencibles - Company: William Russell - Enlistment date: 20 Jan 1815 - Period: 3 Months.

Grinnell, Gordon - Seaman - Major Leonard's Battalion, NY Sea Fencibles.

Griswold, Benjamin - Seaman - Major Fowler's Detachment, NY Sea Fencibles.

Griswold, John H. - Quartermaster Sergeant - Major Leonard's Battalion, NY Sea Fencibles.

Griswold, Samuel L. - Seaman - NY Sea Fencibles - Company: Paul Burrows - Enlistment date: 20 Oct 1814 - Period: 3 Months.

Grover, Joseph - Private - MA Sea Fencibles - Company: Isaac Lyman.

Grygier, Robert - Seaman - Major Leonard's Battalion, NY Sea Fencibles.

Gucher, Charles C. - Ordinary Seaman - Major Leonard's Battalion, NY Sea Fencibles.

Guilson, Thomas - Seaman - Major Leonard's Battalion, NY Sea Fencibles - Company: Alexander Robinson - Enlistment date: 2 Nov 1814 - Period: 3 Months.

Guin, William - Gunner - Major Wooster's Battalion, NY Sea Fencibles.

Gunn, George - Surgeon's Mate - Major Wooster's Battalion, NY Sea Fencibles - Enlistment date: 7 Nov 1814.

Guntz, Francis - Seaman - Major Wooster's Battalion, NY Sea Fencibles - Company: Isaac Silliman -

Served on board a prison ship.

Gurley, Charles - Seaman - Major Leonard's Battalion, NY Sea Fencibles.

Gwin, Peter - Seaman - Major Leonard's Battalion, NY Sea Fencibles - Company: Alexander Robinson - Enlistment date: 2 Nov 1814 - Period: 3 Months.

Hagan, John - Seaman - NY Sea Fencibles - Company: Josiah Ingersoll.

Hagerman, Jacob - Waiter - Major Fowler's Detachment, NY Sea Fencibles.

Hagerman, Jacob - Servant - Major Leonard's Battalion, NY Sea Fencibles.

Hagerman, Matthias - Seaman - Major Fowler's Detachment, NY Sea Fencibles.

Hall, Archibald - Ordinary Seaman - Major Wooster's Battalion, NY Sea Fencibles.

Hall, Archibald - Seaman - Major Fowler's Detachment, NY Sea Fencibles.

Hall, Drew - Seaman - Major Fowler's Detachment, NY Sea Fencibles - Company: James Breath.

Hall, Edward - Private - NH Sea Fencibles - Company: William Marshall - Enlistment date: 27 May 1813 - Discharged on 27 Nov 1813.

Hall, George - Seaman - Major Fowler's Detachment, NY Sea Fencibles.

Hall, Joshua B. - Seaman - NY Sea Fencibles - Company: Josiah Ingersoll - Enlistment date: 30 Dec 1814.

Hall, Stephen - Private - MA Sea Fencibles - Company: Nehemiah Skillings.

Halliman, Henry - Seaman - NY Sea Fencibles - Company: Josiah Ingersoll.

Hamill, John - Waiter - Major Wooster's Battalion, NY Sea Fencibles.

Hamill, John - Seaman - Major Wooster's Battalion, NY Sea Fencibles.

Hamilton, Benjamin - Gunner - NY Sea Fencibles - Company: John Cunningham - Enlistment date: 2 Sep 1814 - Period: 3 Months.

Hamilton, James - Seaman - Major Fowler's Detachment, NY Sea Fencibles - Company: James Breath.

Hamilton, John - Seaman - Major Wooster's Battalion, NY Sea Fencibles.

Hammitt, John - Seaman - Major Wooster's Battalion, NY Sea Fencibles - Company: Isaac Silliman - Enlistment date: 5 Jan 1815 - Period: 1 Yr.

Hankard, Robert - Gunner - Major Fowler's Detachment, NY Sea Fencibles - Company: James Breath.

Hannas, Thomas - Seaman - Major Wooster's Battalion, NY Sea Fencibles.

Hanwige, John - Band - Major Wooster's Battalion, NY Sea Fencibles - Company: Isaac Silliman.

Harden, Jesse - Seaman - Major Leonard's Battalion, NY Sea Fencibles.

Harden, William - Gunner - Major Leonard's Battalion, NY Sea Fencibles.

Hardie, James - Seaman - Major Leonard's Battalion, NY Sea Fencibles.

Harding, John - Quarter Gunner - Major Fowler's Detachment, NY Sea Fencibles.

Harettry, Michael - Seaman - Major Leonard's Battalion, NY Sea Fencibles.

Harkins, John - Quarter Gunner - Major Leonard's Battalion, NY Sea Fencibles.

Harkness, George - Quarter Gunner - Major Fowler's Detachment, NY Sea Fencibles - Company: James

Breath - Pension: Land bounty to Margaret Harkness, widow of George Hardness - BLW 96506-160-55.

Harmon, Benjamin - Private - MA Sea Fencibles - Company: Isaac Lyman.

Harmon, James - Private - MA Sea Fencibles - Company: Isaac Lyman - Born: 25 Jul 1814 - Discharged on 24 Aug 1814.

Harnbrook, Leonard - Seaman - NY Sea Fencibles - Company: John Cunningham - Enlistment date: 4 Sep 1814 - Period: 3 Months.

Harnes, Aimes - Seaman - Major Leonard's Battalion, NY Sea Fencibles.

Harness, John - Seaman - Major Leonard's Battalion, NY Sea Fencibles.

Harnmill, John - Waiter - Major Wooster's Battalion, NY Sea Fencibles - Company: Isaac Silliman.

Harper, Robert - Gunner - Major Wooster's Battalion, NY Sea Fencibles.

Harrass, Michael - Seaman - Major Leonard's Battalion, NY Sea Fencibles.

Harris, David - Gunner - Major Wooster's Battalion, NY Sea Fencibles.

Harris, Thomas - Private - MA Sea Fencibles - Company: Nehemiah Skillings.

Harrison, Jacob - Seaman - NY Sea Fencibles - Company: Josiah Ingersoll.

Harrison, John - Private - NY Sea Fencibles - Company: Paul Burrows - Enlistment date: 5 Mar 1814 - Period: 3 Months.

Harrison, Joseph - Seaman - Major Fowler's Detachment, NY Sea Fencibles.

Harrison, William - Seaman - Major Leonard's Battalion, NY Sea Fencibles.

Harriss, John - Seaman - Major Leonard's Battalion, NY Sea Fencibles.

Hart, Charles - Seaman - Major Leonard's Battalion, NY Sea Fencibles.

Hart, Richard - Seaman - Major Leonard's Battalion, NY Sea Fencibles.

Hartolen, Isaac - Seaman - NY Sea Fencibles - Company: Paul Burrows - Enlistment date: 14 Oct 1814 - Period: 3 Months.

Haskel, David - Private - MA Sea Fencibles - Company: Jeremiah Stickney.

Haskel, Enoch - Private - MA Sea Fencibles - Company: Jeremiah Stickney.

Hassay, Benjamin - Seaman - Major Wooster's Battalion, NY Sea Fencibles - Company: Isaac Silliman - Enlistment date: 4 Jan 1815 - Period: 1 yr.

Hatch, David - Seaman - Major Fowler's Detachment, NY Sea Fencibles - Company: James Breath - Deserted on 1 Nov 1814.

Hathaway, Paul - Seaman - NY Sea Fencibles - Company: Josiah Ingersoll.

Hatter, John - Seaman - Major Wooster's Battalion, NY Sea Fencibles.

Hatthatt, Edward - Gunner - Major Wooster's Battalion, NY Sea Fencibles - Company: John Roorbach.

Hatton, John - Seaman - Major Wooster's Battalion, NY Sea Fencibles.

Hayl, Charles - Private - MA Sea Fencibles - Company: Nehemiah Skillings.

Hays, William H. - Ordinary Seaman - NY Sea Fencibles - Company: Josiah Ingersoll.

Hazard, Alfred U. - Seaman - Major Wooster's Battalion, NY Sea Fencibles.

American Sea Fencibles in the War of 1812

Hazard, Anthony - Seaman - Major Wooster's Battalion, NY Sea Fencibles - Company: Isaac Silliman - Enlistment date: 4 Jan 1815 - Period: 1 Yr.

Hazard, Benjamin - Seaman - Major Wooster's Battalion, NY Sea Fencibles.

Hazard, John - Second Lieutenant - NY Sea Fencibles - Company: Josiah Ingersoll.

Hearin, Patrick - Seaman - Major Wooster's Battalion, NY Sea Fencibles - Company: Isaac Silliman - Enlistment date: 6 Jan 1815 - Period: 1 Yr.

Heddy, Samuel - Seaman - NY Sea Fencibles - Company: Paul Burrows - Enlistment date: 7 Oct 1814 - Period: 3 Months.

Hedges, Thomas - Seaman - Major Wooster's Battalion, NY Sea Fencibles - Company: Lieutenant Benjamin Dayton - Enlistment date: 29 Dec 1814 - Period: 1 Yr - Served on board a prison ship; discharged on 11 Mar 1815.

Helmus, Christopher - Seaman - Major Fowler's Detachment, NY Sea Fencibles - Company: James Breath - Deserted at Blockhouse Constitution on 27 Nov 1814.

Hender, William - Seaman - NY Sea Fencibles - Company: John Cunningham - Enlistment date: 8 Sep 1814 - Period: 3 Months.

Hender, William - Seaman - Major Wooster's Battalion, NY Sea Fencibles - Company: Isaac Silliman - Enlistment date: 7 Jan 1815 - Period: 1 Yr.

Hendrickson, John - Ordinary Seaman - Major Wooster's Battalion, NY Sea Fencibles.

Henery, William - Boatswain - Major Leonard's Battalion, NY Sea Fencibles - Company: William Russell - Enlistment date: 20 Dec 1814 - Period: 3 Months.

Henry, John - Ordinary Seaman - Major Leonard's Battalion, NY Sea Fencibles.

Henry, Robert - Private - MA Sea Fencibles - Company: Nehemiah Skillings.

Herkness, George - Gunner - Major Fowler's Detachment, NY Sea Fencibles - Company: James Breath.

Herringbrook, William - Seaman - Major Wooster's Battalion, NY Sea Fencibles.

Herringon, William L. - Seaman - Major Wooster's Battalion, NY Sea Fencibles.

Herron, Patrick - Seaman - Major Leonard's Battalion, NY Sea Fencibles - Company: William Russell - Enlistment date: 3 Jan 1815 - Period: 3 Months.

Hess Jr., William - Gunner - Major Leonard's Battalion, NY Sea Fencibles.

Hewes, John H. - Seaman - Major Wooster's Battalion, NY Sea Fencibles.

Hewes, John H. - Private - MA Sea Fencibles - Company: Nehemiah Skillings.

Heyer, Henry S. - Ordinary Seaman - Major Leonard's Battalion, NY Sea Fencibles.

Higby, Joshua - Seaman - NY Sea Fencibles - Company: Josiah Ingersoll.

Higby, Leonard - Seaman - NY Sea Fencibles - Company: Josiah Ingersoll.

Higgins, Hiram - Seaman - Major Wooster's Battalion, NY Sea Fencibles.

Higgins, John - Seaman - Major Wooster's Battalion, NY Sea Fencibles.

Highatt, Edward - Gunner - Major Wooster's Battalion, NY Sea Fencibles - Company: Isaac Silliman - Enlistment date: 6 Dec 1814 - Period: 6 Months.

Hill, Daniel - Seaman - Major Wooster's Battalion, NY Sea Fencibles - Company: Isaac Silliman -

Enlistment date: 19 Jan 1815 - Period: 1 Yr.

Hill, Joseph D. - Seaman - Major Leonard's Battalion, NY Sea Fencibles.

Hilliard, John - Private - MA Sea Fencibles - Company: Nehemiah Skillings.

Hilliard, Robert B. - Third Lieutenant - Major Fowler's Detachment, NY Sea Fencibles - Company: James Breath.

Hinckley, Isaac - Private - MA Sea Fencibles - Company: Nehemiah Skillings.

Hinckley, Richard B. - Private - MA Sea Fencibles - Company: Nehemiah Skillings.

Hines, Jacob - Seaman - Major Leonard's Battalion, NY Sea Fencibles.

Hinksman, William - Seaman - Major Leonard's Battalion, NY Sea Fencibles.

Hittkinson, Anthony - Seaman - Major Leonard's Battalion, NY Sea Fencibles - Company: Alexander Robinson - Enlistment date: 4 Oct 1814 - Period: 3 Months.

Hixon, George - Private - MA Sea Fencibles - Company: Nehemiah Skillings.

Hodge, Charles - Third Lieutenant - MA Sea Fencibles - Company: Jeremiah Stickney.

Hodgers, John - Seaman - Major Wooster's Battalion, NY Sea Fencibles - Company: Isaac Silliman - Enlistment date: 5 Jan 1815 - Period: 1 Yr - Deserted on 1 Mar 1815.

Hodgkins, Joseph - Gunner - Major Wooster's Battalion, NY Sea Fencibles - Company: Isaac Silliman - Enlistment date: 4 Jan 1815 - Period: 6 Months.

Hodgkins, Joseph S. - Gunner - Major Wooster's Battalion, NY Sea Fencibles - Company: John Randlet - BLW 82050-40-50, BLW 93028-40-50, BLW 1127-80-55.

Hodgkiss, Philo - Seaman - Major Wooster's Battalion, NY Sea Fencibles.

Hoffman, John - Seaman - Major Leonard's Battalion, NY Sea Fencibles.

Hoffmire, James - Seaman - Major Fowler's Detachment, NY Sea Fencibles.

Holbert, James - Seaman - Major Leonard's Battalion, NY Sea Fencibles.

Holland, Samuel - Private - MA Sea Fencibles - Company: Nehemiah Skillings.

Holley, John - Seaman - Major Fowler's Detachment, NY Sea Fencibles.

Holmes, Bartlett - Private - MA Sea Fencibles - Company: Nehemiah Skillings.

Homer, Jacob - Private - MA Sea Fencibles - Company: Nehemiah Skillings.

Hone, Joshua - Seaman - Major Fowler's Detachment, NY Sea Fencibles.

Hooper, Charles - Seaman - Major Wooster's Battalion, NY Sea Fencibles.

Hopkins, Caleb - Private - MA Sea Fencibles - Company: Nehemiah Skillings.

Hopkins, Henry - Seaman - Major Wooster's Battalion, NY Sea Fencibles.

Hopper, Charles - Seaman - Major Wooster's Battalion, NY Sea Fencibles.

Hopper, James - Seaman - Major Wooster's Battalion, NY Sea Fencibles - Company: John Roorbach.

Hopper, John D. - Seaman - Major Leonard's Battalion, NY Sea Fencibles.

Horton, Timothy - Seaman - Major Fowler's Detachment, NY Sea Fencibles.

Horton, Timothy - Seaman - Major Wooster's Battalion, NY Sea Fencibles - Company: Lieutenant

Benjamin Dayton - Enlistment date: 29 Dec 1814 - Served on board a prison ship.

Howard, William - Private - MA Sea Fencibles - Company: Jeremiah Stickney.

Howe Jr., Edward - Corporal - MA Sea Fencibles - Company: Nehemiah Skillings.

Howell, Henry - Seaman - Major Wooster's Battalion, NY Sea Fencibles - Company: Isaac Silliman - Enlistment date: 13 Jan 1815 - Period: 1 Yr.

Howell, Israel - Private - Major Wooster's Battalion, NY Sea Fencibles - Company: John Roorbach - Enlistment date: 17 Sep 1814 - Pension: Wife Sabrina Porter, SO-20585, SC-15141, WO-12706, WC-17106; married on 15 Nov 1847, Pleasant Mounty, Wayne County, PA; seaman died on 20 Jun 1872 in Smiley, PA - BLW 52807-160-55.

Howland, Rouse - Seaman - NY Sea Fencibles - Company: Josiah Ingersoll.

Hoyt, Samuel - Quartermaster - MA Sea Fencibles - Company: Jeremiah Stickney.

Hulec, Edward - Private - NY Sea Fencibles - Company: Paul Burrows.

Hulsheart, Cornelius B. - Boy - Major Fowler's Detachment, NY Sea Fencibles - Company: James Breath.

Humphrey, John - Seaman - Major Wooster's Battalion, NY Sea Fencibles.

Humphries, James - Seaman - Major Leonard's Battalion, NY Sea Fencibles.

Hunt, Samuel - Seaman - Major Leonard's Battalion, NY Sea Fencibles.

Hunter, William S. - Seaman - Major Wooster's Battalion, NY Sea Fencibles.

Hutchinson, Joseph - Seaman - Major Leonard's Battalion, NY Sea Fencibles.

Hutchinson, Richard - Gunner - NY Sea Fencibles - Company: Paul Burrows - Enlistment date: 19 Sep 1814 - Period: 3 Months.

Hutchison, James - Seaman - NY Sea Fencibles - Company: Josiah Ingersoll.

Huyler, Edward - Seaman - Major Wooster's Battalion, NY Sea Fencibles - Company: Isaac Silliman - Enlistment date: 17 Jan 1815 - Period: 1 Yr.

Huzzy, John - Private - NY Sea Fencibles - Company: Paul Burrows.

Huzzy, Paul - Seaman - NY Sea Fencibles - Company: Paul Burrows - Enlistment date: 7 Oct 1814 - Period: 3 Months.

Hyde, Richard - Seaman - Major Leonard's Battalion, NY Sea Fencibles.

Hyler, Edward - Seaman - NY Sea Fencibles - Company: Paul Burrows - Enlistment date: 12 Oct 1814 - Period: 3 Months.

Hyler, George - Seaman - Major Wooster's Battalion, NY Sea Fencibles - Company: Isaac Silliman - Enlistment date: 11 Jan 1815 - Period: 1 Yr.

Ingall, Thomas - Seaman - Major Leonard's Battalion, NY Sea Fencibles - Company: Alexander Robinson - Enlistment date: 10 Sep 1814 - Period: 3 Months - Discharged before 8 Jan 1815.

Ingersoll, George O. - Private - MA Sea Fencibles - Company: Nehemiah Skillings.

Ingersoll, Josiah - Captain - NY Sea Fencibles - Company: Josiah Ingersoll.

Inglee, Jesse - Private - MA Sea Fencibles - Company: Nehemiah Skillings.

Inglis, John - Seaman - Major Wooster's Battalion, NY Sea Fencibles - Company: John Roorbach.

Innis, Alexander - Gunner - Major Leonard's Battalion, NY Sea Fencibles.

American Sea Fencibles in the War of 1812

Islay, Mathias - Quarter Gunner - Major Wooster's Battalion, NY Sea Fencibles.

Islerman, Reuben - Seaman - Major Wooster's Battalion, NY Sea Fencibles.

Isley, Matthias - Quarter Gunner - Major Wooster's Battalion, NY Sea Fencibles.

Ivers, Thomas - Seaman - Major Fowler's Detachment, NY Sea Fencibles.

Jackson, Abraham - Seaman - Major Leonard's Battalion, NY Sea Fencibles.

Jackson, Benjamin - Seaman - Major Leonard's Battalion, NY Sea Fencibles.

Jackson, John - Seaman - Major Wooster's Battalion, NY Sea Fencibles - Company: John Roorbach.

Jackson, John - Seaman - Major Fowler's Detachment, NY Sea Fencibles - Company: James Breath.

Jackson, John - Seaman - NY Sea Fencibles - Company: Paul Burrows - Enlistment date: 20 Sep 1814 - Period: 3 Months.

Jackson, Morris - Seaman - Major Wooster's Battalion, NY Sea Fencibles.

Jackson, William - Seaman - Major Leonard's Battalion, NY Sea Fencibles - Company: William Russell - Enlistment date: 29 Jan 1815 - Period: 3 Months.

Jacobs, Benjamin - Seaman - Major Fowler's Detachment, NY Sea Fencibles - Company: James Breath - Deserted at Blockhouse Constitution on 3 Dec 1814.

Jacobs, Hans - Seaman - NY Sea Fencibles - Company: Josiah Ingersoll.

Jagger, Cornelius - Seaman - Major Leonard's Battalion, NY Sea Fencibles - Company: Alexander Robinson - Enlistment date: 15 Sep 1814 - Period: 3 Months.

James, Amherst - Seaman - Major Fowler's Detachment, NY Sea Fencibles - Company: James Breath.

James, John - Seaman - Major Leonard's Battalion, NY Sea Fencibles.

James, John - Boy - Major Leonard's Battalion, NY Sea Fencibles - Company: William Russell - Enlistment date: 18 Jan 1815 - Period: 3 Months.

James, John - Seaman - Major Wooster's Battalion, NY Sea Fencibles.

Jardin, Robert - Gunner - NY Sea Fencibles - Company: John Cunningham - Enlistment date: 6 Sep 1814 - Period: 3 Months.

Jelley, Martial - Seaman - NY Sea Fencibles - Company: Josiah Ingersoll.

Jenkins, Eustace - Private - NY Sea Fencibles - Company: Paul Burrows - Enlistment date: 5 Nov 1814 - Deserted on 11 Nov 1814.

Jenkins, Richard - Waiter - Major Leonard's Battalion, NY Sea Fencibles.

Jenkins, Stacey W. - Seaman - NY Sea Fencibles - Company: Paul Burrows - Enlistment date: 23 Sep 1814 - Period: 3 Months - Deserted on 11 Nov 1814.

Jennerson, John S. - Private - MA Sea Fencibles - Company: Nehemiah Skillings.

Jennings, William A. - Seaman - Major Leonard's Battalion, NY Sea Fencibles.

Jeroke, Robert - Seaman - Major Leonard's Battalion, NY Sea Fencibles.

Jervis, Timothy - Seaman - Major Leonard's Battalion, NY Sea Fencibles - Company: Alexander Robinson - Deserted at New York on 28 Oct 1814.

Jester, William - Private - Major Fowler's Detachment, NY Sea Fencibles.

Jewell, William - Seaman - Major Leonard's Battalion, NY Sea Fencibles.

Johnson, Benjamin - Seaman - Major Leonard's Battalion, NY Sea Fencibles.

Johnson, Edward - Seaman - Major Leonard's Battalion, NY Sea Fencibles.

Johnson, Edward - Seaman - Major Wooster's Battalion, NY Sea Fencibles.

Johnson, Green - Sergeant - MA Sea Fencibles - Company: Jeremiah Stickney.

Johnson, Jacob - Seaman - Major Wooster's Battalion, NY Sea Fencibles.

Johnson, Jacob - Seaman - Major Fowler's Detachment, NY Sea Fencibles.

Johnson, James - Seaman - Major Leonard's Battalion, NY Sea Fencibles - Company: William Russell - Enlistment date: 17 Jan 1815 - Period: 3 Months.

Johnson, John - Seaman - Major Wooster's Battalion, NY Sea Fencibles - Company: Isaac Silliman - Enlistment date: 6 Feb 1815 - Period: 1 Yr.

Johnson, John - Seaman - NY Sea Fencibles - Company: John Cunningham - Enlistment date: 5 Sep 1814 - Period: 3 Months.

Johnson, John - Ordinary Seaman - Major Fowler's Detachment, NY Sea Fencibles.

Johnson, John - Seaman - NY Sea Fencibles - Company: Paul Burrows - Enlistment date: 29 Sep 1814 - Period: 3 Months.

Johnson, Lawrence - Seaman - Major Wooster's Battalion, NY Sea Fencibles - Company: Isaac Silliman - Enlistment date: 30 Jun 1815 - Period: 1 Yr.

Johnson, Lawrence - Seaman - Major Leonard's Battalion, NY Sea Fencibles - Company: Alexander Robinson - Enlistment date: 24 Oct 1814 - Period: 3 Months.

Johnson, Leonard - Seaman - Major Wooster's Battalion, NY Sea Fencibles.

Johnson, Thomas - Ordinary Seaman - Major Leonard's Battalion, NY Sea Fencibles.

Johnson, Thomas - Seaman - Major Wooster's Battalion, NY Sea Fencibles.

Johnson, William - Gunner - Major Leonard's Battalion, NY Sea Fencibles.

Johnson, William - Seaman - Major Leonard's Battalion, NY Sea Fencibles - Company: Alexander Robinson - Deserted at New York on 2 Nov 1814.

Johnson, William Wood - Private - Major Wooster's Battalion, NY Sea Fencibles - Company: John Randlet - BLW 1455-120-55.

Johnston, James - Seaman - Major Leonard's Battalion, NY Sea Fencibles.

Johnston, John - Seaman - Major Wooster's Battalion, NY Sea Fencibles.

Jollie, Joan - Seaman - Major Leonard's Battalion, NY Sea Fencibles.

Jolly, James - Seaman - Major Fowler's Detachment, NY Sea Fencibles.

Jonakin, Benjamin - Gunner - Major Wooster's Battalion, NY Sea Fencibles - Company: John Roorbach.

Jones, Charles - Seaman - Major Wooster's Battalion, NY Sea Fencibles.

Jones, George - Gunner - Major Leonard's Battalion, NY Sea Fencibles.

Jones, George G. - Private - MA Sea Fencibles - Company: Nehemiah Skillings.

Jones, James - Servant - Major Fowler's Detachment, NY Sea Fencibles.

American Sea Fencibles in the War of 1812

Jones, James - Private - NY Sea Fencibles - Company: Paul Burrows.

Jones, John - Seaman - Major Fowler's Detachment, NY Sea Fencibles.

Jones, John - Quarter Gunner - Major Leonard's Battalion, NY Sea Fencibles.

Jones, John - Private - Major Leonard's Battalion, NY Sea Fencibles - Company: William Russell - Pension: Land bounty to Mary Jones, widow of John Jones - BLW 95947-160-55.

Jones, Samuel - Seaman - Major Leonard's Battalion, NY Sea Fencibles.

Jones, Sylvester - Seaman - Major Wooster's Battalion, NY Sea Fencibles.

Jones, Thomas - Quarter Gunner - Major Leonard's Battalion, NY Sea Fencibles.

Jones, Thomas - Seaman - Major Wooster's Battalion, NY Sea Fencibles - Company: Isaac Silliman - Enlistment date: 14 Jan 1815 - Period: 1 Yr.

Jones, Thomas - Private - MA Sea Fencibles - Company: Nehemiah Skillings.

Joseph, John - Gunner - Major Leonard's Battalion, NY Sea Fencibles.

Kane, Thomas - Seaman - Major Leonard's Battalion, NY Sea Fencibles - Company: Alexander Robinson - Discharged in New York on 15 Nov 1814.

Kearn, Patrick - Seaman - Major Wooster's Battalion, NY Sea Fencibles.

Kearney, Samuel - Seaman - Major Leonard's Battalion, NY Sea Fencibles.

Kearsing, Henry - Ordinary Seaman - Major Leonard's Battalion, NY Sea Fencibles.

Keech, David - Seaman - Major Fowler's Detachment, NY Sea Fencibles.

Keech, Job - Seaman - Major Leonard's Battalion, NY Sea Fencibles.

Keen, Elisha L. - Second Lieutenant - Major Wooster's Battalion, NY Sea Fencibles.

Keith, William - Seaman - Major Leonard's Battalion, NY Sea Fencibles - Company: Alexander Robinson - Enlistment date: 24 Oct 1814 - Period: 3 Months.

Kelley, John - Seaman - NY Sea Fencibles - Company: Josiah Ingersoll.

Kelly, John - Ordinary Seaman - Major Leonard's Battalion, NY Sea Fencibles.

Kelly, John - Seaman - Major Wooster's Battalion, NY Sea Fencibles.

Kelly, Lewis - Seaman - NY Sea Fencibles - Company: John Cunningham.

Kelly, Mathew - Seaman - NY Sea Fencibles - Company: Paul Burrows - Enlistment date: 1 Oct 1814 - Period: 3 Months.

Kemfield, Edward - Quarter Gunner - NY Sea Fencibles - Company: Josiah Ingersoll.

Kendal, Wilkes - Seaman - Major Fowler's Detachment, NY Sea Fencibles - Company: James Breath.

Kermont, Thomas - Seaman - Major Wooster's Battalion, NY Sea Fencibles.

Kernot, Thomas - Seaman - Major Wooster's Battalion, NY Sea Fencibles - Company: Isaac Silliman - Enlistment date: 30 Jun 1815 - Period: 1 Yr.

Kerr, John T. - Seaman - Major Leonard's Battalion, NY Sea Fencibles - Company: William Russell - Enlistment date: 9 Jan 1815 - Period: 3 Months.

Kerwin, William - Seaman - Major Wooster's Battalion, NY Sea Fencibles - Company: Isaac Silliman - Enlistment date: 6 Jun 1813 - Period: 1 Yr.

Kildier, Barney - Seaman - NY Sea Fencibles - Company: Paul Burrows - Enlistment date: 3 Nov 1814 - Period: 3 Months.

Kimme, Benjamin - Private - NH Sea Fencibles - Company: William Marshall - Enlistment date: 27 May 1813 - Discharged on 31 Aug 1813.

Kimme, William - Private - NH Sea Fencibles - Company: William Marshall - Enlistment date: 27 May 1813 - Discharged on 27 Nov 1813.

King, Samuel - Third Lieutenant - Major Leonard's Battalion, NY Sea Fencibles.

Kingsland, John - Ordinary Seaman - Major Leonard's Battalion, NY Sea Fencibles.

Kingston, Thomas - Ordinary Seaman - Major Leonard's Battalion, NY Sea Fencibles.

Kinnear, Benjamin - Private - NH Sea Fencibles - Company: William Marshall - Enlistment date: 27 Nov 1813 - Discharged on 31 Dec 1813.

Kinout, Thomas - Seaman - Major Leonard's Battalion, NY Sea Fencibles - Company: Alexander Robinson - Enlistment date: 15 Oct 1814 - Period: 3 Months.

Kittle, Thomas S. - Seaman - Major Leonard's Battalion, NY Sea Fencibles.

Kleinham, George - Seaman - Major Leonard's Battalion, NY Sea Fencibles.

Kling, George - Seaman - Major Leonard's Battalion, NY Sea Fencibles.

Knap, Jacob - Private - MA Sea Fencibles - Company: Jeremiah Stickney.

Knapp, Charles - Corporal - MA Sea Fencibles - Company: Nehemiah Skillings.

Knight, Amos - Private - MA Sea Fencibles - Company: Jeremiah Stickney.

Krapff, John C. - Quartermaster - Major Wooster's Battalion, NY Sea Fencibles.

Krapff, John C. - Quartermaster - Major Wooster's Battalion, NY Sea Fencibles - Company: Isaac Silliman - Enlistment date: 26 Sep 1814.

La Rose, Berneil - Band - Major Wooster's Battalion, NY Sea Fencibles - Company: Isaac Silliman.

Lacy, Thomas - Seaman - Major Leonard's Battalion, NY Sea Fencibles - Company: William Russell - Enlistment date: 17 Jan 1815 - Period: 3 Months.

Lafurge, Benjamin - Seaman - Major Leonard's Battalion, NY Sea Fencibles - Company: William Russell - Enlistment date: 18 Jan 1815 - Period: 3 Months - Deserted.

Lambert, Henry - Gunner - Major Leonard's Battalion, NY Sea Fencibles - Company: Alexander Robinson - Enlistment date: 4 Oct 1814 - Period: 3 Months.

Lambert, John - Boatswain - NY Sea Fencibles - Company: John Cunningham - Enlistment date: 2 Sep 1814 - Period: 3 Months.

Lambert, William - Waiter - NY Sea Fencibles - Company: John Cunningham.

Lane, Thomas - Seaman - Major Fowler's Detachment, NY Sea Fencibles.

Langdon, Benjamin - Private - NY Sea Fencibles - Company: John Cunningham - Enlistment date: 5 Sep 1814 - Period: 3 Months.

Langley, Edmund - Seaman - Major Fowler's Detachment, NY Sea Fencibles - Company: James Breath.

Langley, John - Seaman - Major Leonard's Battalion, NY Sea Fencibles.

Larny, John - Seaman - Major Leonard's Battalion, NY Sea Fencibles.

American Sea Fencibles in the War of 1812

Larose, Berrueil - Quarter Gunner - Major Wooster's Battalion, NY Sea Fencibles.

Larus, John - Seaman - Major Leonard's Battalion, NY Sea Fencibles.

Lassell, John - Seaman - NY Sea Fencibles - Company: Josiah Ingersoll.

Lattime, Nicholas - Private - MA Sea Fencibles - Company: Jeremiah Stickney.

Lattimore, Joseph - Seaman - Major Wooster's Battalion, NY Sea Fencibles.

Lattin, Adam - Seaman - Major Fowler's Detachment, NY Sea Fencibles - Company: James Breath.

Laugherty, James - Seaman - Major Leonard's Battalion, NY Sea Fencibles - Company: William Russell - Enlistment date: 12 Jan 1815 - Period: 3 Months.

Laughley, John - Seaman - Major Leonard's Battalion, NY Sea Fencibles.

Lawrence, Benjamin - Seaman - Major Wooster's Battalion, NY Sea Fencibles.

Lawrence, Thomas - Seaman - Major Wooster's Battalion, NY Sea Fencibles - Company: Isaac Silliman - Enlistment date: 6 Jan 1815 - Period: 1 Yr.

Lawton, William - Private - MA Sea Fencibles - Company: Jeremiah Stickney.

Lazare, John - Quarter Gunner - Major Fowler's Detachment, NY Sea Fencibles - Company: James Breath.

Leach, George - Seaman - NY Sea Fencibles - Company: Paul Burrows - Enlistment date: 20 Oct 1814 - Period: 3 Months - Deserted on 18 Nov 1814.

Leach, Samuel - Private - MA Sea Fencibles - Company: Nehemiah Skillings.

Leadbetter, Patrick - Waiter - NY Sea Fencibles - Company: Josiah Ingersoll.

Lear, Benjamin - Private - NH Sea Fencibles - Company: William Marshall - Enlistment date: 27 May 1813 - Discharged on 27 Nov 1813.

Leddy, John - Seaman - NY Sea Fencibles - Company: Josiah Ingersoll.

Ledger, Daniel - Gunner - NY Sea Fencibles - Company: Josiah Ingersoll - Enlistment date: 3 Jan 1815.

Lee, Henry - Seaman - Major Leonard's Battalion, NY Sea Fencibles.

Lee, Robert - Seaman - NY Sea Fencibles - Company: Josiah Ingersoll.

Lee, Samuel - Private - MA Sea Fencibles - Company: Nehemiah Skillings.

Lee, William - Ordinary Seaman - Major Wooster's Battalion, NY Sea Fencibles.

Leonard, James T. - Major - Major Leonard's Battalion, NY Sea Fencibles.

Leonard, Joseph - Seaman - Major Leonard's Battalion, NY Sea Fencibles.

Leonard, William - Seaman - Major Fowler's Detachment, NY Sea Fencibles.

Lester, Platt - Seaman - Major Wooster's Battalion, NY Sea Fencibles.

Letts, Thomas - Seaman - NY Sea Fencibles - Company: Josiah Ingersoll.

Lewis, Eleazer - Private - MA Sea Fencibles - Company: Nehemiah Skillings.

Lewis, James A. - Seaman - Major Leonard's Battalion, NY Sea Fencibles.

Lewis, Jesse - Seaman - NY Sea Fencibles - Company: John Cunningham - Enlistment date: 6 Sep 1814 - Period: 3 Months.

Lewis, Jesse - Seaman - NY Sea Fencibles - Company: Josiah Ingersoll - Enlistment date: 30 Dec 1814.

Lewis, John - Seaman - Major Wooster's Battalion, NY Sea Fencibles - Company: Isaac Silliman - Enlistment date: 14 Jan 1815 - Period: 1 Yr.

Lewis, John - Seaman - NY Sea Fencibles - Company: John Cunningham - Enlistment date: 6 Sep 1814 - Period: 3 Months.

Lewis, John - Ordinary Seaman - Major Leonard's Battalion, NY Sea Fencibles.

Lewis, John - Seaman - Major Fowler's Detachment, NY Sea Fencibles - Company: James Breath.

Lewis, Joseph W. - Private - MA Sea Fencibles - Company: Nehemiah Skillings.

Lewis, Prince - Seaman - Major Leonard's Battalion, NY Sea Fencibles.

Lewis, William - Seaman - Major Fowler's Detachment, NY Sea Fencibles.

Lewis, Winslow - First Lieutenant - MA Sea Fencibles - Company: Nehemiah Skillings.

Lightizer, John - Seaman - Major Fowler's Detachment, NY Sea Fencibles - Company: James Breath.

Likeman, Joseph - Seaman - Major Leonard's Battalion, NY Sea Fencibles.

Lilly, Francis - Seaman - Major Fowler's Detachment, NY Sea Fencibles - Company: James Breath.

Lincoln, James M. - Private - MA Sea Fencibles - Company: Nehemiah Skillings.

Lindsay, Samuel - Private - MA Sea Fencibles - Company: Isaac Lyman - Born: 25 Jul 1814 - Discharged on 24 Aug 1814.

Little, Harry - Servant - Major Fowler's Detachment, NY Sea Fencibles.

Little, John - Seaman - Major Fowler's Detachment, NY Sea Fencibles.

Livingston, Alexander - Private - MA Sea Fencibles - Company: Jeremiah Stickney.

Livingston, John - Seaman - NY Sea Fencibles - Company: Paul Burrows - Enlistment date: 13 Oct 1814 - Period: 3 Months.

Livingston, John - Seaman - Major Leonard's Battalion, NY Sea Fencibles - Company: William Russell - Enlistment date: 19 Jan 1815 - Period: 3 Months - Deserted.

Lloyd, Henry - Seaman - Major Wooster's Battalion, NY Sea Fencibles.

Locke, Daniel - Private - NH Sea Fencibles - Company: William Marshall - Enlistment date: 27 May 1813 - Discharged on 27 Nov 1813.

Locke, Joseph - Sergeant - NH Sea Fencibles - Company: William Marshall - Enlistment date: 27 May 1813 - Discharged on 27 Nov 1813.

Lockwood, William - Seaman - Major Wooster's Battalion, NY Sea Fencibles.

Lord, Samuel L. - Seaman - Major Wooster's Battalion, NY Sea Fencibles.

Losher, Alexander - Seaman - Major Wooster's Battalion, NY Sea Fencibles.

Lougherty, James - Seaman - Major Leonard's Battalion, NY Sea Fencibles.

Louis, John - Seaman - Major Leonard's Battalion, NY Sea Fencibles.

Love, John - Seaman - Major Wooster's Battalion, NY Sea Fencibles - Company: Isaac Silliman.

Lovett, John - Private - Major Leonard's Battalion, NY Sea Fencibles - Company: Alexander Robinson - Pension: Land bounty to Mary Lovett, widow of John Lovett - BLW 64267-160-55.

American Sea Fencibles in the War of 1812

Lovett, John (1) - Seaman - Major Leonard's Battalion, NY Sea Fencibles - Company: Alexander Robinson - Enlistment date: 29 Sep 1814 - Period: 3 Months.

Lovett, John (2) - Seaman - Major Leonard's Battalion, NY Sea Fencibles - Company: Alexander Robinson - Enlistment date: 3 Oct 1814 - Period: 3 Months.

Lovett, John A. - Seaman - Major Leonard's Battalion, NY Sea Fencibles.

Lovett, John I. - Seaman - Major Leonard's Battalion, NY Sea Fencibles.

Lovett, Joseph - Private - MA Sea Fencibles - Company: Jeremiah Stickney.

Low, Abraham - Seaman - Major Wooster's Battalion, NY Sea Fencibles.

Lowndes, Charles - Seaman - NY Sea Fencibles - Company: Josiah Ingersoll - Enlistment date: 5 Jan 1815.

Lowndes, Charles - Seaman - Major Fowler's Detachment, NY Sea Fencibles.

Lowrey, Cornelius - Seaman - NY Sea Fencibles - Company: Josiah Ingersoll.

Lowry, Edward - Seaman - NY Sea Fencibles - Company: Paul Burrows - Enlistment date: 24 Sep 1814 - Period: 3 Months.

Loyd, Daniel - Servant - Major Leonard's Battalion, NY Sea Fencibles.

Loyd, Daniel L. - Seaman - Major Fowler's Detachment, NY Sea Fencibles.

Loyd, Henry - Seaman - Major Wooster's Battalion, NY Sea Fencibles.

Luce, Jasper - Gunner - NY Sea Fencibles - Company: John Cunningham - Enlistment date: 7 Sep 1814 - Period: 3 Months.

Lufkin, David - First Lieutenant - MA Sea Fencibles - Company: Jeremiah Stickney.

Lyman, Christopher - Seaman - NY Sea Fencibles - Company: John Cunningham - Enlistment date: 6 Sep 1814 - Period: 3 Months.

Lyman, Isaac - Captain - MA Sea Fencibles - Company: Isaac Lyman.

Lyons, Charles - Seaman - Major Leonard's Battalion, NY Sea Fencibles.

Lyons, Cornelius S. - Ordinary Seaman - Major Leonard's Battalion, NY Sea Fencibles.

Lyons, Joseph - Seaman - NY Sea Fencibles - Company: John Cunningham - Enlistment date: 3 Sep 1814 - Period: 3 Months.

Mace, Ithamar - Private - NH Sea Fencibles - Company: William Marshall - Enlistment date: 27 May 1813 - Discharged on 27 Nov 1813.

MacKay, George D. - Private - MA Sea Fencibles - Company: Nehemiah Skillings.

MacKay, Joseph - Private - MA Sea Fencibles - Company: Nehemiah Skillings.

Mackie, Thomas - Seaman - Major Leonard's Battalion, NY Sea Fencibles - Company: Alexander Robinson - Enlistment date: 5 Oct 1814 - Period: 3 Months.

Macy, John - Gunner - Major Fowler's Detachment, NY Sea Fencibles - Company: James Breath.

Magee, Patrick - Quarter Gunner - Major Leonard's Battalion, NY Sea Fencibles - Company: William Russell - Enlistment date: 3 Jan 1815 - Period: 3 Months.

Magee, Patrick - Drummer - Major Leonard's Battalion, NY Sea Fencibles.

Maggee, Daniel - Seaman - Major Fowler's Detachment, NY Sea Fencibles.

Magrath, John - Private - NY Sea Fencibles - Company: Paul Burrows.

Malone, Barney - Seaman - Major Wooster's Battalion, NY Sea Fencibles.

Manett, John - Seaman - Major Wooster's Battalion, NY Sea Fencibles.

Manna, Charles - Seaman - Major Leonard's Battalion, NY Sea Fencibles.

Manning, William - Quarter Gunner - NY Sea Fencibles - Company: Josiah Ingersoll.

Mansfield, Adoniah - Seaman - Major Fowler's Detachment, NY Sea Fencibles - Company: James Breath - Enlistment date: 30 Dec 1814.

Mansfield, Adonish - Seaman - NY Sea Fencibles - Company: Josiah Ingersoll.

Mansfield, George - Private - MA Sea Fencibles - Company: Nehemiah Skillings.

Markinson, George - Seaman - Major Leonard's Battalion, NY Sea Fencibles.

Markwood, Joseph - Ordinary Seaman - Major Leonard's Battalion, NY Sea Fencibles.

Marline, John - Seaman - Major Wooster's Battalion, NY Sea Fencibles.

Marlue, John - Seaman - Major Leonard's Battalion, NY Sea Fencibles.

Marshall, William - Captain - NH Sea Fencibles - Company: William Marshall - Enlistment date: 27 May 1813 - Discharged on 27 Nov 1813; served again from 27 Nov 1813 through 31 Dec 1813.

Martin, John - Private - MA Sea Fencibles - Company: Nehemiah Skillings.

Martin, John - Private - NH Sea Fencibles - Company: William Marshall - Enlistment date: 27 May 1813 - Discharged on 27 Nov 1813.

Martin, John N. - Seaman - Major Wooster's Battalion, NY Sea Fencibles.

Marx, George - Seaman - Major Leonard's Battalion, NY Sea Fencibles.

Maryborler, Joseph - Seaman - NY Sea Fencibles - Company: Josiah Ingersoll.

Masey, John - Gunner - Major Fowler's Detachment, NY Sea Fencibles.

Mason, Jacob - Seaman - Major Fowler's Detachment, NY Sea Fencibles - Company: James Breath - Deserted at Blockhouse Constitution on 6 Nov 1814.

Mason, Nicholas - Private - NH Sea Fencibles - Company: William Marshall - Enlistment date: 27 May 1813 - Discharged on 27 Nov 1813.

Massey, James - Gunner - Major Leonard's Battalion, NY Sea Fencibles.

Massey, William - Quarter Gunner - Major Wooster's Battalion, NY Sea Fencibles - Company: Isaac Silliman - Enlistment date: 13 Dec 1814 - Period: 6 Months - Served on gunboat duty at Hurl Gate, NY.

Mattocks, Richard - Seaman - Major Leonard's Battalion, NY Sea Fencibles - Company: James Leonard - Pension: SO-33969.

Maubry, John - Seaman - Major Wooster's Battalion, NY Sea Fencibles.

Maxwell, Charles - Seaman - Major Leonard's Battalion, NY Sea Fencibles.

Maxwell, William - Seaman - Major Fowler's Detachment, NY Sea Fencibles - Company: James Breath.

May, Charles - Private - MA Sea Fencibles - Company: Nehemiah Skillings.

May, George - Seaman - Major Fowler's Detachment, NY Sea Fencibles.

May, William - Private - MA Sea Fencibles - Company: Nehemiah Skillings.

May, William R. - Private - MA Sea Fencibles - Company: Nehemiah Skillings.

Maybe, William H. - Seaman - Major Leonard's Battalion, NY Sea Fencibles.

Mayo, Nicholas - Seaman - Major Wooster's Battalion, NY Sea Fencibles - Company: Isaac Silliman - Enlistment date: 5 Jan 1815 - Period: 1 Yr.

Mayo, Nicholas - Seaman - NY Sea Fencibles - Company: John Cunningham - Enlistment date: 5 Sep 1814 - Period: 3 Months.

McAlpine, John W. - Seaman - Major Wooster's Battalion, NY Sea Fencibles.

McCan, Barney - Seaman - Major Leonard's Battalion, NY Sea Fencibles - Company: William Russell - Enlistment date: 14 Jan 1815 - Period: 3 Months.

McCarthy, Charles - Seaman - Major Leonard's Battalion, NY Sea Fencibles - Company: Alexander Robinson.

McConnel, James - Seaman - Major Leonard's Battalion, NY Sea Fencibles.

McConnell, James - Seaman - NY Sea Fencibles - Company: Paul Burrows - Enlistment date: 24 Sep 1814 - Period: 3 Months - Discharged on 8 Jan 1815.

McCormick, Alexander - Gunner - NY Sea Fencibles - Company: John Cunningham - Enlistment date: 2 Sep 1814 - Period: 3 Months.

McCoy, John - Seaman - Major Fowler's Detachment, NY Sea Fencibles.

McCoy, Thomas - Seaman - Major Wooster's Battalion, NY Sea Fencibles - Company: Isaac Silliman - Enlistment date: 6 Jan 1815 - Period: 1 Yr.

McCreery, Samuel - Seaman - Major Fowler's Detachment, NY Sea Fencibles - Company: James Breath.

McDaniel, James - Private - MA Sea Fencibles - Company: Isaac Lyman - Born: 25 Jul 1814 - Discharged on 24 Aug 1814.

McDonald, John - Seaman - Major Fowler's Detachment, NY Sea Fencibles - Age: 32 - Height: 5' 5 1/2" - Born: Scotland - Trade: Farmer - Enlistment date: 27 Jan 1814.

McElvin, William - Seaman - Major Fowler's Detachment, NY Sea Fencibles - Company: James Breath.

McFarland, William - Seaman - Major Wooster's Battalion, NY Sea Fencibles.

McFarren, John A. - Seaman - Major Wooster's Battalion, NY Sea Fencibles - Company: Isaac Silliman - Enlistment date: 7 Jan 1814 - Period: 1 Yr.

McFurson, John - Ordinary Seaman - Major Wooster's Battalion, NY Sea Fencibles.

McFurson, William - Ordinary Seaman - Major Wooster's Battalion, NY Sea Fencibles.

McGee, Daniel - Seaman - Major Fowler's Detachment, NY Sea Fencibles - Company: James Breath.

McGee, Patrick - Quartermaster Sergeant - Major Leonard's Battalion, NY Sea Fencibles.

McGhaun, Daniel - Seaman - Major Leonard's Battalion, NY Sea Fencibles.

McGinnis, John - Seaman - Major Wooster's Battalion, NY Sea Fencibles.

McGinnis, Michael - Seaman - Major Wooster's Battalion, NY Sea Fencibles - Company: Isaac Silliman - Enlistment date: 4 Jan 1815 - Period: 1 Yr.

McGlaughlin II, James - Seaman - Major Leonard's Battalion, NY Sea Fencibles.

McGlaughlin, Daniel - Seaman - Major Wooster's Battalion, NY Sea Fencibles - Company: Isaac Silliman - Enlistment date: 5 Jan 1815 - Period: 1 Yr.

McGlaughlin, James - Seaman - Major Leonard's Battalion, NY Sea Fencibles.

McGowan, John - Seaman - Major Fowler's Detachment, NY Sea Fencibles - Company: James Breath - Enlistment date: 3 Jan 1815.

McGowan, John - Seaman - NY Sea Fencibles - Company: Josiah Ingersoll.

McGrath, John - Seaman - Major Wooster's Battalion, NY Sea Fencibles - Company: Isaac Silliman - Enlistment date: 7 Feb 1815 - Period: 1 Yr.

McGridge, John - Private - NH Sea Fencibles - Company: William Marshall - Enlistment date: 31 Aug 1813 - Discharged on 27 Nov 1813.

McGroth, John - Seaman - NY Sea Fencibles - Company: Paul Burrows - Enlistment date: 7 Nov 1814 - Period: 3 Months.

McGuire, Patrick - Seaman - Major Wooster's Battalion, NY Sea Fencibles.

McGuire, Patrick - Seaman - NY Sea Fencibles - Company: Josiah Ingersoll - Enlistment date: 4 Jan 1815.

McIntire, Charles - Private - MA Sea Fencibles - Company: Isaac Lyman - Enlistment date: 26 Jul 1814 - Discharged on 23 Sep 1814.

McKann, Barney - Seaman - Major Leonard's Battalion, NY Sea Fencibles.

McKay, George - Ordinary Seaman - Major Wooster's Battalion, NY Sea Fencibles.

McKay, John - Seaman - Major Leonard's Battalion, NY Sea Fencibles.

McKenna, James - Seaman - Major Leonard's Battalion, NY Sea Fencibles.

McKenna, Patrick - Seaman - Major Leonard's Battalion, NY Sea Fencibles.

McKinney, James - Seaman - Major Leonard's Battalion, NY Sea Fencibles - Company: William Russell - Enlistment date: 13 Jan 1814 - Period: 3 Months.

McKoy, Thomas - Seaman - Major Wooster's Battalion, NY Sea Fencibles.

McLain, William - Private - NY Sea Fencibles - Company: Paul Burrows - Enlistment date: 13 Oct 1814 - Period: 3 Months - Deserted on 23 Nov 1814.

McLaughlin I, James - Seaman - Major Leonard's Battalion, NY Sea Fencibles.

McLaughlin II, James - Seaman - Major Leonard's Battalion, NY Sea Fencibles.

McLaughlin III, James - Ordinary Seaman - Major Leonard's Battalion, NY Sea Fencibles.

McLaughlin, Daniel - Private - Major Wooster's Battalion, NY Sea Fencibles.

McLaughlin, Francis - Seaman - Major Leonard's Battalion, NY Sea Fencibles.

McLaughlin, James - Private - Major Leonard's Battalion, NY Sea Fencibles - Company: William Russell - Enlistment date: 16 Jan 1815 - Period: 3 Months.

McLaughlin, James - Seaman - Major Leonard's Battalion, NY Sea Fencibles - Company: William Russell - Enlistment date: 12 Jan 1815 - Period: 3 Months.

McLaughlin, John - Ordinary Seaman - Major Wooster's Battalion, NY Sea Fencibles.

McLaughton, Francis - Seaman - Major Leonard's Battalion, NY Sea Fencibles - Company: Alexander

Robinson - Enlistment date: 2 Nov 1814 - Period: 3 Months.

McMullen, Alexander - Seaman - Major Wooster's Battalion, NY Sea Fencibles - Company: Isaac Silliman - Enlistment date: 11 Jan 1815 - Period: 1 Yr.

McPherson, John - Ordinary Seaman - Major Wooster's Battalion, NY Sea Fencibles.

McRath, John - Private - NY Sea Fencibles - Company: Paul Burrows.

McSweneys, John - Gunner - NY Sea Fencibles - Company: Josiah Ingersoll.

McThay, Thomas - Seaman - Major Leonard's Battalion, NY Sea Fencibles - Company: William Russell - Enlistment date: 3 Jan 1815 - Period: 3 Months - Never joined company.

McWay, John - Seaman - Major Fowler's Detachment, NY Sea Fencibles.

McWharton, John - Second Lieutenant - Major Fowler's Detachment, NY Sea Fencibles.

Mead, John - Seaman - Major Fowler's Detachment, NY Sea Fencibles.

Meakins, John - Gunner - NY Sea Fencibles - Company: John Cunningham - Enlistment date: 2 Sep 1814 - Period: 3 Months.

Meakins, William - Private - NY Sea Fencibles - Company: John Cunningham - Enlistment date: 3 Sep 1814 - Period: 3 Months.

Medley, Enoch - Seaman - NY Sea Fencibles - Company: Josiah Ingersoll.

Megson, Thomas - Seaman - NY Sea Fencibles - Company: John Cunningham - Enlistment date: 3 Sep 1814 - Period: 3 Months.

Mercer, William - Seaman - Major Wooster's Battalion, NY Sea Fencibles - Company: Lieutenant Benjamin Dayton.

Merchant, Joseph - Seaman - Major Fowler's Detachment, NY Sea Fencibles.

Merlue, John - Seaman - Major Leonard's Battalion, NY Sea Fencibles.

Merrihew, William - Gunner - Major Leonard's Battalion, NY Sea Fencibles - Company: Alexander Robinson - Enlistment date: 13 Sep 1814 - Period: 3 Months.

Merriote, Francis - Seaman - Major Wooster's Battalion, NY Sea Fencibles - Company: Isaac Silliman.

Merrow, William - Seaman - Major Leonard's Battalion, NY Sea Fencibles - Company: Alexander Robinson - Enlistment date: 2 Nov 1814 - Period: 3 Months.

Messey, William - Quarter Gunner - Major Wooster's Battalion, NY Sea Fencibles.

Mgham, Daniel - Seaman - Major Leonard's Battalion, NY Sea Fencibles.

Middleton, James - Seaman - Major Wooster's Battalion, NY Sea Fencibles.

Miles, Richard - Seaman - Major Leonard's Battalion, NY Sea Fencibles.

Miller, Alexander - Seaman - Major Wooster's Battalion, NY Sea Fencibles.

Miller, Arthur - Seaman - Major Wooster's Battalion, NY Sea Fencibles.

Miller, Augustus - Seaman - Major Wooster's Battalion, NY Sea Fencibles.

Miller, Henry - Servant - Major Wooster's Battalion, NY Sea Fencibles.

Miller, Isaac - Private - MA Sea Fencibles - Company: Nehemiah Skillings.

Miller, Jacob - Waiter - Major Leonard's Battalion, NY Sea Fencibles.

Miller, James - Quarter Gunner - Major Wooster's Battalion, NY Sea Fencibles.

Miller, Jasper - Seaman - Major Leonard's Battalion, NY Sea Fencibles - Company: Alexander Robinson.

Miller, John - Seaman - Major Wooster's Battalion, NY Sea Fencibles - Company: Lieutenant Benjamin Dayton - Enlistment date: 2 Jan 1815 - Period: 3 Months - Served on board a prison ship.

Miller, John - Quarter Gunner - NY Sea Fencibles - Company: John Cunningham.

Miller, John - Seaman - Major Fowler's Detachment, NY Sea Fencibles.

Miller, John - Seaman - NY Sea Fencibles - Company: Paul Burrows - Enlistment date: 20 Sep 1814 - Period: 3 Months.

Miller, John D. - Seaman - Major Leonard's Battalion, NY Sea Fencibles.

Miller, John G. - Seaman - Major Leonard's Battalion, NY Sea Fencibles.

Miller, Joseph - Seaman - Major Wooster's Battalion, NY Sea Fencibles.

Miller, Thomas - Seaman - Major Fowler's Detachment, NY Sea Fencibles.

Milligan, Basil - Seaman - NY Sea Fencibles - Company: Josiah Ingersoll.

Millis, John - Seaman - Major Leonard's Battalion, NY Sea Fencibles.

Minna, Charles - Seaman - Major Leonard's Battalion, NY Sea Fencibles.

Minns, Jacob - Seaman - Major Fowler's Detachment, NY Sea Fencibles - Company: James Breath.

Minor, Daniel G. - Second Lieutenant - Major Leonard's Battalion, NY Sea Fencibles.

Minor, David G. - Second Lieutenant - Major Leonard's Battalion, NY Sea Fencibles.

Minto, John - Seaman - Major Wooster's Battalion, NY Sea Fencibles.

Mitchell, Henry - Seaman - Major Leonard's Battalion, NY Sea Fencibles - Company: Alexander Robinson - Enlistment date: 12 Oct 1814 - Period: 3 Months.

Mitchell, Henry - Seaman - Major Wooster's Battalion, NY Sea Fencibles - Company: Isaac Silliman - Enlistment date: 7 Feb 1815 - Period: 1 Yr.

Mitchell, Henry - Seaman - NY Sea Fencibles - Company: Paul Burrows - Enlistment date: 4 Nov 1814 - Period: 3 Months.

Mitchell, Walter - Seaman - Major Wooster's Battalion, NY Sea Fencibles.

Moffatt, Samuel - Private - MA Sea Fencibles - Company: Nehemiah Skillings.

Monroe, George - Quarter Gunner - NY Sea Fencibles - Company: Josiah Ingersoll.

Montgomery, Robert - Seaman - Major Leonard's Battalion, NY Sea Fencibles - Company: Alexander Robinson.

Mooberry, John - Seaman - Major Wooster's Battalion, NY Sea Fencibles.

Moody, Charles - Private - MA Sea Fencibles - Company: Isaac Lyman - Enlistment date: 26 Jul 1814 - Discharged on 23 Sep 1814.

Moody, Joseph - Sergeant - MA Sea Fencibles - Company: Isaac Lyman.

Moore, Abraham - Seaman - Major Wooster's Battalion, NY Sea Fencibles.

Moore, George - Private - MA Sea Fencibles - Company: Isaac Lyman.

Moore, John - Seaman - NY Sea Fencibles - Company: John Cunningham - Enlistment date: 3 Sep 1814 -

Period: 3 Months.

Moore, Patrick - Seaman - Major Wooster's Battalion, NY Sea Fencibles.

Moore, Samuel - Private - MA Sea Fencibles - Company: Nehemiah Skillings.

Moores, William - Seaman - Major Leonard's Battalion, NY Sea Fencibles - Company: Alexander Robinson.

Moorfield, James - Private - MA Sea Fencibles - Company: Nehemiah Skillings.

Moorhouse, Marlborough B. - Seaman - NY Sea Fencibles - Company: Paul Burrows - Enlistment date: 27 Sep 1814 - Period: 3 Months.

Mooris, Jacob - Seaman - Major Wooster's Battalion, NY Sea Fencibles.

Moors, Harry - Private - Major Fowler's Detachment, NY Sea Fencibles - Company: James Breath.

Morgan, James - Private - MA Sea Fencibles - Company: Nehemiah Skillings.

Morland, Robert - Private - MA Sea Fencibles - Company: Nehemiah Skillings.

Morrel, Jacob - Seaman - Major Wooster's Battalion, NY Sea Fencibles - Company: Isaac Silliman - Enlistment date: 17 Jan 1815 - Period: 1 Yr.

Morris, Jacob - Seaman - Major Wooster's Battalion, NY Sea Fencibles - Company: Isaac Silliman - Enlistment date: 11 Jan 1815 - Period: 1 Yr.

Morris, Jacob - Seaman - NY Sea Fencibles - Company: Paul Burrows - Enlistment date: 5 Oct 1814 - Period: 3 Months.

Morrison Jr., Thomas - Seaman - Major Leonard's Battalion, NY Sea Fencibles.

Morrison, Charles - Seaman - Major Wooster's Battalion, NY Sea Fencibles - Company: Lieutenant Benjamin Dayton.

Morrison, Henry - Seaman - Major Fowler's Detachment, NY Sea Fencibles - Company: James Breath.

Morrison, John - Servant - Major Leonard's Battalion, NY Sea Fencibles.

Morrison, Robert - Seaman - Major Wooster's Battalion, NY Sea Fencibles.

Morrison, Thomas - Seaman - Major Leonard's Battalion, NY Sea Fencibles - Company: William Russell - Enlistment date: 3 Jan 1815 - Period: 3 Months - Never joined company.

Morrow, William - Seaman - Major Leonard's Battalion, NY Sea Fencibles.

Mosier, Charles - Ordinary Seaman - NY Sea Fencibles - Company: John Cunningham.

Moss, Thomas - Seaman - Major Leonard's Battalion, NY Sea Fencibles.

Moss, William - Seaman - Major Leonard's Battalion, NY Sea Fencibles.

Mott, Charles - Ordinary Seaman - Major Wooster's Battalion, NY Sea Fencibles.

Moylan, Jasper - Boatswain - Major Wooster's Battalion, NY Sea Fencibles.

Muen, William - Seaman - Major Wooster's Battalion, NY Sea Fencibles - Company: Lieutenant Benjamin Dayton - Enlistment date: 29 Dec 1814 - Served on board a prison ship; discharged on 11 Mar 1815.

Mugrige, John - Private - NH Sea Fencibles - Company: William Marshall - Enlistment date: 27 Nov 1813 - Discharged on 31 Dec 1813.

Mulford, Thomas - Seaman - Major Fowler's Detachment, NY Sea Fencibles - Company: James Breath -

Deserted on 7 Nov 1814.

Mullen, James - Private - NH Sea Fencibles - Company: William Marshall - Enlistment date: 27 May 1813 - Discharged on 27 Nov 1813; served again from 27 Nov 1813 through 31 Dec 1813.

Mullen, John - Seaman - NY Sea Fencibles - Company: John Cunningham - Enlistment date: 3 Sep 1814 - Period: 3 Months.

Mullin, John R. - Private - NH Sea Fencibles - Company: William Marshall - Enlistment date: 27 May 1813 - Discharged on 27 Nov 1813; served again from 27 Nov 1813 through 31 Dec 1813.

Munroe, Robert - Seaman - Major Wooster's Battalion, NY Sea Fencibles.

Munson, Peter - Seaman - Major Wooster's Battalion, NY Sea Fencibles - Company: Lieutenant Benjamin Dayton.

Munson, Peter - Seaman - NY Sea Fencibles - Company: John Cunningham - Enlistment date: 3 Sep 18141 - Period: 3 Months - Served on board a prison ship.

Murray, John C. - Seaman - Major Leonard's Battalion, NY Sea Fencibles.

Murray, Lewis - Seaman - Major Wooster's Battalion, NY Sea Fencibles.

Murray, Samuel - Seaman - Major Fowler's Detachment, NY Sea Fencibles - Company: James Breath.

Mutaire, Lewis - Seaman - Major Leonard's Battalion, NY Sea Fencibles.

Muzzy, Benjamin A. - Captain - Major Fowler's Detachment, NY Sea Fencibles - Company: Benjamin Muzzy.

Myers, Jacob - Seaman - Major Fowler's Detachment, NY Sea Fencibles.

Myers, John - Ordinary Seaman - Major Leonard's Battalion, NY Sea Fencibles.

Myers, John - Seaman - NY Sea Fencibles - Company: Paul Burrows - Enlistment date: 11 Oct 1814 - Period: 3 Months - Discharged on 17 Nov 1814.

Myers, Peter - Seaman - Major Leonard's Battalion, NY Sea Fencibles.

Myrick, Charles - First Lieutenant - Major Leonard's Battalion, NY Sea Fencibles - Company: William Russell - Enlistment date: 5 Dec 1814.

Narrell, Samuel - Private - NH Sea Fencibles - Company: William Marshall - Enlistment date: 27 May 1813 - Discharged on 13 Oct 1813.

Nash Jr., Joshua - Private - MA Sea Fencibles - Company: Nehemiah Skillings.

Nash Jr., Moses - Private - MA Sea Fencibles - Company: Nehemiah Skillings.

Nash, Sampson - Seaman - Major Wooster's Battalion, NY Sea Fencibles.

Natvig, George - Third Lieutenant - Major Leonard's Battalion, NY Sea Fencibles.

Natvig, John M. - Seaman - NY Sea Fencibles - Company: Josiah Ingersoll.

Neal Jr., William - Private - NH Sea Fencibles - Company: William Marshall - Enlistment date: 27 May 1813 - Discharged on 27 Nov 1813.

Neal, George - Musician - NH Sea Fencibles - Company: William Marshall - Enlistment date: 27 May 1813 - Discharged on 27 Nov 1813.

Neal, James S. - Quarter Gunner - Major Fowler's Detachment, NY Sea Fencibles.

Neal, William - Private - NH Sea Fencibles - Company: William Marshall - Enlistment date: 27 May

1813 - Discharged on 27 Nov 1813.

Nedson, Edward - Seaman - NY Sea Fencibles - Company: Paul Burrows - Enlistment date: 1 Oct 1814 - Period: 3 Months.

Nedson, Samuel - Seaman - NY Sea Fencibles - Company: Paul Burrows - Enlistment date: 7 Oct 1814 - Period: 3 Months.

Needham, William - Gunner - Major Leonard's Battalion, NY Sea Fencibles - Company: William Russell - Enlistment date: 7 Dec 1814 - Period: 3 Months.

Neil, Henry S. - Seaman - NY Sea Fencibles - Company: Josiah Ingersoll.

Neill, John - Seaman - Major Leonard's Battalion, NY Sea Fencibles.

Nelson, Oliver - Boatswain - NY Sea Fencibles - Company: Josiah Ingersoll.

Nesbit, Edwin - Seaman - Major Fowler's Detachment, NY Sea Fencibles - Company: James Breath - BLW 32578-120-55.

Nevil, Michael - Seaman - Major Wooster's Battalion, NY Sea Fencibles - Company: Isaac Silliman - Enlistment date: 4 Jan 1815 - Period: 1 Yr.

Nevill, Michael - Seaman - NY Sea Fencibles - Company: John Cunningham - Enlistment date: 3 Sep 1814 - Period: 3 Months.

Newlin, Adam - Seaman - Major Wooster's Battalion, NY Sea Fencibles - Company: Isaac Silliman - Enlistment date: 7 Jan 1815 - Period: 1 Yr.

Newson, Samuel - Seaman - Major Fowler's Detachment, NY Sea Fencibles - Company: Benjamin Muzzy.

Nichols, Stephen - Private - NY Sea Fencibles - Company: Paul Burrows - Enlistment date: 5 Oct 1814 - Period: 3 Months.

Nicholson, James - Seaman - Major Fowler's Detachment, NY Sea Fencibles - Company: James Breath - Deserted at Blockhouse Constitution on 4 Dec 1814.

Nicholson, John - Seaman - NY Sea Fencibles - Company: Paul Burrows - Enlistment date: 5 Nov 1814 - Period: 3 Months - Deserted on 7 Nov 1814.

Nickels, Samuel - Private - MA Sea Fencibles - Company: Nehemiah Skillings.

Nickerson, Edward - Seaman - NY Sea Fencibles - Company: John Cunningham - Enlistment date: 2 Sep 1814 - Period: 3 Months.

Niece, Jacob - Seaman - NY Sea Fencibles - Company: Paul Burrows - Enlistment date: 11 Oct 1814 - Period: 3 Months.

Niles, John - Seaman - NY Sea Fencibles - Company: Paul Burrows - Enlistment date: 1 Nov 1814 - Period: 3 Months.

Noble, Francis - Private - MA Sea Fencibles - Company: Nehemiah Skillings.

Nodine, David - Ordinary Seaman - Major Wooster's Battalion, NY Sea Fencibles.

Noland, Peter - Seaman - Major Fowler's Detachment, NY Sea Fencibles - Company: James Breath.

Norris, Coffin - Seaman - Major Wooster's Battalion, NY Sea Fencibles - Company: John Roorbach.

Norton, Stephen - Private - MA Sea Fencibles - Company: Jeremiah Stickney.

Norton, William - Private - MA Sea Fencibles - Company: Jeremiah Stickney.

Notty, William F. - Seaman - NY Sea Fencibles - Company: Josiah Ingersoll.

Nourse, Thomas - Seaman - NY Sea Fencibles - Company: John Cunningham - Enlistment date: 3 Sep 1814 - Period: 3 Months.

Nowell, Silas - Private - MA Sea Fencibles - Company: Jeremiah Stickney.

Oakden, Joseph - Quarter Gunner - Major Leonard's Battalion, NY Sea Fencibles.

O'Brien, Patrick - Seaman - Major Leonard's Battalion, NY Sea Fencibles.

O'Brien, Lawrence - Seaman - Major Wooster's Battalion, NY Sea Fencibles - Company: Isaac Silliman - Enlistment date: 7 Jan 1815 - Period: 1 Yr.

Odiorne, George B. - Private - NH Sea Fencibles - Company: William Marshall - Enlistment date: 27 Nov 1813 - Discharged on 31 Dec 1813.

Odiorne, Samuel - Private - NH Sea Fencibles - Company: William Marshall - Enlistment date: 27 May 1813 - Discharged on 27 Nov 1813.

Ogelsbie, John - Seaman - NY Sea Fencibles - Company: John Cunningham - Enlistment date: 6 Sep 1814 - Period: 3 Months.

Oliver, Benjamin - Private - NH Sea Fencibles - Company: William Marshall - Enlistment date: 27 May 1813 - Discharged on 27 Nov 1813.

Oliver, Thomas - Seaman - NY Sea Fencibles - Company: John Cunningham - Enlistment date: 3 Sep 1814 - Period: 3 Months.

Oliver, William - Seaman - Major Wooster's Battalion, NY Sea Fencibles - Company: Isaac Silliman - Enlistment date: 7 Feb 1815 - Period: 1 Yr.

Olney, Samuel - Seaman - Major Wooster's Battalion, NY Sea Fencibles - Company: Isaac Silliman - Enlistment date: 16 Jan 1815 - Period: 1 Yr.

Onderdonk, Henry L. - Seaman - Major Leonard's Battalion, NY Sea Fencibles.

Orcutt, Stephen - Seaman - Major Wooster's Battalion, NY Sea Fencibles.

Oringer, Robert - Seaman - Major Leonard's Battalion, NY Sea Fencibles - Company: Alexander Robinson - Deserted in New York on 24 Oct 1814.

Osbourn, Charles - Seaman - Major Wooster's Battalion, NY Sea Fencibles - Company: Isaac Silliman - Enlistment date: 13 Jan 1815 - Period: 1 Yr.

Osgood, Samuel W. - Quarter Gunner - Major Leonard's Battalion, NY Sea Fencibles.

Ott, Andrew - Seaman - Major Fowler's Detachment, NY Sea Fencibles.

Otter, James - Third Lieutenant - Major Leonard's Battalion, NY Sea Fencibles.

Owen, George - Seaman - Major Leonard's Battalion, NY Sea Fencibles.

Paddock, Gorham - Seaman - Major Leonard's Battalion, NY Sea Fencibles.

Padock, Graham - Seaman - Major Leonard's Battalion, NY Sea Fencibles - Company: Alexander Robinson - Enlistment date: 20 Sep 1814 - Period: 3 Months - Discharged on 8 Jan 1815.

Paid, Peter - Seaman - Major Leonard's Battalion, NY Sea Fencibles - Company: Alexander Robinson - Enlistment date: 24 Oct 1814 - Period: 3 Months.

Parce, Jonathan - Seaman - Major Leonard's Battalion, NY Sea Fencibles.

Parcel, John H. - Seaman - Major Fowler's Detachment, NY Sea Fencibles.

Pares, Peter - Ordinary Seaman - Major Leonard's Battalion, NY Sea Fencibles.

Park, Isaac - Private - MA Sea Fencibles - Company: Jeremiah Stickney.

Parker, George - Seaman - Major Wooster's Battalion, NY Sea Fencibles - Company: Isaac Silliman - Enlistment date: 25 Jan 1815 - Period: 1 Yr.

Parker, Thomas - Seaman - Major Fowler's Detachment, NY Sea Fencibles.

Parks, Henry - Waiter - NY Sea Fencibles - Company: Paul Burrows - Enlistment date: 1 Oct 1814 - Period: 3 Months.

Parmele, Hayle - Seaman - Major Wooster's Battalion, NY Sea Fencibles.

Parmelee, David - Seaman - NY Sea Fencibles - Company: John Cunningham - Enlistment date: 8 Sep 1814 - Period: 3 Months.

Parrett, Peter - Ordinary Seaman - Major Leonard's Battalion, NY Sea Fencibles.

Parsons, Charles - Private - MA Sea Fencibles - Company: Nehemiah Skillings.

Parsons, Joseph - Private - MA Sea Fencibles - Company: Jeremiah Stickney.

Pascalis, Peter - Seaman - Major Wooster's Battalion, NY Sea Fencibles.

Pasier, John - Servant - NY Sea Fencibles - Company: Josiah Ingersoll.

Patrick, Francis - Quarter Gunner - NY Sea Fencibles - Company: Josiah Ingersoll.

Pattern, Charles - Seaman - NY Sea Fencibles - Company: John Cunningham - Enlistment date: 5 Sep 1814 - Period: 3 Months.

Patterson, Peter - Seaman - Major Wooster's Battalion, NY Sea Fencibles - Company: Isaac Silliman.

Patterson, Peter - Seaman - NY Sea Fencibles - Company: Josiah Ingersoll - Enlistment date: 3 Jan 1815.

Patterson, William - Seaman - Major Leonard's Battalion, NY Sea Fencibles.

Patton, John - Seaman - Major Leonard's Battalion, NY Sea Fencibles - Company: Alexander Robinson - Enlistment date: 29 Oct 1814 - Period: 3 Months.

Paul, Philander - Seaman - NY Sea Fencibles - Company: John Cunningham - Enlistment date: 5 Sep 1814 - Period: 3 Months.

Peabody, Asa - Seaman - Major Fowler's Detachment, NY Sea Fencibles - Company: James Breath.

Pearson, Amos - Private - MA Sea Fencibles - Company: Nehemiah Skillings.

Pearson, Thomas - Private - MA Sea Fencibles - Company: Nehemiah Skillings.

Peaseley, Abiel - Seaman - Major Wooster's Battalion, NY Sea Fencibles.

Peaton, Thomas - Seaman - Major Fowler's Detachment, NY Sea Fencibles.

Penn, William - Private - MA Sea Fencibles - Company: Nehemiah Skillings.

Penn, William - Seaman - Major Wooster's Battalion, NY Sea Fencibles.

Perkins, John - Seaman - Major Leonard's Battalion, NY Sea Fencibles.

Perkins, William - Seaman - Major Wooster's Battalion, NY Sea Fencibles - Company: Isaac Silliman - Enlistment date: 7 Jan 1815 - Period: 1 Yr.

Perkins, Zeph - Seaman - Major Leonard's Battalion, NY Sea Fencibles.

Perry, Robert - Captain - Major Leonard's Battalion, NY Sea Fencibles - Company: Robert Perry.

Perry, William - Seaman - Major Wooster's Battalion, NY Sea Fencibles - Company: John Roorbach - On the boat crew at Fort Sevens, NY.

Peters, John - Seaman - Major Leonard's Battalion, NY Sea Fencibles - Company: Alexander Robinson - Enlistment date: 10 Sep 1814 - Period: 3 Months.

Peters, John - Seaman - Major Fowler's Detachment, NY Sea Fencibles - Company: James Breath - Deserted at Blockhouse Constitution on 30 Sep 1814.

Peterson, Christian - Seaman - NY Sea Fencibles - Company: Josiah Ingersoll.

Peterson, Cornelius - Ordinary Seaman - Major Wooster's Battalion, NY Sea Fencibles.

Peterson, Henry - Private - MA Sea Fencibles - Company: Nehemiah Skillings.

Peterson, John - Servant - Major Fowler's Detachment, NY Sea Fencibles.

Peterson, John - Seaman - Major Fowler's Detachment, NY Sea Fencibles - Company: James Breath.

Peterson, Samuel - Seaman - Major Fowler's Detachment, NY Sea Fencibles - Company: James Breath.

Peterson, Stephen - Seaman - NY Sea Fencibles - Company: Josiah Ingersoll.

Peterson, Thomas - Seaman - Major Wooster's Battalion, NY Sea Fencibles.

Peterson, Thomas - Seaman - Major Fowler's Detachment, NY Sea Fencibles - Company: James Breath.

Phillips, Joseph - Seaman - NY Sea Fencibles - Company: Paul Burrows - Enlistment date: 7 Nov 1814 - Period: 3 Months.

Phillips, Robert - Seaman - NY Sea Fencibles - Company: John Cunningham - Enlistment date: 3 Sep 1814 - Period: 3 Months.

Phillips, William - Seaman - NY Sea Fencibles - Company: Josiah Ingersoll - Enlistment date: 2 Jan 1813.

Picket, Jonathan - Ordinary Seaman - Major Leonard's Battalion, NY Sea Fencibles.

Pitcher, Jonathan - Servant - NY Sea Fencibles - Company: Josiah Ingersoll.

Place, Henry M. - Seaman - Major Leonard's Battalion, NY Sea Fencibles - Company: Alexander Robinson.

Place, William - Seaman - Major Fowler's Detachment, NY Sea Fencibles - Company: James Breath.

Pollo, Peter - Seaman - NY Sea Fencibles - Company: Josiah Ingersoll.

Pommier, George - Private - MA Sea Fencibles - Company: Nehemiah Skillings.

Porter, Abraham - Seaman - Major Fowler's Detachment, NY Sea Fencibles - Company: James Breath.

Porter, John - Waiter - Major Wooster's Battalion, NY Sea Fencibles.

Porter, John - Seaman - Major Wooster's Battalion, NY Sea Fencibles - Company: Isaac Silliman - Enlistment date: 2 Dec 1814 - Dr. Steven's servant.

Posey, John - Servant - NY Sea Fencibles - Company: Josiah Ingersoll.

Post, Archibald L. - Seaman - Major Leonard's Battalion, NY Sea Fencibles - Company: Alexander Robinson - Enlistment date: 28 Oct 1814 - Period: 3 Months.

Post, Edward - Surgeon - Major Leonard's Battalion, NY Sea Fencibles.

Post, Edward - Surgeon - NY Sea Fencibles - Company: Staff.

American Sea Fencibles in the War of 1812

Post, William - Gunner - Major Leonard's Battalion, NY Sea Fencibles - Company: Alexander Robinson - Enlistment date: 10 Sep 1814 - Period: 3 Months.

Powers, Michael - Seaman - NY Sea Fencibles - Company: Paul Burrows - Enlistment date: 1 Nov 1814 - Period: 3 Months.

Pratt, Elihu - Servant - Major Leonard's Battalion, NY Sea Fencibles.

Pratt, Joseph - Private - NY Sea Fencibles - Company: Paul Burrows - Enlistment date: 1 Oct 1814 - Period: 3 Months.

Price, Henry - Quarter Gunner - Major Wooster's Battalion, NY Sea Fencibles.

Prince, George I. - Private - MA Sea Fencibles - Company: Nehemiah Skillings.

Prince, Joseph - Private - MA Sea Fencibles - Company: Jeremiah Stickney.

Proctor, Edward - Private - MA Sea Fencibles - Company: Nehemiah Skillings.

Purcell, Henry - Private - MA Sea Fencibles - Company: Nehemiah Skillings.

Purcell, James - Private - NY Sea Fencibles - Company: Paul Burrows - Enlistment date: 31 Oct 1814 - Period: 3 Months - Deserted on 18 Nov 1814.

Pursell, Joseph - Seaman - Major Leonard's Battalion, NY Sea Fencibles.

Putnam, John - Musician - MA Sea Fencibles - Company: Jeremiah Stickney.

Quereau, Philip I. - Third Lieutenant - Major Fowler's Detachment, NY Sea Fencibles.

Quin, Robert - Waiter - Major Wooster's Battalion, NY Sea Fencibles.

Quin, Robert Arnet - Private - Major Leonard's Battalion, NY Sea Fencibles - Company: Alexander Robinson - BLW 7283-120-55.

Quincy Jr., Samuel - Private - MA Sea Fencibles - Company: Nehemiah Skillings.

Quinn, Robert - Waiter - Major Wooster's Battalion, NY Sea Fencibles - Company: Isaac Silliman.

Quinton, Joshua - Private - NY Sea Fencibles - Company: Josiah Ingersoll - BLW 91086-120-55

Rabbit, Samuel - Seaman - Major Leonard's Battalion, NY Sea Fencibles.

Rafferties, Patrick - Seaman - Major Wooster's Battalion, NY Sea Fencibles.

Rafferty, Patrick - Seaman - Major Wooster's Battalion, NY Sea Fencibles - Company: Isaac Silliman - Enlistment date: 7 Jan 1815 - Period: 1 Yr.

Rafferty, Patrick - Seaman - Major Fowler's Detachment, NY Sea Fencibles.

Rames, David - Waiter - Major Wooster's Battalion, NY Sea Fencibles - Company: Lieutenant Benjamin Dayton - Served on board a prison ship.

Rand, Biel - Seaman - Major Wooster's Battalion, NY Sea Fencibles.

Randall, Henry - Seaman - Major Leonard's Battalion, NY Sea Fencibles - Company: Alexander Robinson - Enlistment date: 2 Nov 1814 - Period: 3 Months.

Randlet, John M. - Captain - Major Wooster's Battalion, NY Sea Fencibles - Company: John Randlet.

Randolph, Francis - Seaman - Major Leonard's Battalion, NY Sea Fencibles - Company: Alexander Robinson - Enlistment date: 24 Oct 1814 - Period: 3 Months.

Rathborne, James - Seaman - Major Fowler's Detachment, NY Sea Fencibles.

Rattee, Charles - Gunner - Major Leonard's Battalion, NY Sea Fencibles - Company: William Russell - Enlistment date: 16 Dec 1814 - Period: 3 Months.

Ratter, John - Seaman - Major Fowler's Detachment, NY Sea Fencibles.

Rattray, John - Seaman - Major Wooster's Battalion, NY Sea Fencibles.

Rea, Hall - Seaman - Major Fowler's Detachment, NY Sea Fencibles.

Read, Charles - Waiter - Major Wooster's Battalion, NY Sea Fencibles.

Read, Thomas - Drummer - Major Wooster's Battalion, NY Sea Fencibles.

Reddin, Morris - Seaman - Major Fowler's Detachment, NY Sea Fencibles.

Redding, James - Gunner - Major Leonard's Battalion, NY Sea Fencibles.

Redin, James - Seaman - Major Wooster's Battalion, NY Sea Fencibles.

Redman, Jesse - Third Lieutenant - NY Sea Fencibles - Company: Paul Burrows - Enlistment date: 16 Sep 1814 - Discharged on 13 Nov 1814.

Redmond, Joseph - Seaman - NY Sea Fencibles - Company: John Cunningham - Enlistment date: 3 Sep 1814 - Period: 3 Months.

Reed, John - Seaman - Major Leonard's Battalion, NY Sea Fencibles.

Reed, John - Seaman - NY Sea Fencibles - Company: Paul Burrows - Enlistment date: 29 Sep 1814 - Period: 3 Months - Deserted on 18 Nov 1814.

Reicke, Nicholas - Gunner - Major Wooster's Battalion, NY Sea Fencibles.

Remsen, Charles - Seaman - Major Wooster's Battalion, NY Sea Fencibles.

Requa, Daniel - Seaman - Major Wooster's Battalion, NY Sea Fencibles.

Reynolds, Justus - Seaman - Major Fowler's Detachment, NY Sea Fencibles.

Rhea, Elisha R. - Ordinary Seaman - Major Leonard's Battalion, NY Sea Fencibles.

Rhine, Calvin - Private - NY Sea Fencibles - Company: Paul Burrows - Enlistment date: 1 Oct 1814 - Period: 3 Months.

Rhodes, Thomas - Seaman - NY Sea Fencibles - Company: Paul Burrows - Enlistment date: 1 Oct 1814 - Period: 3 Months.

Rich, Henry L. - Seaman - Major Fowler's Detachment, NY Sea Fencibles - Company: James Breath.

Richards, Abraham - Seaman - Major Wooster's Battalion, NY Sea Fencibles.

Richards, George - Seaman - Major Leonard's Battalion, NY Sea Fencibles.

Richards, Lewis - Seaman - Major Leonard's Battalion, NY Sea Fencibles.

Richardson, James - Seaman - Major Wooster's Battalion, NY Sea Fencibles - Company: Lieutenant Benjamin Dayton - Enlistment date: 29 Dec 1814 - Period: 1Yr - Served on board a prison ship.

Richardson, Joseph - Private - NY Sea Fencibles - Company: Paul Burrows.

Richardson, William - Seaman - Major Wooster's Battalion, NY Sea Fencibles - Company: Isaac Silliman - Enlistment date: 31 Jan 1815 - Period: 1 Yr.

Richeson, William - Seaman - Major Leonard's Battalion, NY Sea Fencibles - Company: Alexander Robinson - Enlistment date: 25 Oct 1814 - Period: 3 Months.

Richie, John - Gunner - Major Wooster's Battalion, NY Sea Fencibles.

Rickman, Isaac - Seaman - NY Sea Fencibles - Company: John Cunningham - Enlistment date: 3 Sep 1814 - Period: 3 Months.

Riggs, John - Seaman - Major Wooster's Battalion, NY Sea Fencibles.

Rikeman, Isaac - Seaman - Major Wooster's Battalion, NY Sea Fencibles.

Riker, Elijah - Seaman - Major Fowler's Detachment, NY Sea Fencibles - Company: James Breath.

Riker, John - Seaman - Major Wooster's Battalion, NY Sea Fencibles.

Rikerman, Isaac - Seaman - Major Wooster's Battalion, NY Sea Fencibles - Company: Isaac Silliman - Enlistment date: 11 Jan 1815 - Period: 1 Yr.

Rindge, William - Gunner - Major Leonard's Battalion, NY Sea Fencibles.

Ripley, Samuel - Seaman - Major Fowler's Detachment, NY Sea Fencibles.

Ripley, Samuel - Seaman - Major Wooster's Battalion, NY Sea Fencibles - Company: Isaac Silliman - Enlistment date: 17 Jan 1815 - Period: 1 Yr.

Risk, Henry L. - Seaman - Major Fowler's Detachment, NY Sea Fencibles.

Roach, Edward - Seaman - NY Sea Fencibles - Company: Josiah Ingersoll - Enlistment date: 30 Dec 1814.

Robb, Alexander - Gunner - Major Fowler's Detachment, NY Sea Fencibles.

Robb, James - Ordinary Seaman - Major Leonard's Battalion, NY Sea Fencibles.

Robbins, Chandler - Private - MA Sea Fencibles - Company: Nehemiah Skillings.

Robbins, William - Seaman - NY Sea Fencibles - Company: Josiah Ingersoll.

Roberts, Frederick - Ordinary Seaman - Major Wooster's Battalion, NY Sea Fencibles.

Roberts, Joseph - Seaman - Major Leonard's Battalion, NY Sea Fencibles.

Roberts, Michael - Seaman - Major Leonard's Battalion, NY Sea Fencibles.

Roberts, Thomas - Boatswain - Major Wooster's Battalion, NY Sea Fencibles - Company: Isaac Silliman - Enlistment date: 4 Jan 1815 - Period: 6 Months.

Robertson, Bernard - Ordinary Seaman - Major Wooster's Battalion, NY Sea Fencibles.

Robertson, Harrison - Seaman - Major Fowler's Detachment, NY Sea Fencibles.

Robertson, James - Seaman - Major Wooster's Battalion, NY Sea Fencibles.

Robertson, John - Seaman - Major Wooster's Battalion, NY Sea Fencibles.

Robertson, John - Seaman - Major Fowler's Detachment, NY Sea Fencibles - Company: James Breath - Deserted at Blockhouse Constitution on 1 Oct 1814.

Robertson, Robert - Seaman - Major Wooster's Battalion, NY Sea Fencibles.

Robeson, Joseph - Gunner - Major Leonard's Battalion, NY Sea Fencibles.

Robinson, Alexander - Captain - Major Leonard's Battalion, NY Sea Fencibles - Company: Alexander Robinson - Enlistment date: 1 Sep 1814.

Robinson, Hanson - Seaman - Major Fowler's Detachment, NY Sea Fencibles - Company: James Breath.

Robinson, James - Seaman - Major Fowler's Detachment, NY Sea Fencibles - Company: James Breath.

Robinson, James - Seaman - Major Wooster's Battalion, NY Sea Fencibles.

Robinson, James - Seaman - Major Wooster's Battalion, NY Sea Fencibles - Company: Isaac Silliman - Enlistment date: 13 Jan 1815 - Period: 1 Yr.

Robinson, Joseph - Gunner - Major Leonard's Battalion, NY Sea Fencibles - Company: William Russell - Enlistment date: 7 Dec 1814 - Period: 3 Months.

Robinson, Robert - Musician - Major Wooster's Battalion, NY Sea Fencibles.

Robison, John - Musician - Major Wooster's Battalion, NY Sea Fencibles.

Rodden, Michael - Seaman - Major Leonard's Battalion, NY Sea Fencibles.

Rodgers, James - Seaman - Major Wooster's Battalion, NY Sea Fencibles - Company: Isaac Silliman - Enlistment date: 1 Dec 1814 - Period: 6 Months.

Rodgers, John - Gunner - Major Wooster's Battalion, NY Sea Fencibles - Company: Isaac Silliman - Enlistment date: 1 Dec 1814 - Period: 6 Months.

Rodman, Jesse - Third Lieutenant - NY Sea Fencibles - Company: Paul Burrows.

Rodman, Jesse - Seaman - NY Sea Fencibles - Company: Josiah Ingersoll.

Rodman, Jesse - Third Lieutenant - Major Fowler's Detachment, NY Sea Fencibles.

Rodman, Joseph - Seaman - NY Sea Fencibles - Company: John Cunningham.

Roe, Peter - Gunner - Major Leonard's Battalion, NY Sea Fencibles.

Roite, John - Seaman - NY Sea Fencibles - Company: Josiah Ingersoll.

Romaine, Aaron - Seaman - Major Wooster's Battalion, NY Sea Fencibles.

Romer, John - Seaman - Major Wooster's Battalion, NY Sea Fencibles - Company: Isaac Silliman - Enlistment date: 4 Feb 1815 - Period: 1 Yr.

Romer, William I. - Seaman - Major Fowler's Detachment, NY Sea Fencibles.

Rooks, David - Seaman - Major Fowler's Detachment, NY Sea Fencibles.

Roorbach, John O. - Captain - Major Wooster's Battalion, NY Sea Fencibles - Company: John Roorbach.

Rose, John - Seaman - Major Leonard's Battalion, NY Sea Fencibles - Company: Alexander Robinson - Enlistment date: 6 Nov 1814 - Period: 3 Months.

Ross, Robert - Seaman - Major Wooster's Battalion, NY Sea Fencibles - Company: Isaac Silliman - Enlistment date: 1 Feb 1815 - Period: 1 Yr.

Ross, Stephen - Seaman - Major Wooster's Battalion, NY Sea Fencibles.

Rossetor, David - Seaman - NY Sea Fencibles - Company: Paul Burrows - Enlistment date: 18 Oct 1814 - Period: 3 Months.

Rouse, Benjamin - Seaman - Major Wooster's Battalion, NY Sea Fencibles - Company: Isaac Silliman - Enlistment date: 13 Jan 1815 - Period: 1 Yr.

Rousseau, Peter - Private - MA Sea Fencibles - Company: Nehemiah Skillings.

Rowland, John - Seaman - Major Fowler's Detachment, NY Sea Fencibles - Company: James Breath.

Rowling, Charles - Gunner - Major Wooster's Battalion, NY Sea Fencibles.

Rowling, John - Seaman - Major Leonard's Battalion, NY Sea Fencibles.

American Sea Fencibles in the War of 1812

Rowling, John - Seaman - Major Leonard's Battalion, NY Sea Fencibles - Company: Alexander Robinson - Enlistment date: 10 Sep 1814 - Period: 3 Months.

Ruck, John - Ordinary Seaman - Major Wooster's Battalion, NY Sea Fencibles.

Ruck, William - Ordinary Seaman - Major Wooster's Battalion, NY Sea Fencibles.

Ruden, Moors - Surgeon's Mate - NY Sea Fencibles - Company: Josiah Ingersoll.

Ruke, David - Seaman - Major Fowler's Detachment, NY Sea Fencibles.

Ruskee, John - Seaman - NY Sea Fencibles - Company: Paul Burrows - Enlistment date: 14 Oct 1814 - Period: 3 Months.

Russell, John - Seaman - NY Sea Fencibles - Company: Josiah Ingersoll.

Russell, Henry - Sergeant - MA Sea Fencibles - Company: Nehemiah Skillings.

Russell, Robert - Gunner - NY Sea Fencibles - Company: Paul Burrows - Enlistment date: 3 Oct 1814 - Period: 3 Months.

Russell, William - Captain - Major Leonard's Battalion, NY Sea Fencibles - Company: William Russell.

Salter, Samuel - Seaman - Major Leonard's Battalion, NY Sea Fencibles.

Salyar, John - Gunner - Major Leonard's Battalion, NY Sea Fencibles - Company: Alexander Robinson - Enlistment date: 7 Oct 1814 - Period: 3 Months.

Sampson, Isaac - Third Lieutenant - Major Wooster's Battalion, NY Sea Fencibles.

Sampson, Solomon - Seaman - Major Fowler's Detachment, NY Sea Fencibles - Company: James Breath - Deserted at Blockhouse Constitution on 14 Nov 1814.

Sanders, Thomas - Seaman - Major Leonard's Battalion, NY Sea Fencibles - Company: Alexander Robinson - Enlistment date: 26 Sep 1814 - Period: 3 Months.

Sands, Francis - Seaman - Major Fowler's Detachment, NY Sea Fencibles - Company: James Breath.

Sanford, Edward - Seaman - Major Wooster's Battalion, NY Sea Fencibles.

Sangor, Avery - Private - MA Sea Fencibles - Company: Nehemiah Skillings.

Saunders, John - Ordinary Seaman - Major Leonard's Battalion, NY Sea Fencibles.

Saunders, Joseph - Seaman - Major Wooster's Battalion, NY Sea Fencibles.

Savage, John - Seaman - Major Leonard's Battalion, NY Sea Fencibles - Company: Alexander Robinson - Enlistment date: 10 Oct 1814 - Period: 3 Months.

Sawyer, Winthrop - Seaman - NY Sea Fencibles - Company: Paul Burrows - Enlistment date: 1 Oct 1814 - Period: 3 Months.

Sayers, Joseph - Seaman - Major Fowler's Detachment, NY Sea Fencibles - Company: Benjamin Muzzy.

Schenck, Daniel - Seaman - Major Leonard's Battalion, NY Sea Fencibles.

Schenck, Peter D. - Surgeon - Major Leonard's Battalion, NY Sea Fencibles - Company: William Russell - Enlistment date: 7 Dec 1814.

Scheyler, Peter - Second Lieutenant - Major Leonard's Battalion, NY Sea Fencibles - Company: Alexander Robinson - Enlistment date: 13 Sep 1814 - Period: 3 Months.

Schuyler, John - Seaman - NY Sea Fencibles - Company: John Cunningham - Enlistment date: 7 Sep 1814 - Period: 3 Months.

Schuyler, John - Seaman - Major Leonard's Battalion, NY Sea Fencibles.

Schuyler, Peter - Second Lieutenant - Major Leonard's Battalion, NY Sea Fencibles.

Schwitzer, John - Quarter Gunner - Major Wooster's Battalion, NY Sea Fencibles.

Schwitzer, John - Band - Major Wooster's Battalion, NY Sea Fencibles - Company: Isaac Silliman.

Scott, Benjamin - Seaman - Major Wooster's Battalion, NY Sea Fencibles - Company: Isaac Silliman - Enlistment date: 7 Jan 1815 - Period: 1 Yr.

Scott, Edward S. - Corporal - MA Sea Fencibles - Company: Nehemiah Skillings.

Scott, James - Private - Major Fowler's Detachment, NY Sea Fencibles - Company: Benjamin Muzzy - BLW 2868-160-55.

Scott, James - Seaman - Major Leonard's Battalion, NY Sea Fencibles.

Scribner, James - Ordinary Seaman - Major Leonard's Battalion, NY Sea Fencibles.

Seaman, John - Seaman - NY Sea Fencibles - Company: John Cunningham - Enlistment date: 3 Sep 1814.

Seaman, William - Gunner - Major Fowler's Detachment, NY Sea Fencibles.

Seely, Robert - Seaman - Major Fowler's Detachment, NY Sea Fencibles - Company: Benjamin Muzzy - Discharged on 6 Dec 1814.

Selleck, Uriah - Gunner - Major Leonard's Battalion, NY Sea Fencibles.

Seward, Christopher - Seaman - Major Fowler's Detachment, NY Sea Fencibles.

Seward, Thomas - Private - MA Sea Fencibles - Company: Nehemiah Skillings.

Seward, Timothy - Private - MA Sea Fencibles - Company: Nehemiah Skillings.

Sexton, James - Seaman - Major Fowler's Detachment, NY Sea Fencibles.

Seymore, William - Gunner - Major Fowler's Detachment, NY Sea Fencibles.

Seymour, Stephen - Seaman - Major Leonard's Battalion, NY Sea Fencibles.

Shaa, Thomas - Gunner - Major Fowler's Detachment, NY Sea Fencibles.

Shamons, John P. - Seaman - NY Sea Fencibles - Company: John Cunningham.

Shannon, Edward - Private - NH Sea Fencibles - Company: William Marshall - Enlistment date: 27 Nov 1813 - Discharged on 31 Dec 1813.

Shaw, William - Seaman - NY Sea Fencibles - Company: John Cunningham - Enlistment date: 5 Sep 1814 - Period: 3 Months.

Shay, John W. - Seaman - Major Leonard's Battalion, NY Sea Fencibles.

Shearman, John - Seaman - NY Sea Fencibles - Company: John Cunningham - Enlistment date: 6 Sep 1814 - Period: 3 Months.

Sheffield, David S. - Quarter Gunner - Major Leonard's Battalion, NY Sea Fencibles.

Shelbourne, George - Seaman - NY Sea Fencibles - Company: John Cunningham - Enlistment date: 5 Sep 1814 - Period: 3 Months.

Shelbourne, James - Waiter - NY Sea Fencibles - Company: John Cunningham.

Sherman, John - Seaman - Major Fowler's Detachment, NY Sea Fencibles.

Shewlin, John - Seaman - Major Leonard's Battalion, NY Sea Fencibles.

Shields, Patrick - Seaman - Major Leonard's Battalion, NY Sea Fencibles.

Shields, Terrence - Seaman - Major Wooster's Battalion, NY Sea Fencibles - Company: Isaac Silliman - Enlistment date: 5 Jan 1815 - Period: 1 Yr.

Shimell, George - Seaman - Major Wooster's Battalion, NY Sea Fencibles - Company: Isaac Silliman - Enlistment date: 10 Jan 1815 - Period: 1 Yr.

Shoemaker, Benjamin - Servant - Major Wooster's Battalion, NY Sea Fencibles.

Shoemaker, Edward - First Lieutenant - Major Wooster's Battalion, NY Sea Fencibles - Company: Isaac Silliman.

Shortis, James - Gunner - Major Leonard's Battalion, NY Sea Fencibles.

Shortis, James - Seaman - Major Wooster's Battalion, NY Sea Fencibles - Company: Isaac Silliman - Enlistment date: 14 Jan 1815 - Period: 1 Yrs.

Shulan, John - Seaman - Major Leonard's Battalion, NY Sea Fencibles.

Silliman, Isaac - Captain - Major Wooster's Battalion, NY Sea Fencibles - Company: Isaac Silliman.

Silsbee, Benjamin - Private - MA Sea Fencibles - Company: Nehemiah Skillings.

Silva, John - Seaman - Major Leonard's Battalion, NY Sea Fencibles.

Silvary, William - Seaman - Major Leonard's Battalion, NY Sea Fencibles.

Silver, John - Seaman - Major Leonard's Battalion, NY Sea Fencibles.

Silvester, William - Seaman - Major Fowler's Detachment, NY Sea Fencibles - Company: James Breath.

Silvey, John - Gunner - Major Leonard's Battalion, NY Sea Fencibles.

Silvy, John - Gunner - Major Leonard's Battalion, NY Sea Fencibles - Company: William Russell - Enlistment date: 12 Jan 1815 - Period: 3 Months.

Siminson, Richard - Seaman - Major Wooster's Battalion, NY Sea Fencibles.

Simmons, George - Private - NY Sea Fencibles - Company: Paul Burrows - Enlistment date: 7 Oct 1814 - Period: 3 Months - Deserted on 4 Nov 1814.

Simonson, Jacob - Seaman - Major Wooster's Battalion, NY Sea Fencibles.

Simonson, John - Ordinary Seaman - Major Wooster's Battalion, NY Sea Fencibles.

Simonson, Richard - Seaman - Major Wooster's Battalion, NY Sea Fencibles.

Simonson, Samuel - Servant - Major Wooster's Battalion, NY Sea Fencibles.

Simpson, John - Seaman - Major Leonard's Battalion, NY Sea Fencibles.

Simpson, William - Seaman - Major Leonard's Battalion, NY Sea Fencibles.

Simpson, William - Seaman - Major Fowler's Detachment, NY Sea Fencibles.

Sinclair, Daniel - Ordinary Seaman - Major Wooster's Battalion, NY Sea Fencibles.

Siro, Andrew - Seaman - NY Sea Fencibles - Company: John Cunningham - Enlistment date: 3 Sep 1814 - Period: 3 Months.

Skaats, Jacob - Seaman - Major Wooster's Battalion, NY Sea Fencibles.

Skaats, Rinier - Seaman - Major Leonard's Battalion, NY Sea Fencibles.

Skillings, Nehemiah W. - Captain - MA Sea Fencibles - Company: Nehemiah Skillings.

American Sea Fencibles in the War of 1812

Skinner, Pascal - Seaman - Major Leonard's Battalion, NY Sea Fencibles - Company: Alexander Robinson - Enlistment date: 10 Oct 1814 - Period: 3 Months.

Skinner, Thomas - Seaman - Major Leonard's Battalion, NY Sea Fencibles - Company: Alexander Robinson.

Slagle, Peter - Seaman - Major Wooster's Battalion, NY Sea Fencibles - Company: John Roorbach - On the boat crew at Fort Sevens, NY.

Sloan, John - Seaman - Major Leonard's Battalion, NY Sea Fencibles.

Small, Elisha - Private - MA Sea Fencibles - Company: Nehemiah Skillings.

Small, John - Seaman - Major Leonard's Battalion, NY Sea Fencibles - Company: Alexander Robinson.

Small, Robert - Seaman - NY Sea Fencibles - Company: John Cunningham - Enlistment date: 3 Sep 1814 - Period: 3 Months.

Smith I, John - Seaman - NY Sea Fencibles - Company: Josiah Ingersoll.

Smith II, John - Seaman - NY Sea Fencibles - Company: Josiah Ingersoll.

Smith, Abraham - Seaman - NY Sea Fencibles - Company: Josiah Ingersoll.

Smith, Adam - Seaman - NY Sea Fencibles - Company: John Cunningham - Enlistment date: 5 Sep 1814 - Period: 3 Months - Deserted on 27 Oct 1814.

Smith, Carol S. - Seaman - NY Sea Fencibles - Company: Paul Burrows - Enlistment date: 1 Nov 1814 - Period: 3 Months.

Smith, Charles - Quarter Gunner - Major Leonard's Battalion, NY Sea Fencibles - Company: Alexander Robinson.

Smith, Charles - Gunner - Major Fowler's Detachment, NY Sea Fencibles.

Smith, Charles - Quarter Gunner - NY Sea Fencibles - Company: Josiah Ingersoll.

Smith, Charles - Private - MA Sea Fencibles - Company: Nehemiah Skillings.

Smith, George - Private - MA Sea Fencibles - Company: Nehemiah Skillings.

Smith, George N. - Private - MA Sea Fencibles - Company: Nehemiah Skillings.

Smith, Harry - Ordinary Seaman - Major Wooster's Battalion, NY Sea Fencibles.

Smith, Henry - Seaman - NY Sea Fencibles - Company: John Cunningham - Enlistment date: 5 Sep 1814 - Period: 3 Months.

Smith, James - Seaman - Major Leonard's Battalion, NY Sea Fencibles - Company: Alexander Robinson - Enlistment date: 2 Nov 1814 - Period: 3 Months.

Smith, James - Seaman - Major Wooster's Battalion, NY Sea Fencibles - Company: Isaac Silliman - Enlistment date: 11 Jan 1815 - Period: 1 Yr.

Smith, Joel - Musician - MA Sea Fencibles - Company: Jeremiah Stickney.

Smith, John - Corporal - MA Sea Fencibles - Company: Nehemiah Skillings.

Smith, John - Seaman - Major Leonard's Battalion, NY Sea Fencibles.

Smith, John - Seaman - Major Wooster's Battalion, NY Sea Fencibles - Company: Isaac Silliman - Enlistment date: 23 Jan 1815 - Period: 1 YR.

Smith, John - Seaman - NY Sea Fencibles - Company: Josiah Ingersoll - Enlistment date: 30 Dec 1814.

Smith, John G. - Seaman - Major Leonard's Battalion, NY Sea Fencibles - Company: Alexander Robinson - Enlistment date: 4 Oct 1814 - Period: 3 Months.

Smith, Martin - Seaman - Major Wooster's Battalion, NY Sea Fencibles - Company: Isaac Silliman - Enlistment date: 5 Jan 1815 - Period: 1 Yr.

Smith, Melanchthon - Seaman - Major Wooster's Battalion, NY Sea Fencibles - Company: Isaac Silliman - Enlistment date: 19 Jan 1815 - Period: 1 Yr.

Smith, Robert - Seaman - Major Wooster's Battalion, NY Sea Fencibles.

Smith, William - Boy - Major Leonard's Battalion, NY Sea Fencibles.

Smith, William - Seaman - NY Sea Fencibles - Company: Josiah Ingersoll.

Smith, William - Quarter Gunner - MA Sea Fencibles - Company: Nehemiah Skillings.

Smith, William - Quartermaster - MA Sea Fencibles - Company: Nehemiah Skillings.

Smith, William J. - Steward - Major Fowler's Detachment, NY Sea Fencibles - Company: James Breath.

Smithen, Robert - Seaman - Major Leonard's Battalion, NY Sea Fencibles.

Snedecker, Isaac H. - Seaman - Major Wooster's Battalion, NY Sea Fencibles.

Sniffen, James - Seaman - Major Fowler's Detachment, NY Sea Fencibles - Company: James Breath.

Snow, Nathaniel - Third Lieutenant - MA Sea Fencibles - Company: Nehemiah Skillings.

Somers, William - Quarter Gunner - Major Leonard's Battalion, NY Sea Fencibles.

Southerland, Andrew - Seaman - Major Leonard's Battalion, NY Sea Fencibles - Company: William Russell - Enlistment date: 27 Jan 1815 - Period: 3 Months.

Southerland, Daniel - Seaman - Major Wooster's Battalion, NY Sea Fencibles - Company: Isaac Silliman - Enlistment date: 7 Jan 1815 - Period: 1 Yr.

Southward, Cornelius - Seaman - Major Wooster's Battalion, NY Sea Fencibles - Company: Lieutenant Benjamin Dayton - Enlistment date: 29 Dec 1814 - Served on board a prison ship.

Southworth, George A. - Seaman - Major Fowler's Detachment, NY Sea Fencibles.

Sowle, Peleg - Seaman - NY Sea Fencibles - Company: Josiah Ingersoll.

Sparrowhawk, Nathaniel - Seaman - NY Sea Fencibles - Company: Paul Burrows - Enlistment date: 1 Nov 1814 - Period: 3 Months - Deserted on 4 Nov 1814.

Spears, Edward - Seaman - Major Leonard's Battalion, NY Sea Fencibles - Company: Alexander Robinson - Enlistment date: 6 Oct 1814 - Period: 3 Months - Discharged on 8 Jan 1815.

Spencer, John - Seaman - Major Fowler's Detachment, NY Sea Fencibles.

Spock, James - Seaman - Major Fowler's Detachment, NY Sea Fencibles - Company: James Breath.

Spraig, Richard - Seaman - Major Leonard's Battalion, NY Sea Fencibles.

Springsteen, Abraham - Major Wooster's Battalion, NY Sea Fencibles - Company: Isaac Silliman - Pension: Wife Catherine, WO-9998.

Squires, Seth - Seaman - Major Leonard's Battalion, NY Sea Fencibles.

St. Clair, Daniel - Private - Major Wooster's Battalion, NY Sea Fencibles.

Stacey, George - Gunner - NY Sea Fencibles - Company: Paul Burrows - Enlistment date: 20 Sep 1814 - Period: 3 Months.

Stafford, John P. - Quarter Gunner - Major Fowler's Detachment, NY Sea Fencibles - Company: James Breath.

Stallard, Thomas - Private - MA Sea Fencibles - Company: Jeremiah Stickney.

Stannere, James - Seaman - NY Sea Fencibles - Company: Josiah Ingersoll.

Stansbury, Stephen - Third Lieutenant - Major Leonard's Battalion, NY Sea Fencibles - Company: William Russell - Enlistment date: 5 Dec 1814.

Stanton, Elisha - Gunner - Major Fowler's Detachment, NY Sea Fencibles - Company: James Breath.

Stanwood, John - Seaman - Major Leonard's Battalion, NY Sea Fencibles.

Stephens, Alexander H. - Surgeon - Major Wooster's Battalion, NY Sea Fencibles.

Stephens, Thomas - Seaman - Major Leonard's Battalion, NY Sea Fencibles.

Stephenson, William - Seaman - NY Sea Fencibles - Company: Josiah Ingersoll.

Stevens, Alexander - Surgeon - Major Wooster's Battalion, NY Sea Fencibles - Company: Staff - In charge of hospital at Hell Gate; discharged on 5 Apr 1815.

Stevens, H. - Doctor - Major Wooster's Battalion, NY Sea Fencibles - Company: Staff.

Stevens, John - Servant - Major Leonard's Battalion, NY Sea Fencibles.

Stevens, William - Gunner - NY Sea Fencibles - Company: John Cunningham - Enlistment date: 2 Sep 1814 - Period: 3 Months - Pension: Old War IF-27542 - Died on 14 Dec 1826.

Stevenson, Ferdinand - Seaman - Major Leonard's Battalion, NY Sea Fencibles.

Stevenson, Harvey - Seaman - Major Wooster's Battalion, NY Sea Fencibles.

Stevenson, John - Ordinary Seaman - Major Wooster's Battalion, NY Sea Fencibles.

Stewart, William - Servant - Major Fowler's Detachment, NY Sea Fencibles - Company: James Breath.

Stewart, William A. - First Lieutenant - Major Fowler's Detachment, NY Sea Fencibles.

Stickney, Jeremiah - Captain - MA Sea Fencibles - Company: Jeremiah Stickney.

Still, William - Seaman - Major Leonard's Battalion, NY Sea Fencibles - Company: Alexander Robinson - Discharged at New York on 7 Oct 1814.

Stillman, Benjamin M. - Private - MA Sea Fencibles - Company: Nehemiah Skillings.

Stilwell, Samuel - Quarter Gunner - Major Leonard's Battalion, NY Sea Fencibles.

Stilwell, William - Seaman - Major Wooster's Battalion, NY Sea Fencibles.

Stockton, Charles - Gunner - Major Leonard's Battalion, NY Sea Fencibles - Company: Alexander Robinson - Enlistment date: 15 Oct 1814 - Period: 3 Months.

Stoff, Samuel - Ordinary Seaman - Major Wooster's Battalion, NY Sea Fencibles.

Stokes, John - Seaman - Major Leonard's Battalion, NY Sea Fencibles - Company: Alexander Robinson - Deserted at New York City on 6 Nov 1814.

Stone, John - Private - MA Sea Fencibles - Company: Jeremiah Stickney.

Storer, Edward - Seaman - Major Wooster's Battalion, NY Sea Fencibles.

Stoughtenberg, George B. - Seaman - Major Wooster's Battalion, NY Sea Fencibles.

Stover III, Samuel - Private - MA Sea Fencibles - Company: Isaac Lyman - Born: 25 Jul 1814 -

Discharged on 24 Aug 1814.

Stover, Edward - Seaman - Major Wooster's Battalion, NY Sea Fencibles.

Stover, Joseph - Private - MA Sea Fencibles - Company: Jeremiah Stickney.

Stow, Frederick - Seaman - Major Fowler's Detachment, NY Sea Fencibles - Company: James Breath.

Strang, John - Seaman - Major Fowler's Detachment, NY Sea Fencibles.

Striker, Isaac - Seaman - Major Leonard's Battalion, NY Sea Fencibles.

Striker, Jacob - Ordinary Seaman - Major Leonard's Battalion, NY Sea Fencibles.

Strong, John S. - Seaman - Major Wooster's Battalion, NY Sea Fencibles.

Struck, Lawrence - Seaman - Major Fowler's Detachment, NY Sea Fencibles - Company: James Breath.

Sullivan, John - Seaman - NY Sea Fencibles - Company: John Cunningham - Enlistment date: 3 Sep 1814 - Period: 3 Months.

Sullivan, Joseph - Seaman - Major Fowler's Detachment, NY Sea Fencibles - Company: James Breath.

Sunshiman, Henry - Fifer - NY Sea Fencibles - Company: Paul Burrows - Enlistment date: 7 Oct 1814 - Period: 3 Months.

Swain, John - Seaman - Major Leonard's Battalion, NY Sea Fencibles.

Swasey, Samuel - Private - MA Sea Fencibles - Company: Jeremiah Stickney.

Sweasy, Peter - Seaman - Major Leonard's Battalion, NY Sea Fencibles.

Sweeney, John M. - Gunner - NY Sea Fencibles - Company: Josiah Ingersoll.

Sweeny, Hugh - Surgeon's Mate - NY Sea Fencibles - Company: Josiah Ingersoll - Enlistment date: 3 Dec 1814 - Pension: Land bounty to Eliza Ann Sweeny, widow of Hugh Sweeny - BLW 89891-160-55.

Sweeny, Hugh - Surgeon's Mate - NY Sea Fencibles - Company: Josiah Ingersoll.

Swift, Samuel - Private - MA Sea Fencibles - Company: Nehemiah Skillings.

Swim, Richard - Ordinary Seaman - Major Wooster's Battalion, NY Sea Fencibles.

Swinton, Thomas - Seaman - Major Wooster's Battalion, NY Sea Fencibles - Company: John Randlet - Served on General Swift's barge.

Tagiers, Anthony R. - Seaman - Major Leonard's Battalion, NY Sea Fencibles.

Tansell, Nicholas - Seaman - Major Wooster's Battalion, NY Sea Fencibles.

Tapley, James - Ordinary Seaman - NY Sea Fencibles - Company: Josiah Ingersoll.

Tapley, Joseph - Ordinary Seaman - NY Sea Fencibles - Company: Josiah Ingersoll.

Tappan Jr., Benjamin - Private - MA Sea Fencibles - Company: Jeremiah Stickney.

Tarlton, Benjamin - Private - NH Sea Fencibles - Company: William Marshall - Enlistment date: 27 May 1813 - Discharged on 27 Nov 1813.

Tarlton, Joseph - Private - NH Sea Fencibles - Company: William Marshall - Enlistment date: 27 May 1813 - Discharged on 27 Nov 1813; served again from 27 Nov 1813 through 31 Dec 1813.

Tatem, Henry - Seaman - Major Leonard's Battalion, NY Sea Fencibles.

Taylor, Amos - Private - NY Sea Fencibles - Company: Paul Burrows - Enlistment date: 1 Oct 1814 - Period: 3 Months.

American Sea Fencibles in the War of 1812

Taylor, George - Seaman - Major Wooster's Battalion, NY Sea Fencibles.

Taylor, Henry - Seaman - Major Leonard's Battalion, NY Sea Fencibles.

Taylor, Mathew - Gunner - Major Leonard's Battalion, NY Sea Fencibles.

Taylor, Thomas - Private - Major Fowler's Detachment, NY Sea Fencibles - Company: Pexcil Fowler - BLW 90598-160-55.

Taylor, William - Seaman - Major Fowler's Detachment, NY Sea Fencibles.

Taylor, William - Ordinary Seaman - Major Wooster's Battalion, NY Sea Fencibles.

Ten Eyck, Philip - Seaman - Major Leonard's Battalion, NY Sea Fencibles.

Ten Eyck, Philip - Seaman - Major Wooster's Battalion, NY Sea Fencibles - Company: Isaac Silliman - Enlistment date: 4 Jan 1815 - Period: 1 Yr.

Tennery, John - Ordinary Seaman - NY Sea Fencibles - Company: Josiah Ingersoll.

Terry, Ambrose - Seaman - Major Fowler's Detachment, NY Sea Fencibles.

Thaxter, George - Private - MA Sea Fencibles - Company: Nehemiah Skillings.

Thirsby, John - Seaman - Major Wooster's Battalion, NY Sea Fencibles - Company: Isaac Silliman - Enlistment date: 18 Jan 1815 - Period: 1 Yr.

Thomas Jr., John - Private - MA Sea Fencibles - Company: Nehemiah Skillings.

Thomas, Abraham - Seaman - Major Leonard's Battalion, NY Sea Fencibles.

Thomas, Abram - Seaman - Major Leonard's Battalion, NY Sea Fencibles - Company: Alexander Robinson - Enlistment date: 29 Oct 1814 - Period: 3 Months.

Thomas, Adam - Servant - Major Leonard's Battalion, NY Sea Fencibles.

Thomas, Adam William - Seaman - Major Wooster's Battalion, NY Sea Fencibles.

Thomas, Cuff - Seaman - Major Leonard's Battalion, NY Sea Fencibles.

Thomas, Henry - Seaman - NY Sea Fencibles - Company: Paul Burrows - Enlistment date: 4 Nov 1814 - Period: 3 Months.

Thomas, Job - Seaman - Major Wooster's Battalion, NY Sea Fencibles.

Thomas, John - Seaman - Major Leonard's Battalion, NY Sea Fencibles.

Thomas, John - Ordinary Seaman - NY Sea Fencibles - Company: Josiah Ingersoll.

Thomas, John - Seaman - Major Fowler's Detachment, NY Sea Fencibles - Company: Benjamin Muzzy.

Thomas, John - Seaman - Major Fowler's Detachment, NY Sea Fencibles - Company: James Breath.

Thomas, William - Seaman - Major Wooster's Battalion, NY Sea Fencibles - Company: Isaac Silliman.

Thompson, Ellis - Gunner - Major Leonard's Battalion, NY Sea Fencibles.

Thompson, Isaac - Seaman - Major Fowler's Detachment, NY Sea Fencibles - Company: James Breath.

Thompson, James - Seaman - Major Leonard's Battalion, NY Sea Fencibles.

Thompson, John - Quarter Gunner - Major Wooster's Battalion, NY Sea Fencibles.

Thompson, John - Gunner - Major Wooster's Battalion, NY Sea Fencibles - Company: Isaac Silliman - Enlistment date: 4 Jan 1815 - Period: 6 Months.

Thompson, John - Seaman - NY Sea Fencibles - Company: John Cunningham - Enlistment date: 5 Sep 1814 - Period: 3 Months.

Thompson, John - Seaman - Major Fowler's Detachment, NY Sea Fencibles - Company: James Breath.

Thompson, John - Seaman - Major Leonard's Battalion, NY Sea Fencibles.

Thompson, John D. - Sergeant - MA Sea Fencibles - Company: Isaac Lyman - Enlistment date: 25 Jul 1814 - Discharged on 23 Sep 1814.

Thompson, Martin - Private - MA Sea Fencibles - Company: Nehemiah Skillings.

Thompson, Robert - Gunner - Major Wooster's Battalion, NY Sea Fencibles.

Thompson, Samuel - Ordinary Seaman - Major Wooster's Battalion, NY Sea Fencibles.

Thompson, Thomas - Seaman - Major Fowler's Detachment, NY Sea Fencibles - Company: Benjamin Muzzy.

Thompson, William - Seaman - Major Leonard's Battalion, NY Sea Fencibles - Company: Alexander Robinson - Enlistment date: 8 Oct 1814.

Thomson, George - Seaman - Major Fowler's Detachment, NY Sea Fencibles - Company: Benjamin Muzzy.

Thorne, Thomas - Gunner - Major Leonard's Battalion, NY Sea Fencibles.

Thorrington, Samuel - Seaman - NY Sea Fencibles - Company: John Cunningham - Enlistment date: 5 Sep 1814 - Period: 3 Months.

Thrift, William - Seaman - NY Sea Fencibles - Company: Josiah Ingersoll.

Thursby, John - Seaman - Major Wooster's Battalion, NY Sea Fencibles.

Tilbous, James - Seaman - Major Wooster's Battalion, NY Sea Fencibles - Company: Isaac Silliman - Enlistment date: 10 Jan 1815 - Period: 1 Yr.

Tilley, Lewis - Seaman - NY Sea Fencibles - Company: John Cunningham - Enlistment date: 3 Sep 1814 - Period: 3 Months.

Tilton, Daniel - Private - MA Sea Fencibles - Company: Jeremiah Stickney.

Tisdale, James - Seaman - Major Wooster's Battalion, NY Sea Fencibles.

Tisdale, William - Private - MA Sea Fencibles - Company: Nehemiah Skillings.

Titcomb Jr., Jonathan - Private - MA Sea Fencibles - Company: Jeremiah Stickney.

Titcomb, John - Private - MA Sea Fencibles - Company: Jeremiah Stickney.

Titus, George - Servant - Major Fowler's Detachment, NY Sea Fencibles.

Titus, Henry - Seaman - Major Wooster's Battalion, NY Sea Fencibles.

Todd, William F. - Seaman - Major Leonard's Battalion, NY Sea Fencibles.

Tompkins, Enos - Seaman - Major Wooster's Battalion, NY Sea Fencibles.

Tompkins, James - Seaman - Major Fowler's Detachment, NY Sea Fencibles.

Tompkins, Usual - Seaman - Major Leonard's Battalion, NY Sea Fencibles.

Tompkins, William - Seaman - NY Sea Fencibles - Company: John Cunningham - Enlistment date: 3 Sep 1814 - Period: 3 Months.

American Sea Fencibles in the War of 1812

Tonkin, James - Seaman - Major Fowler's Detachment, NY Sea Fencibles.

Totten, William - Seaman - Major Fowler's Detachment, NY Sea Fencibles.

Townsend, Caesar - Seaman - NY Sea Fencibles - Company: John Cunningham - Enlistment date: 5 Sep 1814 - Period: 3 Months.

Townsend, John - Servant - Major Leonard's Battalion, NY Sea Fencibles.

Townsend, Michael - Ordinary Seaman - Major Leonard's Battalion, NY Sea Fencibles.

Tracy, Charles - Second Lieutenant - MA Sea Fencibles - Company: Nehemiah Skillings.

Treadwell, Charles - Seaman - Major Wooster's Battalion, NY Sea Fencibles - Company: Isaac Silliman - Enlistment date: 5 Jan 1815 - Period: 1 Yr.

Treadwell, John - Seaman - Major Wooster's Battalion, NY Sea Fencibles.

Trefethen, Abraham - Private - NH Sea Fencibles - Company: William Marshall - Enlistment date: 27 May 1813 - Discharged on 5 Sep 1813.

Trefethen, Henry - Private - NH Sea Fencibles - Company: William Marshall - Enlistment date: 13 Oct 1813 - Discharged on 27 Nov 1813.

Tripp, John - Gunner - Major Leonard's Battalion, NY Sea Fencibles - Company: Francis Costigan - BLW 37795-160-55.

Trott, James F. - Private - MA Sea Fencibles - Company: Nehemiah Skillings.

Truman, William - Seaman - Major Fowler's Detachment, NY Sea Fencibles - Company: James Breath.

Tuck, Henry - Gunner - Major Leonard's Battalion, NY Sea Fencibles.

Tucker, William - Private - NH Sea Fencibles - Company: William Marshall - Enlistment date: 27 May 1813 - Discharged on 27 Nov 1813.

Tuckerman, BHS - Private - MA Sea Fencibles - Company: Nehemiah Skillings.

Tufts, Robert - Private - MA Sea Fencibles - Company: Nehemiah Skillings.

Tufts, William - Private - MA Sea Fencibles - Company: Nehemiah Skillings.

Tunis, John - Second Lieutenant - Major Leonard's Battalion, NY Sea Fencibles.

Turner, Nathaniel - Seaman - Major Leonard's Battalion, NY Sea Fencibles.

Turner, Robert - Private - MA Sea Fencibles - Company: Nehemiah Skillings.

Turrell, Cales C. - Seaman - Major Leonard's Battalion, NY Sea Fencibles - Company: William Russell - Enlistment date: 23 Jan 1815 - Period: 3 Months.

Tylor, William - Ordinary Seaman - Major Wooster's Battalion, NY Sea Fencibles.

Updike, Reuben - Private - NY Sea Fencibles - Company: Josiah Ingersoll.

Urann, Richard - Private - MA Sea Fencibles - Company: Nehemiah Skillings.

Ustace, James - Seaman - Major Fowler's Detachment, NY Sea Fencibles.

Valentine, John - Seaman - NY Sea Fencibles - Company: John Cunningham - Enlistment date: 5 Sep 1814 - Period: 3 Months.

Valentine, Letting - Seaman - Major Leonard's Battalion, NY Sea Fencibles.

Vallean, Isaiah - Seaman - NY Sea Fencibles - Company: John Cunningham - Enlistment date: 6 Sep

1814 - Period: 3 Months.

Valleau, Isaiah - NY Sea Fencibles - Pension: Wife Ann, WO-11176.

Van Antwerp, Ellis - Seaman - Major Fowler's Detachment, NY Sea Fencibles.

Van Curen, Tobias - Seaman - Major Leonard's Battalion, NY Sea Fencibles - Company: William Russell - Enlistment date: 17 Jan 1815 - Period: 3 Months - Deserted.

Van Derstine, Christopher - Seaman - Major Leonard's Battalion, NY Sea Fencibles - Company: William Russell - Enlistment date: 18 Jan 1815 - Period: 3 Months.

Vanconover, Moses - Seaman - Major Leonard's Battalion, NY Sea Fencibles.

Vancurren, Tobias - Seaman - Major Leonard's Battalion, NY Sea Fencibles.

Vandalson, John - Seaman - Major Wooster's Battalion, NY Sea Fencibles.

Vanderhoff Jr., John - Seaman - Major Wooster's Battalion, NY Sea Fencibles.

Vanderhoff, John - Seaman - Major Wooster's Battalion, NY Sea Fencibles - Company: Isaac Silliman - Enlistment date: 25 Jan 1815 - Period: 1 Yr.

Vanderpool, James - Seaman - Major Leonard's Battalion, NY Sea Fencibles - Company: Alexander Robinson - Enlistment date: 2 Nov 1814 - Period: 3 Months.

Vanderpool, John - Seaman - Major Wooster's Battalion, NY Sea Fencibles - Company: Isaac Silliman - Enlistment date: 18 Feb 1815 - Period: 1 Yr.

Vandine, John - Seaman - NY Sea Fencibles - Company: John Cunningham - Enlistment date: 5 Sep 1814 - Period: 3 Months.

Vandolson, John - Seaman - Major Wooster's Battalion, NY Sea Fencibles - Company: Isaac Silliman - Enlistment date: 7 Jan 1815 - Period: 1 Mo.

Vandorf, William - Seaman - Major Leonard's Battalion, NY Sea Fencibles.

Vanhorn, Cornelius - Ordinary Seaman - Major Leonard's Battalion, NY Sea Fencibles.

Vanorden, John - Seaman - Major Leonard's Battalion, NY Sea Fencibles.

Vanpelt, Dan - Waiter - Major Fowler's Detachment, NY Sea Fencibles.

Vanstram, Nicholas - Seaman - Major Fowler's Detachment, NY Sea Fencibles.

Vanvarrick, Charles - Seaman - Major Fowler's Detachment, NY Sea Fencibles.

Vanzant, Isaac - Seaman - Major Fowler's Detachment, NY Sea Fencibles.

Vanzell, Cornelius - Seaman - Major Leonard's Battalion, NY Sea Fencibles.

Varrell Jr., Solomon - Private - MA Sea Fencibles - Company: Isaac Lyman - Enlistment date: 25 Jul 1814 - Discharged on 24 Aug 1814.

Varrell, Rufus - Private - MA Sea Fencibles - Company: Isaac Lyman - Born: 26 Jul 1814 - Discharged on 23 Sep 1814.

Vaustner, Nicholson - Seaman - Major Fowler's Detachment, NY Sea Fencibles - Company: James Breath.

Vellum, Absalom - Seaman - Major Leonard's Battalion, NY Sea Fencibles - Company: William Russell - Enlistment date: 23 Jan 1815 - Period: 3 Months - Deserted.

Videtts, Ephenetus - Seaman - Major Wooster's Battalion, NY Sea Fencibles.

Vilon, Peter - Seaman - Major Wooster's Battalion, NY Sea Fencibles - Company: Isaac Silliman - Enlistment date: 4 Jan 1815 - Period: 1 Yr.

Vincent, Jacob - Seaman - Major Leonard's Battalion, NY Sea Fencibles - Company: Alexander Robinson - Enlistment date: 24 Oct 1814 - Period: 3 Months.

Voll, Peter - Seaman - NY Sea Fencibles - Company: Josiah Ingersoll.

Votee, Charles - First Lieutenant - NY Sea Fencibles - Company: Paul Burrows - Enlistment date: 16 Sep 1814 - Commissioned as a 2nd Lieutenant on 16 Sep 1814; promoted to 1st Lieutenant on 8 Nov 1814.

Waggsle, Ollins - Private - NY Sea Fencibles - Company: Paul Burrows.

Wainwright, Joshua - Seaman - Major Wooster's Battalion, NY Sea Fencibles - Company: Lieutenant Benjamin Dayton.

Waistcott, Thomas - Seaman - NY Sea Fencibles - Company: Josiah Ingersoll.

Waite, Isaac - First Lieutenant - NY Sea Fencibles - Company: Josiah Ingersoll - Enlistment date: 10 Aug 1814.

Waites, John - Seaman - NY Sea Fencibles - Company: Paul Burrows - Enlistment date: 18 Oct 1814 - Period: 3 Months.

Walden, Benjamin - Gunner - NY Sea Fencibles - Company: John Cunningham - Enlistment date: 6 Sep 1814 - Period: 3 Months.

Waldrom, Elijah - Ordinary Seaman - Major Leonard's Battalion, NY Sea Fencibles.

Waldron, James R. - Private - Major Leonard's Battalion, NY Sea Fencibles - Company: William Russell - BLW 13834-80-55 - Also in Captain Allen's and Rossiter's companies.

Waldron, William - Seaman - Major Leonard's Battalion, NY Sea Fencibles.

Wales, John - Private - MA Sea Fencibles - Company: Nehemiah Skillings.

Walker, Francis H. - Seaman - NY Sea Fencibles - Company: Josiah Ingersoll.

Wall, John - Seaman - NY Sea Fencibles - Company: Josiah Ingersoll.

Wall, Robert - Ordinary Seaman - Major Leonard's Battalion, NY Sea Fencibles.

Wallace, Moses - Seaman - Major Fowler's Detachment, NY Sea Fencibles - Company: James Breath.

Wallace, William - Ordinary Seaman - Major Leonard's Battalion, NY Sea Fencibles.

Wallis, William - Private - MA Sea Fencibles - Company: Nehemiah Skillings.

Walsh, James - Seaman - Major Wooster's Battalion, NY Sea Fencibles.

Walt, John - Gunner - Major Leonard's Battalion, NY Sea Fencibles.

Walton, Samuel - Musician - MA Sea Fencibles - Company: Jeremiah Stickney.

Ward, John - Seaman - Major Wooster's Battalion, NY Sea Fencibles - Company: Isaac Silliman - Age: 33 - Height: 5' 5 1/2" - Born: Ireland - Enlistment date: 3 Jan 1814 - Period: 1 Yr.

Ward, Joseph - Seaman - NY Sea Fencibles - Company: Josiah Ingersoll - Enlistment date: 3 Jan 1815.

Ward, Michael - Seaman - Major Leonard's Battalion, NY Sea Fencibles - Company: Alexander Robinson.

Ward, Stephen - Seaman - NY Sea Fencibles - Company: John Cunningham - Enlistment date: 5 Sep

1814 - Period: 3 Months - Killed by a sentinel on 15 Oct 1814.

Ward, Thomas - Seaman - Major Leonard's Battalion, NY Sea Fencibles.

Ward, William - Corporal - MA Sea Fencibles - Company: Nehemiah Skillings.

Warden, Appleton - Seaman - Major Leonard's Battalion, NY Sea Fencibles - Company: Alexander Robinson.

Warne, Joshua - Seaman - Major Wooster's Battalion, NY Sea Fencibles - Company: Lieutenant Benjamin Dayton - Enlistment date: 29 Dec 1814 - Period: 3 Months - Served on board a prison ship.

Warren, John - Quarter Gunner - Major Leonard's Battalion, NY Sea Fencibles.

Warwick, Isaac - Seaman - Major Wooster's Battalion, NY Sea Fencibles.

Waterbury, Dilas - Seaman - NY Sea Fencibles - Company: Josiah Ingersoll.

Watkins, Andrew - Private - MA Sea Fencibles - Company: Nehemiah Skillings.

Watkins, Osmore - Gunner - Major Wooster's Battalion, NY Sea Fencibles - Company: Isaac Silliman - Enlistment date: 2 Dec 1814 - Period: 6 Months.

Watson, Joshua - Seaman - Major Wooster's Battalion, NY Sea Fencibles.

Watt, John - Gunner - Major Leonard's Battalion, NY Sea Fencibles - Company: Alexander Robinson - Enlistment date: 12 Sep 1814 - Period: 3 Months.

Watterlein, Francis - Quarter Gunner - Major Wooster's Battalion, NY Sea Fencibles.

Waydell, John - Ordinary Seaman - Major Leonard's Battalion, NY Sea Fencibles.

Webb, William - Seaman - Major Leonard's Battalion, NY Sea Fencibles.

Webber, Benjamin - Seaman - Major Wooster's Battalion, NY Sea Fencibles.

Webster, Mark - Private - NH Sea Fencibles - Company: William Marshall - Enlistment date: 27 May 1813 - Discharged on 27 Nov 1813.

Webster, Samuel - Seaman - Major Wooster's Battalion, NY Sea Fencibles.

Webster, William - Seaman - Major Leonard's Battalion, NY Sea Fencibles.

Weeks, Henry - Seaman - Major Wooster's Battalion, NY Sea Fencibles.

Welch, Jonathan - Private - MA Sea Fencibles - Company: Jeremiah Stickney.

Weldon, James - Second Lieutenant - Major Leonard's Battalion, NY Sea Fencibles - Company: Alexander Robinson.

Wendover, Peter W. - Ordinary Seaman - Major Leonard's Battalion, NY Sea Fencibles.

West, James - Seaman - Major Leonard's Battalion, NY Sea Fencibles.

West, Matthew - Seaman - Major Wooster's Battalion, NY Sea Fencibles - Company: Isaac Silliman - Enlistment date: 4 Feb 1815 - Period: 1 Yr.

West, Philip - Seaman - Major Fowler's Detachment, NY Sea Fencibles - Company: James Breath.

West, Reuben - Second Lieutenant - NY Sea Fencibles - Company: Paul Burrows - Enlistment date: 16 Sep 1814 - Period: 3 Months - Former gunner; promoted to 3rd Lieutenant on 8 Nov 1814 and to 2nd Lieutenant on 18 Nov 1814.

West, William - Seaman - Major Fowler's Detachment, NY Sea Fencibles - Company: James Breath -

Deserted at Blockhouse Constitution on 16 Nov 1814.

Westerfeild, Michael - Seaman - Major Leonard's Battalion, NY Sea Fencibles.

Wetsell, Frederick - Seaman - Major Leonard's Battalion, NY Sea Fencibles - Company: William Russell - Enlistment date: 13 Jan 1815 - Period: 3 Months.

Wetterlein, Francis - Band - Major Wooster's Battalion, NY Sea Fencibles - Company: Isaac Silliman.

Wharton, John W. - Second Lieutenant - Major Fowler's Detachment, NY Sea Fencibles - Company: James Breath.

Whaylan, John - Seaman - Major Leonard's Battalion, NY Sea Fencibles - Company: Alexander Robinson - Enlistment date: 26 Oct 1814 - Period: 3 Months.

Wheeler, Henry - Paymaster - Major Leonard's Battalion, NY Sea Fencibles.

Wheelwright, Jeremiah - Sergeant - MA Sea Fencibles - Company: Jeremiah Stickney.

White Jr., Charles - Paymaster - Major Wooster's Battalion, NY Sea Fencibles.

White, Joseph S. - Private - NH Sea Fencibles - Company: William Marshall - Enlistment date: 27 Nov 1813 - Discharged on 31 Dec 1813.

White, Sampson S. - Seaman - Major Wooster's Battalion, NY Sea Fencibles.

White, William - Seaman - Major Wooster's Battalion, NY Sea Fencibles.

Whitman, Nathaniel - Waiter - Major Fowler's Detachment, NY Sea Fencibles.

Whitney, William - Seaman - Major Wooster's Battalion, NY Sea Fencibles - Company: Isaac Silliman - Enlistment date: 4 Jan 1815 - Period: 1 Yr.

Whitney, William - Seaman - NY Sea Fencibles - Company: John Cunningham - Enlistment date: 5 Sep 1814 - Period: 3 Months.

Wicks, Henry - Seaman - Major Wooster's Battalion, NY Sea Fencibles - Company: Isaac Silliman - Pension: Land bounty to Sally Wicks, widow of Henry Wicks - BLW 95685-160-55.

Wier, James - Gunner - Major Fowler's Detachment, NY Sea Fencibles - Company: James Breath.

Wiggins, Benjamin - Seaman - Major Leonard's Battalion, NY Sea Fencibles.

Wilber, Elam - Seaman - NY Sea Fencibles - Company: Paul Burrows - Enlistment date: 1 Oct 1814 - Period: 3 Months.

Wilber, John - Gunner - NY Sea Fencibles - Company: Paul Burrows - Enlistment date: 1 Oct 1814 - Period: 3 Months.

Wilcox, William - Seaman - Major Wooster's Battalion, NY Sea Fencibles.

Wilham, Andrew - Seaman - Major Leonard's Battalion, NY Sea Fencibles.

Wilkes, John - Seaman - Major Wooster's Battalion, NY Sea Fencibles.

Wilkey, Isaiah H. - Seaman - Major Leonard's Battalion, NY Sea Fencibles.

Wilkey, Josiah H. - Seaman - Major Leonard's Battalion, NY Sea Fencibles.

Wilkie, Isaiah - Seaman - Major Leonard's Battalion, NY Sea Fencibles - Company: Alexander Robinson - Enlistment date: 6 Oct 1814 - Period: 3 Months - Deserted.

Will, Andrew - Seaman - NY Sea Fencibles - Company: John Cunningham - Enlistment date: 5 Sep 1814 - Period: 3 Months.

American Sea Fencibles in the War of 1812

Willet, Alexander - Seaman - NY Sea Fencibles - Company: John Cunningham - Enlistment date: 3 Sep 1814 - Period: 3 Months.

Williams, Augustus - Seaman - NY Sea Fencibles - Company: Josiah Ingersoll.

Williams, Augustus - Seaman - Major Fowler's Detachment, NY Sea Fencibles - Company: Benjamin Muzzy - Enlistment date: 30 Dec 1814 - Also served in Captain Josiah Ingersoll's Company.

Williams, Charles - Seaman - NY Sea Fencibles - Company: John Cunningham - Enlistment date: 5 Sep 1814 - Period: 3 Months.

Williams, George - Seaman - Major Wooster's Battalion, NY Sea Fencibles - Company: Isaac Silliman - Enlistment date: 6 Feb 1815 - Period: 1 Yr.

Williams, George - Seaman - Major Fowler's Detachment, NY Sea Fencibles - Company: James Breath.

Williams, James - Seaman - Major Leonard's Battalion, NY Sea Fencibles.

Williams, John - Waiter - Major Wooster's Battalion, NY Sea Fencibles.

Williams, John - Seaman - Major Wooster's Battalion, NY Sea Fencibles - Company: John Roorbach.

Williams, John - Seaman - Major Wooster's Battalion, NY Sea Fencibles.

Williams, John - Seaman - Major Leonard's Battalion, NY Sea Fencibles - Company: Alexander Robinson.

Williams, John - Gunner - Major Leonard's Battalion, NY Sea Fencibles.

Williams, John - Seaman - NY Sea Fencibles - Company: Josiah Ingersoll - Enlistment date: 3 Jan 1815.

Williams, Richard - Private - MA Sea Fencibles - Company: Nehemiah Skillings.

Williams, Robert - Seaman - Major Leonard's Battalion, NY Sea Fencibles.

Williams, Samuel - Ordinary Seaman - Major Wooster's Battalion, NY Sea Fencibles.

Williams, Thomas - Seaman - Major Wooster's Battalion, NY Sea Fencibles.

Williams, William - Ordinary Seaman - Major Wooster's Battalion, NY Sea Fencibles.

Williams, William - Quartermaster - Major Leonard's Battalion, NY Sea Fencibles.

Williams, William - Boatswain - Major Leonard's Battalion, NY Sea Fencibles.

Williamson, Charles - Seaman - Major Wooster's Battalion, NY Sea Fencibles.

Williamson, Daniel - Seaman - Major Wooster's Battalion, NY Sea Fencibles.

Willson, David - Cook - NY Sea Fencibles - Company: Josiah Ingersoll.

Willson, John - Gunner - Major Wooster's Battalion, NY Sea Fencibles - Company: John Roorbach.

Wilson, David - Seaman - NY Sea Fencibles - Company: Josiah Ingersoll - Enlistment date: 30 Dec 1814 - Period: 1 Yr.

Wilson, James - Seaman - Major Wooster's Battalion, NY Sea Fencibles.

Wilson, James - Seaman - Major Leonard's Battalion, NY Sea Fencibles.

Wilson, James - Seaman - Major Leonard's Battalion, NY Sea Fencibles - Company: Alexander Robinson - Enlistment date: 24 Oct 1814 - Period: 3 Months.

Wilson, John - Quarter Gunner - Major Wooster's Battalion, NY Sea Fencibles.

Wilson, Thomas - Seaman - Major Wooster's Battalion, NY Sea Fencibles.

Wiltshire, William - Seaman - Major Fowler's Detachment, NY Sea Fencibles - Company: Benjamin Muzzy - Discharged at Blockhouse Independence on 6 Dec 1814.

Wise, Joseph - Seaman - Major Wooster's Battalion, NY Sea Fencibles.

Wiseburn, Daniel - Seaman - Major Wooster's Battalion, NY Sea Fencibles.

Wiseman, William - Gunner - Major Wooster's Battalion, NY Sea Fencibles.

Withington, James - Gunner - Major Fowler's Detachment, NY Sea Fencibles.

Woggs, Collings - Seaman - NY Sea Fencibles - Company: Paul Burrows - Enlistment date: 7 Oct 1814 - Period: 3 Months.

Wood, Eleazer - Gunner - Major Fowler's Detachment, NY Sea Fencibles - Company: James Breath.

Wood, Francis - Seaman - Major Leonard's Battalion, NY Sea Fencibles.

Wood, Michael - Seaman - Major Leonard's Battalion, NY Sea Fencibles.

Wood, William - Seaman - Major Wooster's Battalion, NY Sea Fencibles.

Woodback, John - Waiter - Major Leonard's Battalion, NY Sea Fencibles.

Woodhull, Isaac - Seaman - Major Wooster's Battalion, NY Sea Fencibles.

Woodman, Jonathan - Private - NH Sea Fencibles - Company: William Marshall - Enlistment date: 27 May 1813 - Discharged on 27 Nov 1813.

Woodruff, Nathaniel - Seaman - Major Wooster's Battalion, NY Sea Fencibles - Company: John Roorbach.

Woodwell, Joseph - Seaman - Major Wooster's Battalion, NY Sea Fencibles.

Woolman, James - Seaman - NY Sea Fencibles - Company: John Cunningham - Enlistment date: 3 Sep 1814 - Period: 3 Months.

Wooster, Charles W. - Major - Major Wooster's Battalion, NY Sea Fencibles - Enlistment date: 1 Sep 1814 - Commanded a battalion of New York Sea Fencibles.

Worth, Barzilla - Paymaster - Major Fowler's Detachment, NY Sea Fencibles.

Wright, Daniel - Seaman - Major Leonard's Battalion, NY Sea Fencibles - Company: William Russell - Enlistment date: 19 Jan 1815 - Period: 3 Months.

Wright, Devit - Seaman - Major Leonard's Battalion, NY Sea Fencibles - Company: Alexander Robinson - Enlistment date: 19 Oct 1814 - Period: 3 Months.

Wright, Edwin - Seaman - Major Wooster's Battalion, NY Sea Fencibles - Company: Isaac Silliman - Enlistment date: 6 Jan 1815 - Period: 1 Yr.

Wyer, John - Private - MA Sea Fencibles - Company: Nehemiah Skillings.

Wynkoop, Peter - Third Lieutenant - NY Sea Fencibles - Company: Josiah Ingersoll.

Yard, Charles - Seaman - NY Sea Fencibles - Company: Josiah Ingersoll.

Yates, Charles - Seaman - Major Leonard's Battalion, NY Sea Fencibles.

Yeaton, Edward - Private - NH Sea Fencibles - Company: William Marshall - Enlistment date: 27 May 1813 - Discharged on 27 Nov 1813; served again from 27 Nov 1813 through 31 Dec 1813.

Yeaton, Isaac S. - Private - NH Sea Fencibles - Company: William Marshall - Enlistment date: 27 May 1813 - Discharged on 27 Nov 1813.

Yeaton, John C. - Private - NH Sea Fencibles - Company: William Marshall - Enlistment date: 27 May 1813 - Discharged on 27 Nov 1813.

Yeaton, Richard - Private - NH Sea Fencibles - Company: William Marshall - Enlistment date: 27 May 1813 - Discharged on 27 Nov 1813; served again from 27 Nov 1813 through 31 Dec 1813.

Young Jr., Jonathan - Private - MA Sea Fencibles - Company: Isaac Lyman - Born: 26 Jul 1814 - Discharged on 23 Sep 1814.

Young, Benjamin - Seaman - Major Leonard's Battalion, NY Sea Fencibles.

Young, John - Private - MA Sea Fencibles - Company: Jeremiah Stickney.

Young, Joseph - Private - MA Sea Fencibles - Company: Isaac Lyman - Born: 26 Jul 1814 - Discharged on 23 Sep 1814.

Young, William - Corporal - MA Sea Fencibles - Company: Jeremiah Stickney.

American Sea Fencibles in the War of 1812

U.S. Sea Fencibles Companies

Unknown Company

Allen, John M.	Private	Harden, Jesse	Private
Azzalell, Dolphus	Private	Hardwick, John	Third Lieutenant
Bailey, Bethel	Gunner	Hardy, Hitch E.	Gunner
Baisard, James	Private	Harris, Elijah	Private
Barell, Francis	Private	Hatch, John	Private
Barnal, John	Private	Hawkins, Isaac	Private
Barras, Waratit	Private	Healey, Joseph	Private
Barren, Francis	Private	Hill, Isaiah	Gunner
Bartlett, William	Private	Hogland, Peter	Private
Barton, John	Private	Horner, Henry	Private
Beacham, Thomas	Private	Hornsby, William	Private
Berkland, Peter	Private	Horton, Alexander	Private
Bions, Caleb	Quarter Gunner	Hubbard, Elias	Private
Bonner, John	Third Lieutenant	Hubbard, Joseph	Private
Brantly, James	Private	Ireland, John	Private
Bridges, James	Private	Ivy, Reuben	Private
Briggs, Spencer	Second Lieutenant	James, James	Private
Brown, Francis	Private	Jeter, Jesse	Private
Burrall, Lewis	Private	Johnson, Michael	Private
Bursley, Samuel C.	Private	Jones, John	Gunner
Butler, William	Private	Jones, Samuel	Private
Case, Hyman St.	Private	Keeny, John	Private
Coats, Thomas G.	Private	Knowles, Benjamin	Private
Coles, John	Private	Leach, Benjamin	Quarter Gunner
Connaway, Charles	Private	Litig, George	Private
Corcoran, John	Seaman	Livermore, John	Private
Corherson, John	Private	Loftes, Samuel	Private
Cottingham, Michael	Waiter	MacAarel, John	Private
Couturier, John Julius	First Lieutenant	Mathis, Jesse	Quarter Gunner
Coward, John	Private	McCally, Neal	Private
Cowdery, Isaac	Private	McCasstler, Jacob	Private
Culberhouse, Charles	Private	McClanning, Benjamin	Private
Cumming, James J.	First Lieutenant	McGill, Dubao	Private
Dauel, Simeon	Private	McIntosh, Lacklan	Second Lieutenant
Easter, James	Private	Miles, James	Private
Edmonds, Peter	Private	Miller, Jeremiah	Boatswain
Farrington, Gilbert	Second Lieutenant	Mills, John B.	Private
Ferguson, John	Private	Myers, Casten	Private
Fields, Horatio	Private	Myers, Richard	Private
Finch, William	Private	Neal, William	Private
Flinn, James	Private	Nesbit, Isaac	Private
Fredericks, George	Private	Newman, James	Second Lieutenant
Fuller, Solomon	Private	Norris, Luke	Private
Gibbs, Christian	Private	O'Donnel, John	Private
Gibbs, Pardon	Private	O'Neal, Levy	Private
Gibbs, Seth	Private	Oram, Josiah	Private
Gilbert, Martin	Private	Pattillo, George	Private
Gilman, John	Waiter	Payne, Harry	Private
Gladge, Thomas	Private	Pongers, Peter	Private
Goldson, John	Private	Potter, Robert	Private
Goodwin, Jesse	Private	Quill, William	Gunner
Green, Anson	Private	Quinton, John F.	Private
Green, George W.	First Lieutenant	Rabbs, William	Private
Green, John	Seaman	Richards, Samuel	Private
Greene, Georgia	Private	Rogers, John	Private
Hague, Joseph	Servant	Rose, Horatio	Private
Hall, George	Gunner	Russell, George J.	Private
		Russell, William H.	First Lieutenant

American Sea Fencibles in the War of 1812

Unknown Company (Continued)
Scott, Elijah	Private
Scott, Henry	Private
Scurlock, Eli	Private
Shaw, Thomas	Private
Sibbels, John	Private
Skelton, Abel	Private
Slade, Benjamin	Private
Sorter, John	Private
Spangler, George	Private
Spencer, Henry	Private
Stewart, John	Gunner
Stiron, Wallis	Private
Stiverson, John	Private
Swinson, Nicholas	Private
Taber, Charles	Waiter
Taber, Joseph	Waiter
Tabor, Pardon T.	Second Lieutenant
Thomas, Peter	Sergeant
Thompson, John	Private
Tonison, Jones	Private
Tucker, Mary	Washerwoman
Tyson, John William	Gunner
Umphris, William	Private
Vaughn, Francis	Private
Vinning, Shaderick	Private
Whitaker, John	Private
Wilkerson, Edward	Private
Wilkerson, John	Private
Williams, George	Private
Williams, John	Private
Williams, Stephen	First Lieutenant
Willis, John	Private
Willley, John E.	Waiter
Winstraw, Charles	Private
Winters, Isaac	Private
Wormesdorff, John	Private

Captain Benjamin Pearce's Company
Bates, John	Seaman
Baxter, Benjamin	Seaman
Briggs, Jonathan	Seaman
Brownell, Isaac	Seaman
Brownell, Lawton	Seaman
Bumpus, Etsiel	Seaman
Bumpus, Perez	Seaman
Bumpus, Warren	Seaman
Bumpus, Willard	Seaman
Clarke Jr., Ebenezer	Seaman
Clarke Sr., Ebenezer	Gunner
Clarke, Stephen	Quarter Gunner
DeFord, George Washington	Seaman
Elden, William	Seaman
Gibbs, Joshua	Quarter Gunner
Holmes, Peter	Seaman
Hopkins, Isaac	Seaman
Hull, Daniel	Seaman
Laridon, William	Seaman
Leonard, Ichabod	Gunner
Munroe, William	Second Lieutenant
Nye, Benjamin	Gunner
Pearce, Benjamin	Captain
Perry, John	Quarter Gunner
Potter, Walter	Gunner
Russell, James	Seaman
Smith, Martin	Seaman
Smith, Whellen	Quarter Gunner
Turner, John	Seaman
Tyler, Cornelius	Seaman
White, Ebenezer	First Lieutenant
Yeomans Jr., John	Third Lieutenant
Young, John	Seaman

Captain Frederick Brooks' Company
Adams, John	Seaman
Anderson, James	Seaman
Anthmans, Emanuel	Seaman
Archibald, Samuel	Seaman
Archibald, William	Seaman
Arnold, Ambrose	Seaman
Arnold, George Washington	Seaman
Bailey, Arthur	Seaman
Barrett, Horatio	Seaman
Bayner, Richard	First Lieutenant
Beachman, Jesse	Seaman
Bell, Eleazer	Seaman
Bell, Mathew	Gunner
Bigelow, William H.	Seaman
Britts, John F.	Seaman
Brooks, Frederick	Captain
Brooks, Stephen	Seaman
Brown, Noah	Seaman
Cason, William	Seaman
Clarke, Thomas L.	Seaman
Cole, Jacob	Gunner
Congleton, George	Seaman
Crawford, William	Seaman
Creamer, James	Seaman
Dange, Samuel	Seaman
Easters, William	Seaman
Floyd, Bazil	Seaman
Floyd, Miles S.	Seaman
Fulcher, Francis	Seaman
Gautier, Francis	Seaman
Gautier, Joseph B.	Seaman
Green, Joseph H.	Seaman
Griffin, Henry	Seaman
Hardison, Henry	Seaman
Homes, Henry	Seaman
Jester, Ebenezer	Seaman
Linton, James	Seaman
Mahoney, Miles	Seaman
Mason, Edward S.	Seaman
Masters, Joseph	Seaman
May, Joseph S.	Seaman
McKeal, Richard	Seaman
McMahone, James	Seaman
Mitchell, Byrd B.	Second Lieutenant

Captain Brooks' Company (Continued)

Nelson, Benjamin	Seaman
Newby, John	Seaman
Owens, James	Seaman
Pinkham, William	Seaman
Pollard, Hiram	Seaman
Pollard, Jesse	Seaman
Rawls, William	Seaman
Rue, John J.	Seaman
Scarborough, Jacob	Seaman
Silverthorn, Derison	Seaman
Silverthorn, Guilford	Seaman
Smith, Samuel	Seaman
Tooley, Anson	Seaman
Tooley, Atkins	Seaman
Tooley, Jonathan	Seaman
Tooley, Laban	Seaman
Townsend, John	Seaman
Tyson, William	Seaman
Welch, Mathew	Seaman
White, George	Seaman
Williams, Mathew	Seaman
Worner, Joseph	Seaman

Captain John Davis' Company

Adams, Aaron	Seaman
Adams, William P.	First Lieutenant
Bachelder, William	Seaman
Bean, Obadiah	Seaman
Berry, Isaac	Seaman
Broughton, John	Seaman
Brown, Thomas	Seaman
Burnham, Dudley	Seaman
Claridge, Stephen T.	Seaman
Clark, David E.	Seaman
Cushing, Caleb S.	Gunner
Daniels, John	Seaman
Davis, John S.	Captain
Davis, Oliver	Seaman
Davis, Owen	Seaman
Davis, Robert	Gunner
Davis, Samuel	Seaman
Downing, Jonathan	Seaman
Drown, Peter	Gunner
Fair, John	Seaman
Fernald, Benjamin	Seaman
Fernald, Robert	Seaman
Fernald, William M.	Seaman
Gay, Isaac J.	Seaman
Gilman, Nehemiah	Waiter
Greenough, Francis L.	Seaman
Haley, William	Seaman
Hastings, Thomas	Seaman
Hefers, William	Seaman
Hill, John P.	Seaman
Hill, John S.	Seaman
Hill, John T.	Seaman
Hill, Joshua B.	Seaman
Horn, John	Seaman
Hutchings, Samuel	Seaman
Jeffrey, James	Seaman
Jenkins Jr., Thomas	Quarter Gunner
Jenkins, John	Seaman
Johnson, John	Seaman
Kaine, John	Gunner
Keen, Joseph	Seaman
Kerswell, Joshua	Seaman
King, Robert R.	Seaman
Leavitt, Thomas	Seaman
Lovering, Nathaniel	Seaman
Lunt, Amos	Seaman
Magee, James	Seaman
Maling, Thomas	Gunner
Morris, Thomas	Seaman
Morrison, Nathan	Seaman
Richardson, Edward	Seaman
Ricker, Charles	Seaman
Rowell, John P.	Seaman
Rymes, George	Seaman
Saunders, Charles	Seaman
Sheriff, Henry A.	Seaman
Simpson, Robert	Seaman
Tarlton, William S.	Seaman
Tilton, John	Seaman
Tilton, Winthrop	Waiter
Tod, Rebecca	Washerwoman
Tuck, Josiah	Seaman
Tucker, Henry	Seaman
Underhill, David	Seaman
Wallace, Simon	Seaman
Welch, Samuel	Seaman
Willey, Robert	Seaman
Wilson, Aaron	Seaman

Captain John DuBose's Company

Adams, John	Seaman
Adams, William	Quarter Gunner
Barfield, Asa	Seaman
Barwick, William	Seaman
Bennett, William H.	Seaman
Clements, George	Boatswain
Dickson, James	Gunner
DuBose, John	Captain
Griffin, James	Seaman
Griffin, Mrs.	Washerwoman
Guinott, John	Seaman
Jannett, John	Gunner
Luile, William	Gunner
Potter, Levi	Gunner
Stewart, John	Seaman
Taylor, John	Gunner
Williams, James	Seaman
Wright, Jonathan	Seaman

Captain John Gill's Company

Alford, Thomas	Seaman
Askew, Charles	Seaman
Aull, James	Seaman

American Sea Fencibles in the War of 1812

Captain Gill's Company (Continued)

Baker, Asa H.	Seaman
Bowers, Daniel	Seaman
Bradford, William	Seaman
Buzzard, Michael	Seaman
Caffrey, John R.	Seaman
Carey, Dennis	Seaman
Carr, George	Seaman
Caspost, Jeremiah	Seaman
Childes, James	Seaman
Clark, Peter	Seaman
Conrad, John	Seaman
Cook, Samuel	Seaman
Craig, John	Seaman
Dalton, Edward	Seaman
Dawson, James	Seaman
Day, Cornelius	Seaman
Dedmont, Edward	Seaman
Dellsher, George	Seaman
Dorsey, Henry K.	Seaman
Elliott, Benjamin	Seaman
Fife, Andrew H.	Gunner
Forbes, William	Seaman
Freeman, William	Seaman
Gardiner, Samuel	Seaman
George, Ezekiel C.	Seaman
George, James	Seaman
Gibbs, Levin	Seaman
Gill, John	Captain
Gleason, John	Seaman
Gosswel, Anthony	Seaman
Hall Jr., Caleb	Seaman
Hambley, James	Seaman
Hanson, William	Quarter Gunner
Henry, John	Seaman
Hutton, Samuel	Seaman
Hutton, William	Seaman
Izer, Joshua	Seaman
James, William	Seaman
Kane Jr., Jacob	Seaman
Keplinger, George	Seaman
Kim, John	Seaman
Letts, Thomas	Seaman
Limmer, Terrance	Seaman
Locey, William	Seaman
McCrackin, James	Seaman
McDonald, Samuel	Gunner
McDowell, Thomas	Seaman
Morgan, John	Seaman
Nary, Michael	Seaman
Patterson, William	Seaman
Peregoy, William	Gunner
Redman, James	Seaman
Redman, Joshua	Seaman
Rick, John	Seaman
Rooke, John A.	Gunner
Sales, John B.	Seaman
Scott, Richard	Seaman
Shayack, Samuel	Seaman
Shipper, David	Seaman
Shorben, John	Seaman
Simons, James	Seaman
Sinton, Francis	Seaman
Slaker, Zacheus	Gunner
Smith, William	Seaman
Smithson, Luther	Seaman
Stevens, James L.	Gunner
Stinson, Stephen	Seaman
Stout, John	Seaman
Swift, John	Seaman
Trimble, John	Quarter Gunner
Tucker, Joshua	Seaman
Warrick, John	Seaman
Welch, Moses	Seaman
Westwood, Thomas	Seaman
White, William N.	Seaman

Captain John Marley's Company

Marley, John	Captain

Captain John Nicholson's Company

Allan, James	Seaman
Brown, Barnabas	Quarter Gunner
Brown, John	Seaman
Brown, Thomas	Seaman
Carlisle, Edward	Seaman
Carlisle, Jesse	Seaman
Carlisle, Robert	Seaman
Carter, Frederick	Seaman
Cartwright, Henry N.	Private
Champean, Jeremiah	Seaman
Champeon, James	Private
Chaves, Asgad	Seaman
Chaves, John	Seaman
Clark, Needham	Private
Coleman, Jonas	Private
Coleman, Joseph	Seaman
Coly, Wright	Seaman
Cook, Johnson	Seaman
Cooper, Joseph	Private
Cooper, Josiah	Seaman
Cribb, Jonathan	Seaman
Cribb, Jonathan	Seaman
Cribb, Shadrach	Seaman
Daughtry, William	Private
David, Turner	Seaman
Davis, Caleb	Seaman
Davis, John	Seaman
Davis, Julius	Private
Davis, Turner	Private
Davis, William	Seaman
Elwell, Benjamin	Seaman
Glover, Joseph	Seaman
Grant, John	Private
Grimes, Mercer	Seaman
Hardy, Arthur	Seaman
Irvin, James	Seaman
Jackson, James	Seaman

American Sea Fencibles in the War of 1812

Captain Nicholson's Company (Continued)

Jenkins, Henry	Seaman
Jonas, Jones	Seaman
Jones, Jonathan	Seaman
Jones, Shadrick	Seaman
Jordan, John	Seaman
Kellyhan, Cornelius	Seaman
Kellyhan, Neil	Private
Lardy, Arthur	Seaman
Love, John	Seaman
Lytle, Robert	First Lieutenant
MacLenman, Moran	Seaman
MacMillan, Neill	Seaman
Martin, Martin	Private
Mathews, Neil	Seaman
McCrumin, Roderick	Seaman
McDonald, Daniel	Seaman
McDonald, John	Seaman
McFatter, Alexander	Seaman
McFatter, Nivan	Seaman
McIntyre, Daniel	Seaman
McLellan, Moran	Seaman
McLellan, Samuel	Seaman
McNeill, Neil	Seaman
McRae, Alexander	Seaman
Molsbay, James	Seaman
Morgan, William	Seaman
Nicholson, John	Captain
Parham, Matthew	Private
Perry, John	Seaman
Pooll, Samuel	Seaman
Priest, Neil	Seaman
Revells, Henry	Seaman
Riverbank, Frederick	Private
Russ, John M.	Seaman
Russ, Josiah	Seaman
Russ, Thomas	Seaman
Shaw, Donald	Seaman
Smith, John	Seaman
Smith, Neil	Seaman
Smith, Thomas	Seaman
Spencer, Thomas L.	Seaman
Stephens, Levi	Seaman
Stiner, Joseph	Private
Stuart, John	Seaman
Thompson, William	Seaman
Tison, Aaron	Seaman
Venters, Francis	Private
Wane, John	Seaman
West, Samuel	Private
White, David J.	Seaman
White, William	Seaman
Wiggins, Elijah	Seaman
Wilkinson, James	Seaman
Wilkison, Thomas	Seaman
Wright, Thomas	Seaman
Yates, Ignatius	Private
Yates, Uriah G.	Seaman

Captain Lemuel Morris' Company

Andrews, John	Seaman
Andrews, Nathaniel	Seaman
Antone, Joseph	Seaman
Atkins, George	Seaman
Barnett, John	Seaman
Belfour, Azabell	Seaman
Brady, William	Quarter Gunner
Bredging, Andrew	Seaman
Brown, John	Seaman
Brown, Peter	Seaman
Brown, Thomas	Seaman
Cameron, Alexander	Seaman
Cammell, Richard	Gunner
Campbell, Richard	Seaman
Carberry, John	Seaman
Cassady, Andrew	Seaman
Cathcart, Robert	Seaman
Clarkson, John	Seaman
Clements, Peter	Seaman
Clinton, James	Quarter Gunner
Cochran, John	Seaman
Coffin, Daniel	Seaman
Cole, Benjamin	Seaman
Conger, David	Gunner
Cooper, Samuel	Seaman
Corcheran, John	Seaman
Cottingham, William	Seaman
Craig, John	Seaman
Cullin, Terrance	Seaman
Cummings, Robert	Seaman
Custis, Watt	Seaman
Dill, Isaiah	Quarter Gunner
Drummond, Aaron	Seaman
Duffey, James	Seaman
Dunlavey, John	Seaman
Dunwell, William	Servant
Edgecomb, William	Seaman
Edson, John M.	Seaman
Egbert, Daniel	Seaman
Fargo, Mathew	Seaman
Farrell, John	Seaman
Farrell, Peter	Gunner
Fowler, Nicholas	Seaman
Fowler, William	Gunner
Francis, James	Seaman
Fredericks, Charles	Seaman
Gardiner, Thomas	Seaman
Gazzam, William	Seaman
Gilmore, Stephen	Seaman
Gordon, George	Seaman
Greene, John	Seaman
Hall, Thomas	Seaman
Haskett, William	Seaman
Hill, Daniel	Seaman
Hughes, John	Seaman
Hunter, William	Seaman
Hutton, James	Seaman
Hybert, Augustus	Seaman

American Sea Fencibles in the War of 1812

Captain Morris' Company (Continued)
Hyde, Charles	Quarter Gunner
Irwin, William	Seaman
Johnson, John	Seaman
Johnson, John	Seaman
Johnson, John	Seaman
Jones, James	Seaman
Jones, Thomas	Seaman
Jones, William	Gunner
Kenny, John	Seaman
Landsdown, Edward	Seaman
Lawrence, Elisha	Seaman
Lester, Platt	Seaman
Lester, Smith	Quarter Gunner
Liddle, Archibald	Gunner
MacKerall, John	Seaman
Maples, Charles	Seaman
Marley, John	Seaman
Marsh, Phineas	Seaman
McKnell, John	Seaman
McMillen, Alexander	Seaman
McNeil, Samuel	Seaman
McPherson, John	Second Lieutenant
Merrick, Joseph	Seaman
Miller, Abraham	Seaman
Morris, Lemuel	Captain
Morrison, Joseph	Quarter Gunner
Myers, George	Seaman
Myers, John	Seaman
Oliver, William	Seaman
Patton, Robert	Seaman
Pearce, Charles	Gunner
Pearce, Thomas	Seaman
Pell, Thomas	Seaman
Peters, John	Seaman
Robertson, John	Seaman
Robertson, Robert	Seaman
Robinson, James A.	Seaman
Scissell, Joseph	Seaman
Shay, Thomas	Seaman
Smith, Charles	Seaman
Smith, James	Seaman
Smith, John	Seaman
Smith, John	Seaman
Snale, Robert	Gunner
Southerland, Thomas	Seaman
Spence, John	Seaman
Stephens, George B.	Seaman
Steward, Charles	Seaman
Taggart, James	Seaman
Taylor, William	Gunner
Thompson, Joseph	Seaman
Turner, Thomas	Seaman
Vanalstine, Christopher	Seaman
Walker, John	Seaman
Walker, Thomas	Seaman
Walmsby, James	Seaman
Walters, William	Seaman
Ward Jr., John	Seaman
Wheaton, Henry	Seaman
White, John	Gunner

Captain McQueen McIntosh's Company
Biseman, David	Gunner
Carlisle, Robert	Seaman
Carroll, David	Sergeant
Cline, David	Seaman
Gray, Gabriel	Seaman
Hargrove, Britton	Seaman
Lee, Joseph	Seaman
McIntosh, McQueen	Captain
Padrick, John	Seaman
Priest, Archibald	Gunner
Rodgers, David	Seaman
Runalds, Danny	Seaman
Russ, James	Seaman
Searles, Edward	Seaman
Shaw, Daniel	Seaman
West, Gibson	Seaman

Captain Noah Terry's Company
Alben, Zerah	Seaman
Aldridge, Howell	Seaman
Anderson, Stephen B.	Seaman
Baker, Clothier H.	Gunner
Baker, John	Seaman
Baker, Nathaniel	Seaman
Bennett, Edward	Seaman
Bennett, Gamiliel	Seaman
Bennett, Lester	Seaman
Bennett, Samuel	Seaman
Brown, Daniel	Gunner
Brown, David	Boatswain
Brown, Leander	Seaman
Brown, Orin D.	Seaman
Brown, Samuel	Seaman
Bryam, Eliab	Gunner
Case, Samuel H.	Seaman
Coles, Thaddeus	Seaman
Coles, William	Quarter Gunner
Collins Jr., Samuel	Seaman
Collins, Samuel	Seaman
Cooper, Elias M.	Seaman
Corey, John O.	Quarter Gunner
Corey, Stephen	Seaman
Cornwall, Hewlett	Seaman
Crowell, Mark S.	Seaman
Crowell, Paul	Seaman
Daily, Henry	Seaman
Davis, Jonathan	Seaman
Duvall, John	Seaman
Edwards Jr., John	Seaman
Eldridge, Benjamin G.	Seaman
Fanning, James	Seaman
Fordham, Daniel	Gunner
Fordham, James	Gunner
Freeman, John	Quarter Gunner
Gann, John	Seaman

American Sea Fencibles in the War of 1812

Captain Terry's Company (Continued)

Gardiner, Jeremiah	Quarter Gunner
German, Robert	Seaman
Gray, James	Seaman
Hallock, Sydney C.	Gunner
Hamilton, Benjamin	Seaman
Hannis, Thomas	Seaman
Harris, Thomas R.	Seaman
Havens, Jacob	Seaman
Havens, Nathaniel T.	Seaman
Havens, William H.	Seaman
Haynes, David	Captain
Hedges, Jared	Seaman
Hicks, William	Seaman
Howell, Usher H.	Seaman
Howell, William	Seaman
Isaacs, John M.	Third Lieutenant
Jane, John	Seaman
Jessup, Frederick	Seaman
Jones, Lewis	Seaman
King, Clark	Seaman
King, David	Seaman
King, Hubbard	Seaman
King, John	Seaman
King, Richard	Seaman
Langdon, David	Seaman
Leek, Abraham	Seaman
Leek, Jacob	Gunner
Lester, Nathaniel	Seaman
Lewis, Thomas	Seaman
L'Hommeron, Jabez F.	Seaman
Loper, Abraham	Seaman
Loper, Amos	Seaman
McGran, John	Seaman
Miller, Eleazer	Seaman
Miller, Isaac W.	Seaman
Miller, Jonathan	Seaman
Miller, Jonathan J.	Seaman
Miller, King	Seaman
Miller, Samuel	Seaman
Mott, Young	Seaman
Myers, John F.	Seaman
Niles, George	Seaman
Niles, Peleg	Seaman
Nostrand, John	Seaman
Osborn, Samuel	Seaman
Overton, Mattiah	Seaman
Payne, Harvey	Seaman
Payne, Rufus	Seaman
Petty, William	Seaman
Pierson, John	Seaman
Racket, David	Seaman
Raymond, George	Waiter
Rodgers, Apollo	Seaman
Rose, Hosea	Seaman
Ruland, Israel	Seaman
Sammis, Daniel	Seaman
Sandford, Jesse	Seaman
Shearman, John	Seaman
Sherman, John	Seaman
Sherry, William	Servant
Smith, Benjamin	Seaman
Smith, Eldridge	Seaman
Smith, Judah	Seaman
Smith, Lewis	Seaman
Stansborough, David	Seaman
Stansborough, Isaac	Seaman
Stewart, Silas	Gunner
Stiverson, Allen	Seaman
Stringham, John	Seaman
Sweezy, Nathan B.	Seaman
Terry, Amon	Servant
Terry, Noah	Captain
Terry, Shadrach	Seaman
Tillotson, David	Seaman
Tuthill, Joshua	Seaman
Watts, John	Seaman
White, Elias	Seaman
Williamson, John M.	First Lieutenant
Wilmot, Henry	Seaman
Young, Samuel	Seaman

Captain Peleg Barker's Company

Barker, Peleg	Captain
Barstow, Solomon	Seaman
Bates, John	Seaman
Bates, Joshua T.	Seaman
Bradford, Henry	Gunner
Caswell, Daniel	Seaman
Dillingham, Benjamin	Quarter Gunner
Drew, Edward	Seaman
Foster, Robert	Seaman
Glover, Charles G.	Gunner
Harper, Peter	Gunner
Hitch, Hardy E.	Gunner
Hussey, Peter	Quarter Gunner
Kalm, John	First Lieutenant
Kulgars, Dirk	Seaman
Morris, George S.	Seaman
Nichols, Edward	Seaman
Rice, John	Seaman
Riddle, Joshua	Gunner
Snow, Nathaniel	Seaman
Stevens, Thomas	Seaman
Swain, Benjamin	Boatswain
Symmes, Isaac	Seaman
Tabu, William	Waiter
Thomas, John	Seaman
Tupper, Peleg	Gunner
Wadsworth, John	Seaman
Wadsworth, Seth	Seaman
Wallis, John	Seaman
Waters, William	Seaman
West, Edward B.	Gunner
West, Thomas	Quarter Gunner

Captain Simmones Bunbury's Company

Bailey, Esma	Seaman

American Sea Fencibles in the War of 1812

Captain Bunbury's Company (Continued)

Barbine, Charles	Seaman
Bennett, Freeman	Seaman
Bhare, Charles	Seaman
Blunt, Joseph	Seaman
Bosley, Thomas	Servant
Boyd, John	Gunner
Brinkman, John	Seaman
Brook, William	Seaman
Brown, James	Servant
Brown, John	Seaman
Brown, John	Seaman
Brown, Thomas	Quarter Gunner
Bunbury, Matthew Simmones	Captain
Bussel, George	Gunner
Concklin, John	Seaman
Connally, James	Seaman
Connally, John	Seaman
Coomes, John	Gunner
Cooper, John	Seaman
Cordery, Isaac	Seaman
Crea, Hugh	Seaman
Curtis, William	Seaman
Dear, Isaac	Seaman
Devon, William J.	Seaman
Dickerson, James	Seaman
Drear, Joseph	Seaman
Edmunds, Abijah	Seaman
Evans, Patrick	Seaman
Fletcher, John	Seaman
Forsey, Elias P.	Seaman
Foy, Gregory	First Lieutenant
Fredericks, Paul	Seaman
Gibson, Thomas	Seaman
Glenn, James	Seaman
Goodmanson, Peter	Seaman
Gorsuch, Gerard	Third Lieutenant
Green, Anthony	Seaman
Green, John	Seaman
Green, Robert	Seaman
Guess, Thomas	Seaman
Hall, Caleb	Seaman
Hall, Joseph	Seaman
Hanes, James	Seaman
Harrington, Robert	Gunner
Hash, Peter	Seaman
Hayes, Adam	Seaman
Herd, Samuel	Servant
Higby, Noah	Gunner
Hooper, Erestus	Seaman
Hush, Peter	Seaman
Jackson, John	Seaman
Johnson, Henry	Seaman
Jones, William	Seaman
Kildue, George M.	Seaman
Kincaid, Myers	Seaman
Knower, John	Seaman
Koog, Martin	Seaman
Lawrence, James	Boatswain
Linnenburger, John	Seaman
Linsey, Joseph	Seaman
Lives, William G.	Seaman
Lough, Michael	Seaman
Luley, Charles	Seaman
Manson, Henry	Seaman
Marshall, Elias	Seaman
Mason, Henry	Seaman
McKnight, Lewis	Seaman
Meeks, James P.	Seaman
Montgomery, Archibald	Seaman
Morris, George	Seaman
Morris, George	Seaman
Morrow, William	Seaman
Oram, Isaiah	Seaman
Oram, John	Seaman
Page, Jenkin	Seaman
Patterson, Thomas G.	Seaman
Reynolds, Pierce	Servant
Richardson, William	Seaman
Robertson, Thomas	Seaman
Robinson, Thomas	Seaman
Rogers, Joseph	Seaman
Ross, Samuel S.	Seaman
Scracklin, Lewis	Seaman
Sherman, Lewis J.	Seaman
Smith, Alexander	Seaman
Smith, Peter	Seaman
Smother, Aderick	Servant
Smothers, John	Servant
Sparks, William	Seaman
Stephens, Timothy	Seaman
Sterrett, Robert	Seaman
Talbot, Joseph	Seaman
Thompson, Elisha	Seaman
Thompson, Richard	Seaman
Todd, George	Seaman
Tranquille, Lewis	Seaman
Travelles, John	Seaman
Travlot, John	Seaman
Tyler, John	Seaman
Valiant, John	Gunner
Warfield, George	Seaman
Welsh, John	Seaman
Welsh, Pierce	Seaman
Whailing, Timothy	Servant
White, Benjamin	Quarter Gunner
White, Charles	Seaman
White, Joseph P.	Gunner
Williams, James	Seaman
Williams, James	Seaman
Wilson, George C.	Gunner
Wilson, William	Gunner
Wood, John	Seaman
Woods, Lewis	Seaman
Young, Peter	Quarter Gunner

Captain Thomas Newell's Company

Brant, Solomon	Seaman

American Sea Fencibles in the War of 1812

Captain Newell's Company (Continued)

Carny, John	Seaman
Castillaw, Henry	Gunner's Mate
Hewitt, John	Gunner
Hill, James	Seaman
Johnson, George	Seaman
Johnson, James	Boatswain
Johnson, John	Seaman
Johnson, Tuhail	Seaman
Jones, Charles	Seaman
Jones, Henry B.	Third Lieutenant
Leach, B. W.	Seaman
Newell, Thomas M.	Captain
Nichols, Abraham	First Lieutenant
O'Neal, Ferdinand Armstrong	Second Lieutenant
Paten, John	Seaman
Ramsdale, James	Seaman
Rhodes, Thomas	Seaman
Robertson, Robert	Seaman
Tarbox, Thomas	Seaman

Captain William Addison's Company

Addison, William H.	Captain
Alford, Jacob	Musician
Barnhart, Henry	Seaman
Bebee, Edward	Seaman
Belott, William	Seaman
Bongers, Peter C.	Seaman
Cary, Dennis	Seaman
Clark, James M.	Seaman
Cooper, Hezekiah	Seaman
Crocker, James	Seaman
Curtis, John	Seaman
Evins, David	Seaman
Gordon, John	Seaman
Griffiths, Thomas B.	Seaman
Hadley, Joseph	Seaman
Hamilton, John	Seaman
Hanalin, Patrick	Gunner
Hands, Ephraim	Seaman
Hands, Nicholas	Seaman
Hane Jr., Jacob	Seaman
Harris, John	Seaman
Hollings, John	Seaman
Ing, John	Seaman
Jordan, Samuel	Quarter Gunner
Lacey, William	Seaman
Lewis, Barall	Seaman
MacKey, Robert	Seaman
McComas, Charles	Seaman
McCoy, Alexander	Seaman
McCracken, John	Quarter Gunner
McNeir, George	Third Lieutenant
Mestler, Coonrod	Seaman
Miles, John	Seaman
Newit, Edward	Seaman
Peters, William	Seaman
Potter, Thomas	Servant
Robinson, Caleb R.	Second Lieutenant
Rook, John	Seaman
Sadler, Augustus	Seaman
Scott, Joseph	Seaman
Shartle, Henry	Seaman
Shehey, Michael	Seaman
Stephens, James L.	Gunner
Stoke, Zacheous	Gunner
Vinyard, James	Seaman
Wallace, James	Seaman
Walsh, Moses	Seaman
Whetson, George	Seaman
Williams, Job	Servant
Williams, Richard	Seaman
Williams, William	Seaman
Wilson, Charles	Seaman

American Sea Fencibles in the War of 1812

State Sea Fencibles Companies

Massachusetts Sea Fencibles

Captain Isaac Lyman's Company
Blaisdell, David	Private
Donnell, Henry	Private
Donnell, Nathaniel	Private
Gilman, George	Private
Goodwin, Abiel	Private
Grover, Joseph	Private
Harmon, Benjamin	Private
Harmon, James	Private
Lindsay, Samuel	Private
Lyman, Isaac	Captain
McDaniel, James	Private
McIntire, Charles	Private
Moody, Charles	Private
Moody, Joseph	Sergeant
Moore, George	Private
Stover III, Samuel	Private
Thompson, John D.	Sergeant
Varrell Jr., Solomon	Private
Varrell, Rufus	Private
Young Jr., Jonathan	Private
Young, Joseph	Private

Captain Jeremiah Stickney's Company
Adams, Thomas	Private
Aubin, Joseph	Corporal
Bartlett Jr., William	Sergeant
Bassett, Christopher	Private
Bayley, Moses	Musician
Blanchard Jr., Jeremiah	Private
Boardman, Thomas	Private
Boddery, John	Private
Brown, Nathan	Private
Buntin, Joseph	Sergeant
Call, Charles	Private
Coffin Jr., David	Private
Coffin, Hector	Second Lieutenant
Cook, Charles	Corporal
Couch, John	Private
Cummings, James	Private
Dennis, Amos	Private
Dole, John	Private
Francis, James	Corporal
Friend, William	Private
Furlong, Henry	Private
Gerrish, Enoch	Private
Gerrish, Mays	Private
Haskel, David	Private
Haskel, Enoch	Private
Hodge, Charles	Third Lieutenant
Howard, William	Private
Hoyt, Samuel	Quartermaster
Johnson, Green	Sergeant
Knap, Jacob	Private
Knight, Amos	Private
Lattime, Nicholas	Private
Lawton, William	Private
Livingston, Alexander	Private
Lovett, Joseph	Private
Lufkin, David	First Lieutenant
Norton, Stephen	Private
Norton, William	Private
Nowell, Silas	Private
Park, Isaac	Private
Parsons, Joseph	Private
Prince, Joseph	Private
Putnam, John	Musician
Smith, Joel	Musician
Stallard, Thomas	Private
Stickney, Jeremiah	Captain
Stone, John	Private
Stover, Joseph	Private
Swasey, Samuel	Private
Tappan Jr., Benjamin	Private
Tilton, Daniel	Private
Titcomb Jr., Jonathan	Private
Titcomb, John	Private
Walton, Samuel	Musician
Welch, Jonathan	Private
Wheelwright, Jeremiah	Sergeant
Young, John	Private
Young, William	Corporal

Captain Nehemiah Skillings's Company
Adams, Atkins	Private
Adamson, John	Private
Aires, Frederick W.	Private
Allen, James A.	Private
Atkins, Isaac	Private
Austin, William	Private
Bany, Nicholas C.	Private
Bertody, Charles	Private
Blair, Victor	Private
Blanchard, Andrew	Private
Blanchard, Charles	Private
Boyer, Daniel	Private
Bradstreet, Samuel H.	Private
Bronson, Shubael G.	Private
Burnham, F. A.	Private
Burrows, William	Private
Butler, Francis C.	Private
Butody, Chs.	Private
Callender, Joseph	Sergeant
Carter, Robert	Private
Chapman, Edward	Private
Chapman, Nathaniel	Private
Clap, Edward	Private
Cobb, Lom	Private
Crooker, Tilden	Private
Curtis, Caleb	Corporal

Captain Skilling's Company (Continued)

Name	Rank
Curtis, Theodore	Private
Davis, Joseph	Private
Dennis, Thomas	Private
Dewson, Francis	Private
Dickson, Joshua D.	Private
Doak, John	Private
Edes, Robert B.	Private
Endicott Jr., William	Private
Field, Josiah	Private
Gardner, Benjamin	Private
Getty, Francis	Private
Glover, Russell	Sergeant
Glover, Stephen	Private
Goodwin, Timothy	Private
Gorham, Benjamin	Private
Griffin, William	Private
Hall, Stephen	Private
Harris, Thomas	Private
Hayl, Charles	Private
Henry, Robert	Private
Hewes, John H.	Private
Hilliard, John	Private
Hinckley, Isaac	Private
Hinckley, Richard B.	Private
Hixon, George	Private
Holland, Samuel	Private
Holmes, Bartlett	Private
Homer, Jacob	Private
Hopkins, Caleb	Private
Howe Jr., Edward	Corporal
Ingersoll, George O.	Private
Inglee, Jesse	Private
Jennerson, John S.	Private
Jones, George G.	Private
Jones, Thomas	Private
Knapp, Charles	Corporal
Leach, Samuel	Private
Lee, Samuel	Private
Lewis, Eleazer	Private
Lewis, Joseph W.	Private
Lewis, Winslow	First Lieutenant
Lincoln, James M.	Private
MacKay, George D.	Private
MacKay, Joseph	Private
Mansfield, George	Private
Martin, John	Private
May, Charles	Private
May, William	Private
May, William R.	Private
Miller, Isaac	Private
Moffatt, Samuel	Private
Moore, Samuel	Private
Moorfield, James	Private
Morgan, James	Private
Morland, Robert	Private
Nash Jr., Joshua	Private
Nash Jr., Moses	Private
Nickels, Samuel	Private
Noble, Francis	Private
Parsons, Charles	Private
Pearson, Amos	Private
Pearson, Thomas	Private
Penn, William	Private
Peterson, Henry	Private
Pommier, George	Private
Prince, George I.	Private
Proctor, Edward	Private
Purcell, Henry	Private
Quincy Jr., Samuel	Private
Robbins, Chandler	Private
Rousseau, Peter	Private
Russell, Henry	Sergeant
Sangor, Avery	Private
Scott, Edward S.	Corporal
Seward, Thomas	Private
Seward, Timothy	Private
Silsbee, Benjamin	Private
Skillings, Nehemiah W.	Captain
Small, Elisha	Private
Smith, Charles	Private
Smith, George	Private
Smith, George N.	Private
Smith, John	Corporal
Smith, William	Quarter Gunner
Smith, William	Quartermaster
Snow, Nathaniel	Third Lieutenant
Stillman, Benjamin M.	Private
Swift, Samuel	Private
Thaxter, George	Private
Thomas Jr., John	Private
Thompson, Martin	Private
Tisdale, William	Private
Tracy, Charles	Second Lieutenant
Trott, James F.	Private
Tuckerman, BHS	Private
Tufts, Robert	Private
Tufts, William	Private
Turner, Robert	Private
Urann, Richard	Private
Wales, John	Private
Wallis, William	Private
Ward, William	Corporal
Watkins, Andrew	Private
Williams, Richard	Private
Wyer, John	Private

American Sea Fencibles in the War of 1812

New Hampshire Sea Fencibles

Captain William Marshall's Company

Bell, Meshack	Private
Card, John	Private
Davis, Samuel P.	Private
Dunking, Samuel	Private
Farneil, Ebing	Private
Farniel, Samuel	Private
Foss, Benjamin	Private
Foss, Samuel	Musician
Foy, John	Ensign
Hall, Edward	Private
Kimme, Benjamin	Private
Kimme, William	Private
Kinnear, Benjamin	Private
Lear, Benjamin	Private
Locke, Daniel	Private
Locke, Joseph	Sergeant
Mace, Ithamar	Private
Marshall, William	Captain
Martin, John	Private
Mason, Nicholas	Private
McGridge, John	Private
Mugrige, John	Private
Mullen, James	Private
Mullin, John R.	Private
Narrell, Samuel	Private
Neal Jr., William	Private
Neal, George	Musician
Neal, William	Private
Odiorne, George B.	Private
Odiorne, Samuel	Private
Oliver, Benjamin	Private
Shannon, Edward	Private
Tarlton, Benjamin	Private
Tarlton, Joseph	Private
Trefethen, Abraham	Private
Trefethen, Henry	Private
Tucker, William	Private
Webster, Mark	Private
White, Joseph S.	Private
Woodman, Jonathan	Private
Yeaton, Edward	Private
Yeaton, Isaac S.	Private
Yeaton, John C.	Private
Yeaton, Richard	Private

New York Sea Fencibles

Unknown Company

Acker, Abraham	Seaman
Burrows, Berndt J.	Lieutenant
Cook, Richard A.	Private
Valleau, Isaiah	

Captain Christopher Colles' Company

Colles, Christopher	Captain

Captain John Cunningham's Company

Aykins, William	Seaman
Bailey, Richard	Seaman
Bakeman, John	Seaman
Baker, Francis	Seaman
Barnes, John	Seaman
Barry, John	Quarter Gunner
Beekman, John	Seaman
Bliss, John	Private
Borches, Jenny	Seaman
Boyd, William	Private
Brown, Gilbert	First Lieutenant
Brown, Samuel	Second Lieutenant
Brown, Walter S.	Third Lieutenant
Brush, William	Private
Burrows, Ebenezer	Seaman
Campbell, John	Private
Carpenter, John	Surgeon
Clark, James	Private
Clark, William	Private
Cock, Robert	Private
Conner, Thomas	Gunner
Connurl, John	Seaman
Cook, Patrick	Waiter
Culleday, James	Private
Culler, James	Seaman
Cunningham, John	Captain
Dennis, John	Private
Dixon, Thomas	Seaman
Duke, James	Gunner
Egbert, Frederick	Seaman
Elwill, George P.	Ordinary Seaman
Ennis, Benjamin	Private
Evans, William	Gunner
Fisher, John	Seaman
Fisley, Richard	Seaman
Francis, John	Gunner
Franklin, William	Private
Frazier, James	Seaman
Freeman, John	Private
Frisby, Richard	Seaman
Frogwell, Edward	Private
Gabriel, Ross	Seaman
Gibson, James	Private
Goodman, Thomas	Seaman
Griffith, Henry	Private
Hamilton, Benjamin	Gunner
Harnbrook, Leonard	Seaman
Hender, William	Seaman
Jardin, Robert	Gunner
Johnson, John	Seaman

American Sea Fencibles in the War of 1812

Captain Cunningham's Company (Continued)

Kelly, Lewis	Seaman
Lambert, John	Boatswain
Lambert, William	Waiter
Langdon, Benjamin	Private
Lewis, Jesse	Seaman
Lewis, John	Seaman
Luce, Jasper	Gunner
Lyman, Christopher	Seaman
Lyons, Joseph	Seaman
Mayo, Nicholas	Seaman
McCormick, Alexander	Gunner
Meakins, John	Gunner
Meakins, William	Private
Megson, Thomas	Seaman
Miller, John	Quarter Gunner
Moore, John	Seaman
Mosier, Charles	Ordinary Seaman
Mullen, John	Seaman
Munson, Peter	Seaman
Nevill, Michael	Seaman
Nickerson, Edward	Seaman
Nourse, Thomas	Seaman
Ogelsbie, John	Seaman
Oliver, Thomas	Seaman
Parmelee, David	Seaman
Pattern, Charles	Seaman
Paul, Philander	Seaman
Phillips, Robert	Seaman
Redmond, Joseph	Seaman
Rickman, Isaac	Seaman
Rodman, Joseph	Seaman
Schuyler, John	Seaman
Seaman, John	Seaman
Shamons, John P.	Seaman
Shaw, William	Seaman
Shearman, John	Seaman
Shelbourne, George	Seaman
Shelbourne, James	Waiter
Siro, Andrew	Seaman
Small, Robert	Seaman
Smith, Adam	Seaman
Smith, Henry	Seaman
Stevens, William	Gunner
Sullivan, John	Seaman
Thompson, John	Seaman
Thorrington, Samuel	Seaman
Tilley, Lewis	Seaman
Tompkins, William	Seaman
Townsand, Caesar	Seaman
Valentine, John	Seaman
Vallean, Isaiah	Seaman
Vandine, John	Seaman
Walden, Benjamin	Gunner
Ward, Stephen	Seaman
Whitney, William	Seaman
Will, Andrew	Seaman
Willet, Alexander	Seaman
Williams, Charles	Seaman
Woolman, James	Seaman

Captain Josiah Ingersoll's Company

Ackerley, Frederick	Ordinary Seaman
Adams, John	Ordinary Seaman
Aherly, Frederick	Ordinary Seaman
Airhart, James	Seaman
Alpheus, John	Seaman
Armstrong, Archibald	Seaman
Arthur, John	Private
Baker, Ephraim	Seaman
Baker, William	Servant
Barkley, William	Seaman
Barlow, Edward	Seaman
Barry, John	Seaman
Bass, George	Gunner
Benian, William	Seaman
Bergenny, Renny	Quarter Gunner
Bond, Nathaniel J.	Seaman
Bool, Joseph	Seaman
Bramer, John	Seaman
Brant, Christopher	Seaman
Bruce, Henry	Quarter Gunner
Cahill, Thomas	Ordinary Seaman
Cannon, Robert	Seaman
Carlow, William	Seaman
Carman, John B.	Hospital Ward Master
Carman, Robert	Seaman
Carroll, William	Seaman
Cartange, James	Ordinary Seaman
Cheeny Jr., Abiel	Seaman
Cheney, Abiel	Seaman
Cinefield, Edward	Gunner
Clark, Chester	Seaman
Clason, Henry	Private
Cline, Jacob	Seaman
Coleman, Silas	Seaman
Craig, Matthew	Seaman
Crosby, James M.	Seaman
Davis, Lewis	Seaman
Denny, William	Gunner
Dimorest, Daniel	Seaman
Dixon, William	Seaman
Dunnica, Edward	Seaman
Finnegan, John	Seaman
Fish, James G.	Seaman
Flinn, Henry	Seaman
Fowler, Abraham	Waiter
Francis, John	Seaman
Gale, Joseph	Seaman
Gellis, Marshall	Seaman
Glauseau, John	Seaman
Gould, John	Seaman
Hagan, John	Seaman
Hall, Joshua B.	Seaman
Halliman, Henry	Seaman
Harrison, Jacob	Seaman
Hathaway, Paul	Seaman
Hays, William H.	Ordinary Seaman

American Sea Fencibles in the War of 1812

Captain Ingersoll's Company (Continued)
Hazard, John	Second Lieutenant
Higby, Joshua	Seaman
Higby, Leonard	Seaman
Howland, Rouse	Seaman
Hutchison, James	Seaman
Ingersoll, Josiah	Captain
Jacobs, Hans	Seaman
Jelley, Martial	Seaman
Kelley, John	Seaman
Kemfield, Edward	Quarter Gunner
Lassell, John	Seaman
Leadbetter, Patrick	Waiter
Leddy, John	Seaman
Ledger, Daniel	Gunner
Lee, Robert	Seaman
Letts, Thomas	Seaman
Lewis, Jesse	Seaman
Lowndes, Charles	Seaman
Lowrey, Cornelius	Seaman
Manning, William	Quarter Gunner
Mansfield, Adonish	Seaman
Maryborler, Joseph	Seaman
McGowan, John	Seaman
McGuire, Patrick	Seaman
McSweneys, John	Gunner
Medley, Enoch	Seaman
Milligan, Basil	Seaman
Monroe, George	Quarter Gunner
Natvig, John M.	Seaman
Neil, Henry S.	Seaman
Nelson, Oliver	Boatswain
Notty, William F.	Seaman
Pasier, John	Servant
Patrick, Francis	Quarter Gunner
Patterson, Peter	Seaman
Peterson, Christian	Seaman
Peterson, Stephen	Seaman
Phillips, William	Seaman
Pitcher, Jonathan	Servant
Pollo, Peter	Seaman
Posey, John	Servant
Quinton, Joshua	Private
Roach, Edward	Seaman
Robbins, William	Seaman
Rodman, Jesse	Seaman
Roite, John	Seaman
Ruden, Moors	Surgeon's Mate
Russel, John	Seaman
Smith I, John	Seaman
Smith II, John	Seaman
Smith, Abraham	Seaman
Smith, Charles	Quarter Gunner
Smith, John	Seaman
Smith, William	Seaman
Sowle, Peleg	Seaman
Stannere, James	Seaman
Stephenson, William	Seaman
Sweeney, John M.	Gunner
Sweeny, Hugh	Surgeon's Mate
Sweeny, Hugh	Surgeon's Mate
Tapley, James	Ordinary Seaman
Tapley, Joseph	Ordinary Seaman
Tennery, John	Ordinary Seaman
Thomas, John	Ordinary Seaman
Thrift, William	Seaman
Updike, Reuben	Private
Voll, Peter	Seaman
Waistcott, Thomas	Seaman
Waite, Isaac	First Lieutenant
Walker, Francis H.	Seaman
Wall, John	Seaman
Ward, Joseph	Seaman
Waterbury, Dilas	Seaman
Williams, Augustus	Seaman
Williams, John	Seaman
Willson, David	Cook
Wilson, David	Seaman
Wynkoop, Peter	Third Lieutenant
Yard, Charles	Seaman

Captain Paul Burrows' Company
Alley, James	Quarter Gunner
Ames, Thomas	Private
Anderson, John	Boatswain
Anderson, John	Quarter Gunner
Ashby, Henry	Waiter
Ashley, Denison	Private
Bailey, Henry	Private
Baker, Paul	Private
Barker, James	Private
Bates, Benjamin	Private
Brown, James	Private
Brown, Peter	Quarter Gunner
Brushel, Moses	Private
Bunt, William	Private
Burrows Jr., Paul	Captain
Burrows, Benjamin	Gunner
Burrows, Frederick	Waiter
Burrows, George	Quarter Gunner
Burrows, James	Musician
Burt, William	Private
Carr, Richard	Private
Cary, Nathaniel	Private
Caswell, Lewin	Quarter Gunner
Choat, Ebenezer	Private
Clark, James	Private
Concklin, John	Private
Concklin, Samuel	Private
Cooper, James	Private
Cottrell, Shephard	Private
Crocker, Ichabod	Private
Crocker, Joseph	Private
Cunningham, Owen	Private
Curtis, Joseph	Private
Curtis, Josiah	Private
Dailey, John	Private
Daniels, James	Private

Captain Burrows' Company (Continued)

Delany, Peter	Private
Devorix, Robert	Private
Dewey, John	Private
Downing, Elisha	Private
Dunham, John	Private
Ellingham, John	Seaman
Ellis, Samuel	Private
Fellows, George	First Lieutenant
Fish, Coddington B.	Seaman
Fish, Sprague	Gunner
Golett, John	Private
Gould, George	Seaman
Griswold, Samuel L.	Seaman
Harrison, John	Private
Hartolen, Isaac	Seaman
Heddy, Samuel	Seaman
Hulec, Edward	Private
Hutchinson, Richard	Gunner
Huzzy, John	Private
Huzzy, Paul	Seaman
Hyler, Edward	Seaman
Jackson, John	Seaman
Jenkins, Eustacey	Private
Jenkins, Stacey W.	Seaman
Johnson, John	Seaman
Jones, James	Private
Kelly, Mathew	Seaman
Kildier, Barney	Seaman
Leach, George	Seaman
Livingston, John	Seaman
Lowry, Edward	Seaman
Magrath, John	Private
McConnell, James	Seaman
McGroth, John	Seaman
McLain, William	Private
McRath, John	Private
Miller, John	Seaman
Mitchell, Henry	Seaman
Moorhouse, Marlborough B.	Seaman
Morris, Jacob	Seaman
Myers, John	Seaman
Nedson, Edward	Seaman
Nedson, Samuel	Seaman
Nichols, Stephen	Private
Nicholson, John	Seaman
Niece, Jacob	Seaman
Niles, John	Seaman
Parks, Henry	Waiter
Phillips, Joseph	Seaman
Powers, Michael	Seaman
Pratt, Joseph	Private
Purcell, James	Private
Redman, Jesse	Third Lieutenant
Reed, John	Seaman
Rhine, Calvin	Private
Rhodes, Thomas	Seaman
Richardson, Joseph	Private
Rodman, Jesse	Third Lieutenant
Rossetor, David	Seaman
Ruskee, John	Seaman
Russell, Robert	Gunner
Sawyer, Winthrop	Seaman
Simmons, George	Private
Smith, Carol S.	Seaman
Sparrowhawk, Nathaniel	Seaman
Stacey, George	Gunner
Sunshiman, Henry	Fifer
Taylor, Amos	Private
Thomas, Henry	Seaman
Votee, Charles	First Lieutenant
Waggsle, Ollins	Private
Waites, John	Seaman
West, Reuben	Second Lieutenant
Wilber, Elam	Seaman
Wilber, John	Gunner
Woggs, Collings	Seaman

Staff

Post, Edward	Surgeon

New York Sea Fencibles
Major Fowler's Detachment

Unknown Company

Adams, Thomas D.	Seaman
Adams, Thomas S.	Gunner
Allen Jr., William	Seaman
Andrews, John	Seaman
Archer, Charles	Sergeant
Astran, John	Seaman
Bankoff, James	Quarter Gunner
Barnes, Henry	Seaman
Beck, Frederick	Seaman
Bell, John	Seaman
Bennett, James	Seaman
Birch, John I.	Seaman
Bishop, Reuben	Seaman
Bisset, Isaac	Seaman
Black, Bristol	Servant
Blanche, Anthony	Quarter Gunner
Bogardus, Richard	Seaman
Bowen, Benjamin G.	Seaman
Bower, Benjamin	Seaman
Bowers, George	Seaman
Bowne, Benjamin J.	Seaman
Brown, Charles	Seaman
Brown, John	Second Lieutenant
Bruce, John	Seaman
Bryan, John	Seaman
Bunshane, Francis	Boatswain
Byrns, George	Seaman

American Sea Fencibles in the War of 1812

Unknown Company

Camp, Alexander	Gunner
Campbell, John	Boatswain
Carson, Andrew	Seaman
Case, Peter	Gunner
Caudle, Wilkes	Seaman
Clark, John	Seaman
Clawson, Henry	Seaman
Collens, Thomas	Seaman
Collins, Michael	Seaman
Connelly, Thomas	Seaman
Cowan, Andrew	Gunner
Crery, Samuel	Sergeant
Cure, Robert	Seaman
Curran, Nicholas	Seaman
Davis, William	Seaman
Dempsey, Charles D.	Seaman
Deweize, John	Seaman
Dobbing, Samuel	Seaman
Douglass, William	Drummer
Ely, Charles	Seaman
Eustace, Ames	Seaman
Fowler, Adam	Seaman
Fowler, Pexcel	Major
Francis, John	Seaman
Frennon, Harvy	Seaman
Frennon, Henry	Seaman
Funk, Nathaniel	Seaman
Gammon, William	Seaman
Gilbert, Henry	Seaman
Gillis, John	Quarter Gunner
Gould, John	Seaman
Griswold, Benjamin	Seaman
Hagerman, Jacob	Waiter
Hagerman, Matthias	Seaman
Hall, Archibald	Seaman
Hall, George	Seaman
Harding, John	Quarter Gunner
Harrison, Joseph	Seaman
Hoffmire, James	Seaman
Holley, John	Seaman
Hone, Joshua	Seaman
Horton, Timothy	Seaman
Ivers, Thomas	Seaman
Jester, William	Private
Johnson, Jacob	Seaman
Johnson, John	Ordinary Seaman
Jolly, James	Seaman
Jones, James	Servant
Jones, John	Seaman
Keech, David	Seaman
Lane, Thomas	Seaman
Leonard, William	Seaman
Lewis, William	Seaman
Little, Harry	Servant
Little, John	Seaman
Lowndes, Charles	Seaman
Loyd, Daniel L.	Seaman
Maggee, Daniel	Seaman
Masey, John	Gunner
May, George	Seaman
McCoy, John	Seaman
McDonald, John	Seaman
McWay, John	Seaman
McWharton, John	Second Lieutenart
Mead, John	Seaman
Merchant, Joseph	Seaman
Miller, John	Seaman
Miller, Thomas	Seaman
Myers, Jacob	Seaman
Neal, James S.	Quarter Gunner
Ott, Andrew	Seaman
Parcel, John H.	Seaman
Parker, Thomas	Seaman
Peaton, Thomas	Seaman
Peterson, John	Servant
Quereau, Philip I.	Third Lieutenant
Rafferty, Patrick	Seaman
Rathborne, James	Seaman
Ratter, John	Seaman
Rea, Hall	Seaman
Reddin, Morris	Seaman
Reynolds, Justus	Seaman
Ripley, Samuel	Seaman
Risk, Henry L.	Seaman
Robb, Alexander	Gunner
Robertson, Harrison	Seaman
Rodman, Jesse	Third Lieutenant
Romer, William I.	Seaman
Rooks, David	Seaman
Ruke, David	Seaman
Seaman, William	Gunner
Seward, Christopher	Seaman
Sexton, James	Seaman
Seymore, William	Gunner
Shaa, Thomas	Gunner
Sherman, John	Seaman
Simpson, William	Seaman
Smith, Charles	Gunner
Southworth, George A.	Seaman
Spencer, John	Seaman
Stewart, William A.	First Lieutenant
Strang, John	Seaman
Taylor, William	Seaman
Terry, Ambrose	Seaman
Titus, George	Servant
Tompkins, James	Seaman
Tonkin, James	Seaman
Totten, William	Seaman
Ustace, James	Seaman
Van Antwerp, Ellis	Seaman
Vanpelt, Dan	Waiter
Vanstram, Nicholas	Seaman
Vanvarrick, Charles	Seaman
Vanzant, Isaac	Seaman
Whitman, Nathaniel	Waiter
Withington, James	Gunner
Worth, Barzilla	Paymaster

American Sea Fencibles in the War of 1812

Captain Benjamin Muzzy's Company

Astreen, John	Private
Cannon, David	Private
Davis, John	Seaman
Grant, George	Seaman
Muzzy, Benjamin A.	Captain
Newson, Samuel	Seaman
Sayers, Joseph	Seaman
Scott, James	Private
Seely, Robert	Seaman
Thomas, John	Seaman
Thompson, Thomas	Seaman
Thomson, George	Seaman
Williams, Augustus	Seaman
Wiltshire, William	Seaman

Captain James Breath's Company

Ackley, Stephen	Boy
Allen, William	Private
Ames, James	Private
Andra, John	Private
Augustus, Peter	Private
Breath, James	Captain
Brothers, Siah	Seaman
Brown, William	Private
Collins, Thomas	Private
Conklin, Jacob	Seaman
Conner, John	Seaman
Cooper, James	Private
Copper, Elisha	Private
Cornish, Isaac	Seaman
Cosse, Peter	Quarter Gunner
Culver, William	Gunner
Curtis, Benjamin	Gunner
Dickinson, John	Seaman
Dorsey, James	Seaman
Downs, Francis	Seaman
Dubois, Cato	Seaman
Eeason, James	Seaman
Ephraim, Stephen	Private
Golly, James	Seaman
Gordon, James	Seaman
Gray, John	Seaman
Gregory, Prince	Seaman
Hall, Drew	Seaman
Hamilton, James	Seaman
Hankard, Robert	Gunner
Harkness, George	Quarter Gunner
Hatch, David	Seaman
Helmus, Christopher	Seaman
Herkness, George	Gunner
Hilliard, Robert B.	Third Lieutenant
Hulsheart, Cornelius B.	Boy
Jackson, John	Seaman
Jacobs, Benjamin	Seaman
James, Amherst	Seaman
Kendal, Wilkes	Seaman
Langley, Edmund	Seaman
Lattin, Adam	Seaman
Lazare, John	Quarter Gunner
Lewis, John	Seaman
Lightizer, John	Seaman
Lilly, Francis	Seaman
Macy, John	Gunner
Mansfield, Adoniah	Seaman
Mason, Jacob	Seaman
Maxwell, William	Seaman
McCreery, Samuel	Seaman
McElvin, William	Seaman
McGee, Daniel	Seaman
McGowan, John	Seaman
Minns, Jacob	Seaman
Moors, Harry	Private
Morrison, Henry	Seaman
Mulford, Thomas	Seaman
Murray, Samuel	Seaman
Nesbit, Edwin	Seaman
Nicholson, James	Seaman
Noland, Peter	Seaman
Peabody, Asa	Seaman
Peters, John	Seaman
Peterson, John	Seaman
Peterson, Samuel	Seaman
Peterson, Thomas	Seaman
Place, William	Seaman
Porter, Abraham	Seaman
Rich, Henry L.	Seaman
Riker, Elijah	Seaman
Robertson, John	Seaman
Robinson, Hanson	Seaman
Robinson, James	Seaman
Rowland, John	Seaman
Sampson, Solomon	Seaman
Sands, Francis	Seaman
Silvester, William	Seaman
Smith, William J.	Steward
Sniffen, James	Seaman
Spock, James	Seaman
Stafford, John P.	Quarter Gunner
Stanton, Elisha	Gunner
Stewart, William	Servant
Stow, Frederick	Seaman
Struck, Lawrence	Seaman
Sullivan, Joseph	Seaman
Thomas, John	Seaman
Thompson, Isaac	Seaman
Thompson, John	Seaman
Truman, William	Seaman
Vaustner, Nicholson	Seaman
Wallace, Moses	Seaman
West, Philip	Seaman
West, William	Seaman
Wharton, John W.	Second Lieutenant
Wier, James	Gunner
Williams, George	Seaman
Wood, Eleazer	Gunner

American Sea Fencibles in the War of 1812

Captain Pexcil Fowler's Company
Taylor, Thomas — Private

Staff
Aymar, Benjamin — Quartermaster

New York Sea Fencibles
Major Leonard's Battalion

Unknown Company

Name	Rank
Abdel, John	Ordinary Seaman
Adlington, Thomas	Seaman
Anderan, Aaron	Seaman
Anderson, James	Seaman
Anderson, William	Quarter Gunner
Andrews, William	Seaman
Antonie, Mark	Seaman
Antons, Robert	Seaman
Armstrong, James	Ordinary Seaman
Arnold, Effingham W.	Ordinary Seaman
Arnott, Shelby	Seaman
Atkinson, Anthony H.	Seaman
Atkinson, John H.	Seaman
Bacon, Benjamin	Seaman
Bailey Sr., Benjamin	Seaman
Bain, Daniel	Gunner
Balls, William	Gunner
Bantan, John	Ordinary Seaman
Bantz, John T.	Ordinary Seaman
Barker, James	Seaman
Barrell, John	Seaman
Barrett, John	Seaman
Bates, Andrew	Gunner
Bates, Ashel C.	Seaman
Batricks, John	Ordinary Seaman
Batricks, Robert	Seaman
Bellancy, William	Private
Bellands, Paul	Treasurer
Belmount, Charlie	Seaman
Benjamin, Parchal	Seaman
Bergen, Hugh	Seaman
Bice, Joseph	Drummer
Billard, William	Seaman
Billings, Henry	Seaman
Bird, Robertson	Seaman
Black, Joseph	Seaman
Blanchard, David	Seaman
Bloome, Joseph	Seaman
Blume, Joseph	Seaman
Bogardus, Abraham	Boatswain
Bogart, Daniel	Seaman
Bogert, John	Seaman
Bomer, William	Seaman
Booth, Joseph	Seaman
Bounds, William	Seaman
Bowers, John	Seaman
Bowley, Jay	Seaman
Brady, Francis	Seaman
Brady, John	Seaman
Bray, George	Seaman
Brigham, Dexter	Seaman
Brimont, Charles	Seaman
Broderick, John	Seaman
Brooks, Thomas	Seaman
Brown, Ackman	Seaman
Brown, George	Seaman
Brown, John	Waiter
Brown, Thomas	Seaman
Brown, William	Servant
Bull, Thomas	Seaman
Bunker, John	Seaman
Burns, James	Quarter Gunner
Burns, Thomas	Seaman
Califlower, Edward	Seaman
Calligan, John	Second Lieutenant
Campbell, John	Seaman
Cannon, Jacob	Seaman
Carter, George	Seaman
Chambers, Andrew	Quarter Gunner
Chessey, John Francis	Seaman
Chubb, David	Seaman
Clark, James A.	Seaman
Clarke, Henry	Seaman
Clarke, John A.	Seaman
Cleves, Charles	Seaman
Cline, Frederick	Seaman
Colton, William	Private
Conover, Joseph I.	Seaman
Corbett, Charles	Seaman
Corbil, Charles	Seaman
Corby, Seph	Boatswain
Corley, Joseph	Private
Corry, William	Seaman
Costigan, Samuel Fisker	Ordinary Seaman
Cotton Jr., William M.	Seaman
Cox, Miles	Seaman
Crane, James	Seaman
Crawford, Peter	Seaman
Cuffee, Amos	Seaman
Cummings, George	Seaman
Cunningham, James	Gunner
Curren, John	Seaman
Dauson, Robert	Seaman
Davis, William	Seaman
Delaware, Thomas	Seaman
Dickson, William	Seaman
Dixon, Richards	Seaman
Dixon, Thomas	First Lieutenant
Dominick, John W.	Gunner
Donohue, John	Ordinary Seaman
Dorimus, George G.	Seaman
Dougherty, Philip	Ordinary Seaman
Duryee, George	Seaman

American Sea Fencibles in the War of 1812

Unknown Company

Duvault, Jacob	Seaman
Earles, Cornelius	Seaman
Earles, James	Seaman
Edwards, Shelby	Seaman
Egburt, Daniel	Seaman
Elder, Jacob	Seaman
Elliott, Charles	Quarter Gunner
Elliott, Nicholas	Seaman
Ellis, Thomas	Ordinary Seaman
Elsworth, Arthur	Ordinary Seaman
Elsworth, Francis	Seaman
England, William	Quarter Gunner
Enney, Jacob	Seaman
Evans, Robert	Ordinary Seaman
Fennell, James	Gunner
Fields, Samuel	Ordinary Seaman
Finch, John	Ordinary Seaman
Flanagan, Hugh	Seaman
Flinn, Edwards	Seaman
Flocker, John	Seaman
Francis, Peter	Seaman
Frazier, James	Quarter Gunner
Fredericks, Andrew	Seaman
Fricks, Richard	Quarter Gunner
Fulton, Eliakim	Ordinary Seaman
Gallagher, James	Seaman
Gallagher, Thomas	Seaman
Gammon, Ralph	Seaman
Gardner, Henry	Seaman
Gerisher, Charles	Ordinary Seaman
Glover, Edward	Seaman
Godwin, Thomas	Ordinary Seaman
Goldsmith, Silas H.	Seaman
Goodwin, Thomas	Private
Gould, Robert	Ordinary Seaman
Grally, Nicholas	Seaman
Greefield, William	Seaman
Grennell, Jordan	Seaman
Griffith, George	Gunner
Grinnell, Gordon	Seaman
Griswold, John H.	Quartermaster Sergeant
Grygier, Robert	Seaman
Gucher, Charles C.	Ordinary Seaman
Gurley, Charles	Seaman
Hagerman, Jacob	Servant
Harden, Jesse	Seaman
Harden, William	Gunner
Hardie, James	Seaman
Harettry, Michael	Seaman
Harkins, John	Quarter Gunner
Harnes, Aimes	Seaman
Harness, John	Seaman
Harrass, Michael	Seaman
Harrison, William	Seaman
Harriss, John	Seaman
Hart, Charles	Seaman
Hart, Richard	Seaman
Henry, John	Ordinary Seaman
Hess Jr., William	Gunner
Heyer, Henry S.	Ordinary Seaman
Hill, Joseph D.	Seaman
Hines, Jacob	Seaman
Hinksman, William	Seaman
Hoffman, John	Seaman
Holbert, James	Seaman
Hopper, John D.	Seaman
Humphries, James	Seaman
Hunt, Samuel	Seaman
Hutchinson, Joseph	Seaman
Hyde, Richard	Seaman
Innis, Alexander	Gunner
Jackson, Abraham	Seaman
Jackson, Benjamin	Seaman
James, John	Seaman
Jenkins, Richard	Waiter
Jennings, William A.	Seaman
Jeroke, Robert	Seaman
Jewell, William	Seaman
Johnson, Benjamin	Seaman
Johnson, Edward	Seaman
Johnson, Thomas	Ordinary Seaman
Johnson, William	Gunner
Johnston, James	Seaman
Jollie, Joan	Seaman
Jones, George	Gunner
Jones, John	Quarter Gunner
Jones, Samuel	Seaman
Jones, Thomas	Quarter Gunner
Joseph, John	Gunner
Kearney, Samuel	Seaman
Kearsing, Henry	Ordinary Seaman
Keech, Job	Seaman
Kelly, John	Ordinary Seaman
King, Samuel	Third Lieutenant
Kingsland, John	Ordinary Seaman
Kingston, Thomas	Ordinary Seaman
Kittle, Thomas S.	Seaman
Kleinham, George	Seaman
Kling, George	Seaman
Langley, John	Seaman
Larny, John	Seaman
Larus, John	Seaman
Laughley, John	Seaman
Lee, Henry	Seaman
Leonard, James T.	Major
Leonard, Joseph	Seaman
Lewis, James A.	Seaman
Lewis, John	Ordinary Seaman
Lewis, Prince	Seaman
Likeman, Joseph	Seaman
Lougherty, James	Seaman
Louis, John	Seaman
Lovett, John A.	Seaman
Lovett, John I.	Seaman
Loyd, Daniel	Servant
Lyons, Charles	Seaman
Lyons, Cornelius S.	Ordinary Seaman

American Sea Fencibles in the War of 1812

Unknown Company
Magee, Patrick	Drummer
Manna, Charles	Seaman
Markinson, George	Seaman
Markwood, Joseph	Ordinary Seaman
Marlue, John	Seaman
Marx, George	Seaman
Massey, James	Gunner
Maxwell, Charles	Seaman
Maybe, William H.	Seaman
McConnel, James	Seaman
McGee, Patrick	Quartermaster Sergeant
McGhaun, Daniel	Seaman
McGlaughlin II, James	Seaman
McGlaughlin, James	Seaman
McKann, Barney	Seaman
McKay, John	Seaman
McKenna, James	Seaman
McKenna, Patrick	Seaman
McLaughlin I, James	Seaman
McLaughlin II, James	Seaman
McLaughlin III, James	Ordinary Seaman
McLaughlin, Francis	Seaman
Merlue, John	Seaman
Mgham, Daniel	Seaman
Miles, Richard	Seaman
Miller, Jacob	Waiter
Miller, John D.	Seaman
Miller, John G.	Seaman
Millis, John	Seaman
Minna, Charles	Seaman
Minor, Daniel G.	Second Lieutenant
Minor, David G.	Second Lieutenant
Morrison Jr., Thomas	Seaman
Morrison, John	Servant
Morrow, William	Seaman
Moss, Thomas	Seaman
Moss, William	Seaman
Murray, John C.	Seaman
Mutaire, Lewis	Seaman
Myers, John	Ordinary Seaman
Myers, Peter	Seaman
Natvig, George	Third Lieutenant
Neill, John	Seaman
Oakden, Joseph	Quarter Gunner
O'Brien, Patrick	Seaman
Onderdonk, Henry L.	Seaman
Osgood, Samuel W.	Quarter Gunner
Otter, James	Third Lieutenant
Owen, George	Seaman
Paddock, Gooham	Seaman
Parce, Jonathan	Seaman
Pares, Peter	Ordinary Seaman
Parrett, Peter	Ordinary Seaman
Patterson, William	Seaman
Perkins, John	Seaman
Perkins, Zeph	Seaman
Picket, Jonathan	Ordinary Seaman
Post, Edward	Surgeon
Pratt, Elihu	Servant
Pursell, Joseph	Seaman
Rabbit, Samuel	Seaman
Redding, James	Gunner
Reed, John	Seaman
Rhea, Elisha R.	Ordinary Seaman
Richards, George	Seaman
Richards, Lewis	Seaman
Rindge, William	Gunner
Robb, James	Ordinary Seaman
Roberts, Joseph	Seaman
Roberts, Michael	Seaman
Robeson, Joseph	Gunner
Rodden, Michael	Seaman
Roe, Peter	Gunner
Rowling, John	Seaman
Salter, Samuel	Seaman
Saunders, John	Ordinary Seaman
Schenck, Daniel	Seaman
Schuyler, John	Seaman
Schuyler, Peter	Second Lieutenant
Scott, James	Seaman
Scribner, James	Ordinary Seaman
Selleck, Uriah	Gunner
Seymour, Stephen	Seaman
Shay, John W.	Seaman
Sheffield, David S.	Quarter Gunner
Shewlin, John	Seaman
Shields, Patrick	Seaman
Shortis, James	Gunner
Shulan, John	Seaman
Silva, John	Seaman
Silvary, William	Seaman
Silver, John	Seaman
Silvey, John	Gunner
Simpson, John	Seaman
Simpson, William	Seaman
Skaats, Rinier	Seaman
Sloan, John	Seaman
Smith, John	Seaman
Smith, William	Boy
Smithen, Robert	Seaman
Somers, William	Quarter Gunner
Spraig, Richard	Seaman
Squires, Seth	Seaman
Stanwood, John	Seaman
Stephens, Thomas	Seaman
Stevens, John	Servant
Stevenson, Ferdinand	Seaman
Stilwell, Samuel	Quarter Gunner
Striker, Isaac	Seaman
Striker, Jacob	Ordinary Seaman
Swain, John	Seaman
Sweasy, Peter	Seaman
Tagiers, Anthony R.	Seaman
Tatem, Henry	Seaman
Taylor, Henry	Seaman
Taylor, Mathew	Gunner
Ten Eyck, Philip	Seaman

American Sea Fencibles in the War of 1812

Unknown Company

Thomas, Abraham	Seaman
Thomas, Adam	Servant
Thomas, Cuff	Seaman
Thomas, John	Seaman
Thompson, Ellis	Gunner
Thompson, James	Seaman
Thompson, John	Seaman
Thorne, Thomas	Gunner
Todd, William F.	Seaman
Tompkins, Usual	Seaman
Townsend, John	Servant
Townsend, Michael	Ordinary Seaman
Tuck, Henry	Gunner
Tunis, John	Second Lieutenant
Turner, Nathaniel	Seaman
Valentine, Letting	Seaman
Vanconover, Moses	Seaman
Vancurren, Tobias	Seaman
Vandorf, William	Seaman
Vanhorn, Cornelius	Ordinary Seaman
Vanorden, John	Seaman
Vanzell, Cornelius	Seaman
Waldrom, Elijah	Ordinary Seaman
Waldron, William	Seaman
Wall, Robert	Ordinary Seaman
Wallace, William	Ordinary Seaman
Walt, John	Gunner
Ward, Thomas	Seaman
Warren, John	Quarter Gunner
Waydell, John	Ordinary Seaman
Webb, William	Seaman
Webster, William	Seaman
Wendover, Peter W.	Ordinary Seaman
West, James	Seaman
Westerfeild, Michael	Seaman
Wheeler, Henry	Paymaster
Wiggins, Benjamin	Seaman
Wilham, Andrew	Seaman
Wilkey, Isaiah H.	Seaman
Wilkey, Josiah H.	Seaman
Williams, James	Seaman
Williams, John	Gunner
Williams, Robert	Seaman
Williams, William	Boatswain
Williams, William	Quartermaster
Wilson, James	Seaman
Wood, Francis	Seaman
Wood, Michael	Seaman
Woodback, John	Waiter
Yates, Charles	Seaman
Young, Benjamin	Seaman

Captain Alexander Robinson's Company

Abrams, William	Private
Anderson, William	Third Lieutenant
Arthur, John	Private
Bailey Jr., Benjamin	Private
Brown, Andrew	Private
Carpenter, Walter	Seaman
Carroll, Charles	Private
Carroll, James	Private
Case, Joseph	Private
Case, Thomas	Seaman
Cavannah, Stephen	Seaman
Chase, Samuel	Private
Clark, Peter G.	Seaman
Colberth, John	Private
Colles, David	Private
Connor, Thomas	Gunner
Corbey, Joseph	Boatswain
Cox, Samuel G.	Boatswain
Cranston, William	First Lieutenant
Currier, William	Seaman
Dansh, John	Seaman
Delaplain, William B.	Seaman
Ewen, George W.	Seaman
Foster, Nathan	Gunner
Fullum, Thomas	Seaman
Gardner, Gilbert C.	Seaman
Garrison, Peter	Seaman
George, William	Seaman
Gham, Daniel M.	Seaman
Green, John	Third Lieutenant
Greenfield, William	Seaman
Guilson, Thomas	Seaman
Gwin, Peter	Seaman
Hittkinson, Anthony	Seaman
Ingall, Thomas	Seaman
Jagger, Cornelius	Seaman
Jervis, Timothy	Seaman
Johnson, Lawrence	Seaman
Johnson, William	Seaman
Kane, Thomas	Seaman
Keith, William	Seaman
Kinout, Thomas	Seaman
Lambert, Henry	Gunner
Lovett, John	Private
Lovett, John (1)	Seaman
Lovett, John (2)	Seaman
Mackie, Thomas	Seaman
McCarthy, Charles	Seaman
McLaughton, Francis	Seaman
Merrihew, William	Gunner
Merrow, William	Seaman
Miller, Jasper	Seaman
Mitchell, Henry	Seaman
Montgomery, Robert	Seaman
Moores, William	Seaman
Oringer, Robert	Seaman
Padock, Graham	Seaman
Paid, Peter	Seaman
Patton, John	Seaman
Peters, John	Seaman
Place, Henry M.	Seaman
Post, Archibald L.	Seaman
Post, William	Gunner
Quin, Robert Arnet	Private

American Sea Fencibles in the War of 1812

Captain Robinson's Company (Continued)

Randall, Henry	Seaman
Randolph, Francis	Seaman
Richeson, William	Seaman
Robinson, Alexander	Captain
Rose, John	Seaman
Rowling, John	Seaman
Salyar, John	Gunner
Sanders, Thomas	Seaman
Savage, John	Seaman
Scheyler, Peter	Second Lieutenant
Skinner, Pascal	Seaman
Skinner, Thomas	Seaman
Small, John	Seaman
Smith, Charles	Quarter Gunner
Smith, James	Seaman
Smith, John G.	Seaman
Spears, Edward	Seaman
Still, William	Seaman
Stockton, Charles	Gunner
Stokes, John	Seaman
Thomas, Abram	Seaman
Thompson, William	Seaman
Vanderpool, James	Seaman
Vincent, Jacob	Seaman
Ward, Michael	Seaman
Warden, Appleton	Seaman
Watt, John	Gunner
Weldon, James	Second Lieutenant
Whaylan, John	Seaman
Wilkie, Isaiah	Seaman
Williams, John	Seaman
Wilson, James	Seaman
Wright, Devit	Seaman

Captain Francis Costigan's Company

Baker, James McLaughlin	Private
Costigan, Francis	Captain
Tripp, John	Gunner

Captain James Leonard's Company

Mattocks, Richard	Seaman

Captain Robert Perry's Company

Perry, Robert	Captain

Captain William Russell's Company

Adams, William	Servant
Allen, William	Quarter Gunner
Anderson, Hans J.	Gunner
Angles, Lewis D.	Seaman
Brown, John	Private
Bruorson, Elisha	Servant
Carver, William	Seaman
Clark, John	Quarter Gunner
Coles, John	Gunner
Collier, Hezekiah	First Lieutenant
Colligan, Edward	Seaman
Colwell, Thomas D.	Gunner
Cotton, William	Seaman
Crone, Thomas	Seaman
Curran, James	Seaman
Daniels, William	Boy
Davis, John	Quarter Gunner
Delafield, Edward	Surgeon
Dix, West	Seaman
Donnelly, Owen	Seaman
Doran, Patrick	Seaman
Dougherty, William	Seaman
Dugan, James	Seaman
Garrisher, Charles	Seaman
Gedney, John	Seaman
Gilbert, Peter	Seaman
Gilligan, Martin	Seaman
Grimes, William	Boy
Henery, William	Boatswain
Herron, Patrick	Seaman
Jackson, William	Seaman
James, John	Boy
Johnson, James	Seaman
Jones, John	Private
Kerr, John T.	Seaman
Lacy, Thomas	Seaman
Lafurge, Benjamin	Seaman
Laugherty, James	Seaman
Livingston, John	Seaman
Magee, Patrick	Quarter Gunner
McCan, Barney	Seaman
McKinney, James	Seaman
McLaughlin, James	Private
McLaughlin, James	Seaman
McThay, Thomas	Seaman
Morrison, Thomas	Seaman
Myrick, Charles	First Lieutenant
Needham, William	Gunner
Rattee, Charles	Gunner
Robinson, Joseph	Gunner
Russell, William	Captain
Schenck, Peter D.	Surgeon
Silvy, John	Gunner
Southerland, Andrew	Seaman
Stansbury, Stephen	Third Lieutenant
Turrell, Cales C.	Seaman
Van Curen, Tobias	Seaman
Van Derstine, Christopher	Seaman
Vellum, Absalom	Seaman
Waldron, James R.	Private
Wetsell, Frederick	Seaman
Wright, Daniel	Seaman

American Sea Fencibles in the War of 1812

New York Sea Fencibles
Major Wooster's Battalion

Unknown Company
Adams, John	First Lieutenant
Adams, John	Servant
Adams, Rufus	Seaman
Albert, Sebastian	Quarter Gunner
Allen, James	Seaman
Alveridge, Sylvester	Seaman
Andrews, David	Seaman
Arnet, John	Third Lieutenant
Atkinson, John	Seaman
Austin, James	Seaman
Bain, John	Ordinary Seaman
Baker, John	Ordinary Seaman
Baker, William	Seaman
Barbier, Joseph	Quarter Gunner
Barnard, George	Ordinary Seaman
Barnes, John	Sergeant
Barnet, George	Ordinary Seaman
Barton, Peter	Seaman
Bates, Thomas F.	Seaman
Battis, John	Seaman
Beatty, Thomas	Seaman
Beckman, Charles	Seaman
Benstead, Richard	Seaman
Berger, Hugh	Seaman
Bergmar, Frederick A.	Gunner
Berry, George	Seaman
Biles, Joseph	Seaman
Billings, Harry	Seaman
Bilson, John	Seaman
Blackley, William	Gunner
Blank, Jacob	Seaman
Blow, Samuel	Seaman
Bopp, Baptist	Gunner
Borchard, John B.	Quarter Gunner
Boston, Isaac	Seaman
Botchford, Richard	Seaman
Bradford, John	Ordinary Seaman
Brewer, Edward	Seaman
Briggs, John	Quarter gunner
Brown, Francis	Boatswain
Brown, Lewis	Ordinary Seaman
Brown, William	Waiter
Browning, Isaac	Gunner
Brunow, Bernett J.	First Lieutenant
Brush, James	Seaman
Bull, Thomas	Gunner
Burgess, Thomas	Gunner
Burr, David	Ordinary Seaman
Butler, Fortune	Seaman
Butler, John	Seaman
Cady, Arnold	Seaman
Caffrey, Francis	Seaman
Call, John	Seaman
Calmell, Paul	Seaman
Campbell, John	Seaman
Cannel, John	Seaman
Carman, John B.	Ward master
Carpenter, Samuel	Ordinary Seaman
Carragan, Haugh	Seaman
Carragan, Patrick	Seaman
Carso, Daniel	Gunner
Ceaser, Friend	Seaman
Churchill, John	Seaman
Clifton, Thomas	Seaman
Coats, John	Captain's servant
Cobbs, Clenezer	Sergeant
Colburn, Hugh	Seaman
Connelly, Francis	Seaman
Craig, Robert	Ordinary Seaman
Crane, Philip	Seaman
Creeley, Nicholas	Seaman
Cromwell, Ephraim	Musician
Crosdale, William Henry	Second Lieutenant
Culoris, Charles	Ordinary Seaman
Curry, James	Seaman
Curry, William	Seaman
Dark, Nicholas A.	Seaman
Davis, Aaron	Seaman
Davis, David	Seaman
Davis, James	Seaman
Davis, John	Seaman
Dawson, John	Seaman
Dickson, John	Seaman
Dow, Joseph	Seaman
Downing, William	Quarter Gunner
Drake, William	Seaman
Driver, Samuel	Seaman
Duggin, James	Seaman
Dumm, Edward	Seaman
Dunlap, James	Seaman
Dunn, Samuel	Seaman
Edwards, John	Seaman
Elliston, William	Seaman
Ellit, Thomas	Seaman
Ellston, William	Seaman
Etsell, Richard	Seaman
Evans, John	Seaman
Evas, Henry	Seaman
Ewing, Thomas	Gunner
Ferguson, George	Seaman
Fitch, Richard	Waiter
Fortune, Julius	Seaman
Fougeret, Fils	Musician
Fowler, James H.	Seaman
Fowler, Levi	Seaman
Fowler, Nicholas	Seaman
Francis, John	Waiter
Freeman, William	Seaman
Fritzh, John	Seaman

American Sea Fencibles in the War of 1812

Unknown Company

Front, Andrew	Seaman	Kelly, John	Seaman
Fuller, Zachers R.	Quarter Gunner	Kermont, Thomas	Seaman
Furman, Daniel	Seaman	Krapff, John C.	Quartermaster
Furrill, Caleb C.	Seaman	Larose, Berrueil	Quarter Gunner
Gantz, Francis	Seaman	Lattimore, Joseph	Seaman
Gardinier, Thomas	Quarter Gunner	Lawrence, Benjamin	Seaman
Garrett, John	Seaman	Lee, William	Ordinary Seaman
Gazzam, William	Seaman	Lester, Platt	Seaman
Genn, William	Gunner	Lloyd, Henry	Seaman
Gibbons, Andrew	Seaman	Lockwood, William	Seaman
Giles, Joh	Seaman	Lord, Samuel L.	Seaman
Giles, William	Ordinary Seaman	Losher, Alexander	Seaman
Glantein, Thomas	Seaman	Low, Abraham	Seaman
Glanter, Thomas	Seaman	Loyd, Henry	Seaman
Greene, John	Seaman	Malone, Barney	Seaman
Greene, William	Gunner	Manett, John	Seaman
Greenleaf, Charles	Ordinary Seaman	Marline, John	Seaman
Greenwich, John	Seaman	Martin, John N.	Seaman
Grim, Peter	Seaman	Maubry, John	Seaman
Guin, William	Gunner	McAlpine, John W.	Seaman
Gunn, George	Surgeon's Mate	McFarland, William	Seaman
Hall, Archibald	Ordinary Seaman	McFurson, John	Ordinary Seaman
Hamill, John	Seaman	McFurson, William	Ordinary Seaman
Hamill, John	Waiter	McGinnis, John	Seaman
Hamilton, John	Seaman	McGuire, Patrick	Seaman
Hannas, Thomas	Seaman	McKay, George	Ordinary Seaman
Harper, Robert	Gunner	McKoy, Thomas	Seaman
Harris, David	Gunner	McLaughlin, Daniel	Private
Hatter, John	Seaman	McLaughlin, John	Ordinary Seaman
Hatton, John	Seaman	McPherson, John	Ordinary Seaman
Hazard, Alfred U.	Seaman	Messey, William	Quarter Gunner
Hazard, Benjamin	Seaman	Middleton, James	Seaman
Hendrickson, John	Ordinary Seaman	Miller, Alexander	Seaman
Herringbrook, William	Seaman	Miller, Arthur	Seaman
Herringon, William L.	Seaman	Miller, Augustus	Seaman
Hewes, John H.	Seaman	Miller, Henry	Servant
Higgins, Hiram	Seaman	Miller, James	Quarter Gunner
Higgins, John	Seaman	Miller, Joseph	Seaman
Hodgkiss, Philo	Seaman	Minto, John	Seaman
Hooper, Charles	Seaman	Mitchell, Walter	Seaman
Hopkins, Henry	Seaman	Mooberry, John	Seaman
Hopper, Charles	Seaman	Moore, Abraham	Seaman
Humphrey, John	Seaman	Moore, Patrick	Seaman
Hunter, William S.	Seaman	Mooris, Jacob	Seaman
Islay, Mathias	Quarter Gunner	Morrison, Robert	Seaman
Islerman, Reuben	Seaman	Mott, Charles	Ordinary Seaman
Isley, Matthias	Quarter Gunner	Moylan, Jasper	Boatswain
Jackson, Morris	Seaman	Munroe, Robert	Seaman
James, John	Seaman	Murray, Lewis	Seaman
Johnson, Edward	Seaman	Nash, Sampson	Seaman
Johnson, Jacob	Seaman	Nodine, David	Ordinary Seaman
Johnson, Leonard	Seaman	Orcutt, Stephen	Seaman
Johnson, Thomas	Seaman	Parmele, Hayle	Seaman
Johnston, John	Seaman	Pascalis, Peter	Seaman
Jones, Charles	Seaman	Peaseley, Abiel	Seaman
Jones, Sylvester	Seaman	Penn, William	Seaman
Kearn, Patrick	Seaman	Peterson, Cornelius	Ordinary Seaman
Keen, Elisha L.	Second Lieutenant	Peterson, Thomas	Seaman
		Porter, John	Waiter

American Sea Fencibles in the War of 1812

Unknown Company
Price, Henry	Quarter Gunner
Quin, Robert	Waiter
Rafferties, Patrick	Seaman
Rand, Biel	Seaman
Rattray, John	Seaman
Read, Charles	Waiter
Read, Thomas	Drummer
Redin, James	Seaman
Reicke, Nicholas	Gunner
Remsen, Charles	Seaman
Requa, Daniel	Seaman
Richards, Abraham	Seaman
Richie, John	Gunner
Riggs, John	Seaman
Rikeman, Isaac	Seaman
Riker, John	Seaman
Roberts, Frederick	Ordinary Seaman
Robertson, Bernard	Ordinary Seaman
Robertson, James	Seaman
Robertson, John	Seaman
Robertson, Robert	Seaman
Robinson, James	Seaman
Robinson, Robert	Musician
Robison, John	Musician
Romaine, Aaron	Seaman
Ross, Stephen	Seaman
Rowling, Charles	Gunner
Ruck, John	Ordinary Seaman
Ruck, William	Ordinary Seaman
Sampson, Isaac	Third Lieutenant
Sanford, Edward	Seaman
Saunders, Joseph	Seaman
Schwitzer, John	Quarter Gunner
Shoemaker, Benjamin	Servant
Siminson, Richard	Seaman
Simonson, Jacob	Seaman
Simonson, John	Ordinary Seaman
Simonson, Richard	Seaman
Simonson, Samuel	Servant
Sinclair, Daniel	Ordinary Seaman
Skaats, Jacob	Seaman
Smith, Harry	Ordinary Seaman
Smith, Robert	Seaman
Snedecker, Isaac H.	Seaman
St. Clair, Daniel	Private
Stephens, Alexander H.	Surgeon
Stevenson, Harvey	Seaman
Stevenson, John	Ordinary Seaman
Stilwell, William	Seaman
Stoff, Samuel	Ordinary Seaman
Storer, Edward	Seaman
Stoughtenberg, George B.	Seaman
Stover, Edward	Seaman
Strong, John S.	Seaman
Swim, Richard	Ordinary Seaman
Tansell, Nicholas	Seaman
Taylor, George	Seaman
Taylor, William	Ordinary Seaman
Thomas, Adam William	Seaman
Thomas, Job	Seaman
Thompson, John	Quarter Gunner
Thompson, Robert	Gunner
Thompson, Samuel	Ordinary Seaman
Thursby, John	Seaman
Tisdale, James	Seaman
Titus, Henry	Seaman
Tompkins, Enos	Seaman
Tredwell, John	Seaman
Tylor, William	Ordinary Seaman
Vandalson, John	Seaman
Vanderhoff Jr., John	Seaman
Videtts, Ephenetus	Seaman
Walsh, James	Seaman
Warwick, Isaac	Seaman
Watson, Joshua	Seaman
Watterlein, Francis	Quarter Gunner
Webber, Benjamin	Seaman
Webster, Samuel	Seaman
Weeks, Henry	Seaman
White Jr., Charles	Paymaster
White, Sampson S.	Seaman
White, William	Seaman
Wilcox, William	Seaman
Wilkes, John	Seaman
Williams, John	Seaman
Williams, John	Waiter
Williams, Samuel	Ordinary Seaman
Williams, Thomas	Seaman
Williams, William	Ordinary Seaman
Williamson, Charles	Seaman
Williamson, Daniel	Seaman
Wilson, James	Seaman
Wilson, John	Quarter Gunner
Wilson, Thomas	Seaman
Wise, Joseph	Seaman
Wiseburn, Daniel	Seaman
Wiseman, William	Gunner
Wood, William	Seaman
Woodhull, Isaac	Seaman
Woodwell, Joseph	Seaman
Wooster, Charles W.	Major

Captain Isaac Silliman's Company
Anthony, Robert	Seaman
Arnet, Joseph	Third Lieutenant
Candle, Thomas	Seaman
Caragher, Patrick	Seaman
Carragher, Hugh	Seaman
Cary, Nathan	Private
Clark, Moses	Waiter
Clough, Nathaniel	Second Lieutenant
Conover, Joseph J.	Seaman
Crandle, Silas	Seaman
Cuffee, Amos	Seaman
Culbert, John	Seaman
Cunningham, James	Seaman
Dall, James L.	Quarter gunner

American Sea Fencibles in the War of 1812

Captain Silliman's Company (Continued)

Daniels, James	Seaman
Daniels, John	Seaman
Darrah, John	Seaman
Derrick, Cornelius	Gunner
Dewint, Henry	Seaman
Dwart, Nicholas	Seaman
Fanqeret, Nicholas	Band
Fowler, Noah	Seaman
Furgusson, George	Seaman
Gibbs, Thomas	Seaman
Guntz, Francis	Seaman
Hammitt, John	Seaman
Hanwige, John	Band
Harnmill, John	Waiter
Hassay, Benjamin	Seaman
Hazard, Anthony	Seaman
Hearin, Patrick	Seaman
Hender, William	Seaman
Highatt, Edward	Gunner
Hill, Daniel	Seaman
Hodgers, John	Seaman
Hodgkins, Joseph	Gunner
Howell, Henry	Seaman
Huyler, Edward	Seaman
Hyler, George	Seaman
Johnson, John	Seaman
Johnson, Lawrence	Seaman
Jones, Thomas	Seaman
Kernot, Thomas	Seaman
Kerwin, William	Seaman
Krapff, John C.	Quartermaster
La Rose, Berneil	Band
Lawrence, Thomas	Seaman
Lewis, John	Seaman
Love, John	Seaman
Massey, William	Quarter Gunner
Mayo, Nicholas	Seaman
McCoy, Thomas	Seaman
McFarren, John A.	Seaman
McGinnis, Michael	Seaman
McGlaughlin, Daniel	Seaman
McGrath, John	Seaman
McMullen, Alexander	Seaman
Merriote, Francis	Seaman
Mitchell, Henry	Seaman
Morrel, Jacob	Seaman
Morris, Jacob	Seaman
Nevil, Michael	Seaman
Newlin, Adam	Seaman
O'Brion, Lawrence	Seaman
Oliver, William	Seaman
Olney, Samuel	Seaman
Osbourn, Charles	Seaman
Parker, George	Seaman
Patterson, Peter	Seaman
Perkins, William	Seaman
Porter, John	Seaman
Quinn, Robert	Waiter
Rafferty, Parick	Seaman
Richardson, William	Seaman
Rikerman, Isaac	Seaman
Ripley, Samuel	Seaman
Roberts, Thomas	Boatswain
Robinson, James	Seaman
Rodgers, James	Seaman
Rodgers, John	Gunner
Romer, John	Seaman
Ross, Robert	Seaman
Rouse, Benjamin	Seaman
Schwitzer, John	Band
Scott, Benjamin	Seaman
Shields, Terrence	Seaman
Shimell, George	Seaman
Shoemaker, Edward	First Lieutenant
Shortis, James	Seaman
Silliman, Isaac	Captain
Smith, James	Seaman
Smith, John	Seaman
Smith, Martin	Seaman
Smith, Melancton	Seaman
Southerland, Daniel	Seaman
Springsteen, Abraham	
Ten Eyck, Philip	Seaman
Thirsby, John	Seaman
Thomas, William	Seaman
Thompson, John	Gunner
Tilbous, James	Seaman
Tredwell, Charles	Seaman
Vanderhoff, John	Seaman
Vanderpool, John	Seaman
Vandolson, John	Seaman
Vilon, Peter	Seaman
Ward, John	Seaman
Watkins, Osmore	Gunner
West, Matthew	Seaman
Wetterlein, Francis	Band
Whitney, William	Seaman
Wicks, Henry	Seaman
Williams, George	Seaman
Wright, Edwin	Seaman

Captain John Randlet's Company

Ackley, John	Private
Carlock, William	Seaman
Davis, George	Seaman
Evertson, Alexander	Seaman
Fitzsimmons, William	Seaman
Hodgkins, Joseph S.	Gunner
Johnson, William Wood	Private
Randlet, John M.	Captain
Swinton, Thomas	Seaman

Captain John Roorbach's Company

Carlock, John	Seaman
DeForrest, William T.	Private
Dunn, E.	Seaman
Garrison, William	Seaman

Captain Roorbach's Company (Continued)

Gracie, Edward G.	Third Lieutenant	Dayton, Benjamin G.	Lieutenant
Hatthatt, Edward	Gunner	Dobbins, Samuel	Seaman
Hopper, James	Seaman	Gantz, Gabriel	Seaman
Howell, Israel	Private	Hedges, Thomas	Seaman
Inglis, John	Seaman	Horton, Timothy	Seaman
Jackson, John	Seaman	Mercer, William	Seaman
Jonakin, Benjamin	Gunner	Miller, John	Seaman
Norris, Coffin	Seaman	Morrison, Charles	Seaman
Perry, William	Seaman	Muen, William	Seaman
Roorbach, John O.	Captain	Munson, Peter	Seaman
Slagle, Peter	Seaman	Rames, David	Waiter
Williams, John	Seaman	Richardson, James	Seaman
Willson, John	Gunner	Southward, Cornelius	Seaman
Woodruff, Nathaniel	Seaman	Wainwright, Joshua	Seaman
		Warne, Joshua	Seaman

Lieutenant Benjamin Dayton's Detachment

Baptist, John	Cook		
Bowman, John	Drummer		
Brower, Jeremiah	Gunner		

Staff

Stevens, Alexander	Surgeon
Stevens, H.	Doctor
Fougerat, Fitz	Boy

Bibliography

American Commercial and Daily Advertiser, Baltimore, MD.

American State Papers, Military Affairs, Volume III, (Gales & Seaton: Washington, DC, 1860).

Bayler, William H. and Oliver O. Jones, *History of the Marine Society of Newburyport, Massachusetts*, 1906.

British and Foreign State Papers 1816-1817, British Foreign Office, (James Ridgway and Sons: Piccadilly, England, 1836).

Davenport, Charles Benedict, *Naval Officers, Their Heredity and Development*, (Carnegie Institution of Washington: Washington, DC, 1919).

Documents of the Senate of the State of New York, 127th Session, Volume VIII, Number 2, Part 5, 1904, (Oliver A. Quayle, State Printers: Albany, NY, 1904).

Guernsey, R. S., *New York City and Vicinity during the War of 1812-1815*, volume II, (Charles L. Woodward, Bookseller: New York, NY, 1895).

Heitman, Francis B., *Historical Register and Dictionary of the United States Army From Its Organization, September 29, 1789, to March 2, 1903*, Volume I and II, (Genealogical Publishing Company, Baltimore, Maryland: 1994).

History of the Connecticut Valley in Massachusetts, Volume II, (Louis H. Everts: Philadelphia, PA, 1879).

Laws of the State of New Hampshire passed from December session 1805 to June session 1810, (Isaac Hill Printers: Concord, NH, 1811).

Laws of the State of New York Passed at the Thirty-Eighth Session of the Legislature, (J. Buel, Printer to the State: Albany, NY 1815), thirty-eighth session.

Marine, William M., *The British Invasion of Maryland 1812-1815*, (Society of the War of 1812 in Maryland: Baltimore, MD, 1913).

Military History of the State of New Hampshire, Part II, (C. E. Potter, McFarland & Jenkins: Concord, NH, 1866).

Muster Rolls of the Soldiers of the War of 1812 detached from the Militia of North Carolina in 1812-1814, (North Carolina Adjutant General's Office: Raleigh, 1851).

Pearson, Brigadier General Gardner W., *Records of the Massachusetts Volunteer Militia*, (Wright & Potter Printing Co.: Boston, MA, 1913).

Presto Press, Mattapoisett, MA, volume XVII, number 9, 26 Feb 1969, page 14, History of Fort Phoenix, by Donald R. Bernard, part XV.

Proceedings of the Bostonian Society at the Annual Meeting, January 10, 1899, (Order of the Society: Old State House, Boston, 1899).

Public Statutes at Large of the United States of America, volume III, (Boston: Charles C. Little and James Brown, 1846), Thirteenth Congress.

Register of Enlistments in the U.S. Army, 1798-1914; (Washington, DC: National Archives Microfilm Publication M233, 81 rolls); Records of the Adjutant General's Office, 1780's-1917, Record Group 94.

Report from the Secretary of War in Obedience to the Resolutions of the Senate of the 5th and 30th of June, 1834, and the 3rd of March, 1835, in Relation to the Pension Establishment of the United States, (1835 Pension Rolls), (Duff Green, Washington, D.C.: 1835).

The Sag-Harbor Express, Sag Harbor, Suffolk County, NY, Thursday, 30 Apr 1891, volume XXXII, number 42.

United States. Bureau of Land Management, General Land Office Records, Automated Records Project; *Federal Land Patents*, State Volumes, http://www.glorecords.blm.gov/, Springfield, Virginia: Bureau of Land Management, Eastern States, 2007.

War of 1812 Military Bounty Land Warrants, 1815-1858; National Archives Microfilm Publication M848; Records of the Bureau of Land Management, Record Group 49; National Archives, Washington, D.C.

War of 1812 Pension Applications; National Archives Microfilm Publication M313; Records of the Department of Veterans Affairs, Record Group Number 15; National Archives, Washington D.C.

Whitehorne, Joseph A., *The Battle for Baltimore 1814*, (The Nautical & Aviation Publishing Company of America: Baltimore, MD, 1997).

www.ingramcontent.com/pod-product-compliance
Lightning Source LLC
Chambersburg PA
CBHW080815190426
43197CB00041B/2832